NIGHT MARY™

rick remender   kieron dwyer

STORY & SCRIPT BY RICK REMENDER
STORY & ART BY KIERON DWYER

LETTERS BY ROBBIE ROBBINS
& TOM B. LONG

EDITS BY CHRIS RYALL

DESIGN BY ROBBIE ROBBINS

www.idwpublishing.com

ISBN: 978-1-933239-27-9
11 10 09 08   2 3 4 5

IDW Publishing: **Operations**: Moshe Berger, Chairman • Ted Adams, President • Matthew Ruzicka, CPA, Controller • Alan Payne, VP of Sales • Lorelei Bunjes, Dir. of Digital Services • Marci Hubbard, Executive Assistant • Alonzo Simon, Shipping Manager • **Editorial**: Chris Ryall, Publisher/Editor-in-Chief • Scott Dunbier, Editor, Special Projects • Andy Schmidt, Senior Editor • Justin Eisinger, Editor • Kris Oprisko, Editor/Foreign Lic. • Denton J. Tipton, Editor • Tom Waltz, Editor • Mariah Huehner, Assistant Editor • **Design**: Robbie Robbins, EVP/Sr. Graphic Artist • Ben Templesmith, Artist/Designer • Neil Uyetake, Art Director • Chris Mowry, Graphic Artist • Amauri Osorio, Graphic Artist

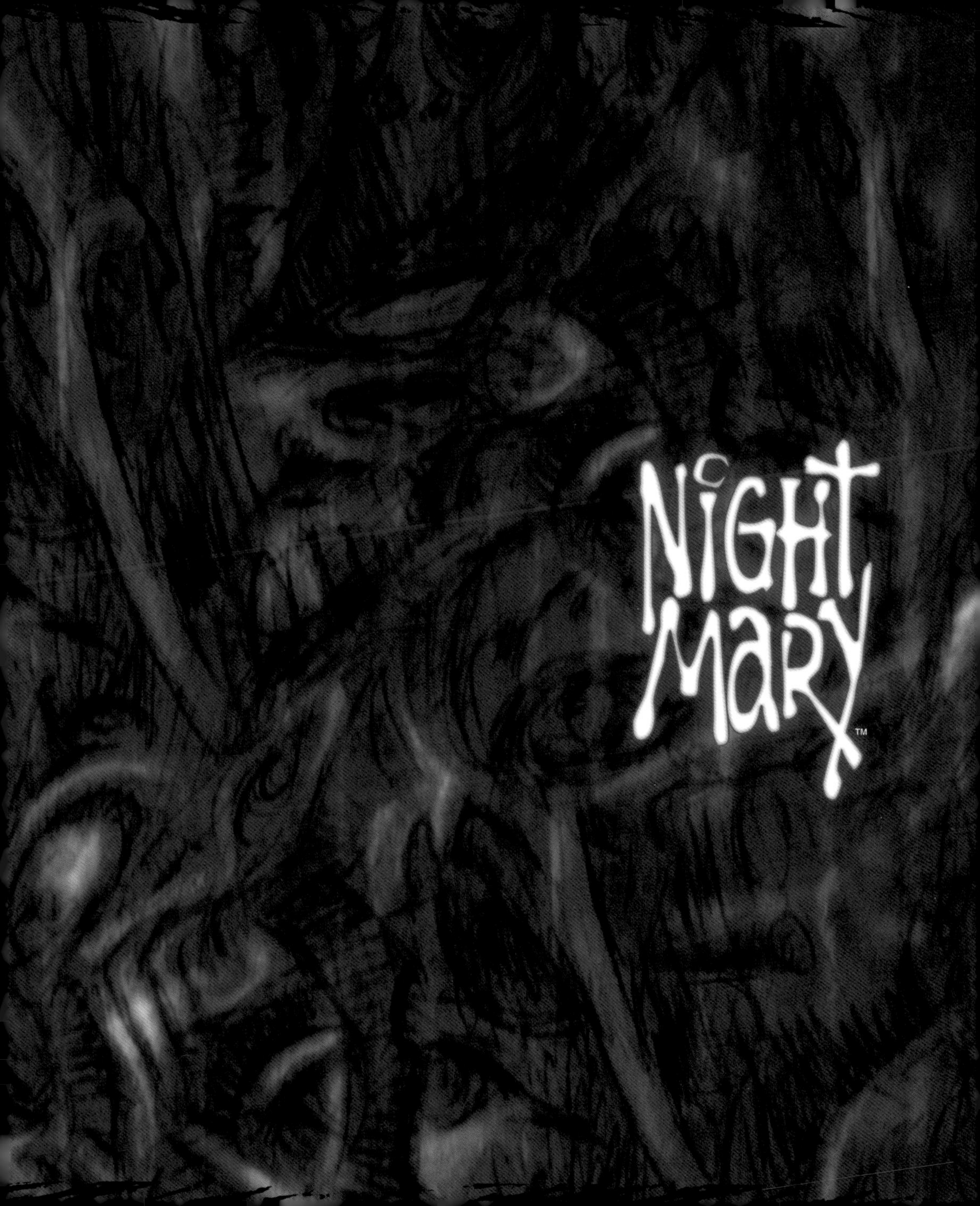
NIGHT MARY™

Night Mary

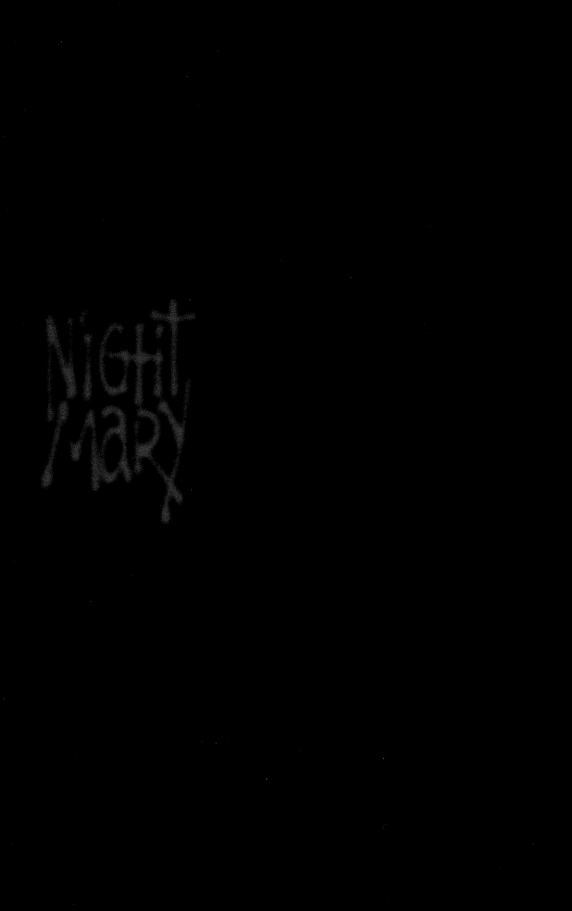

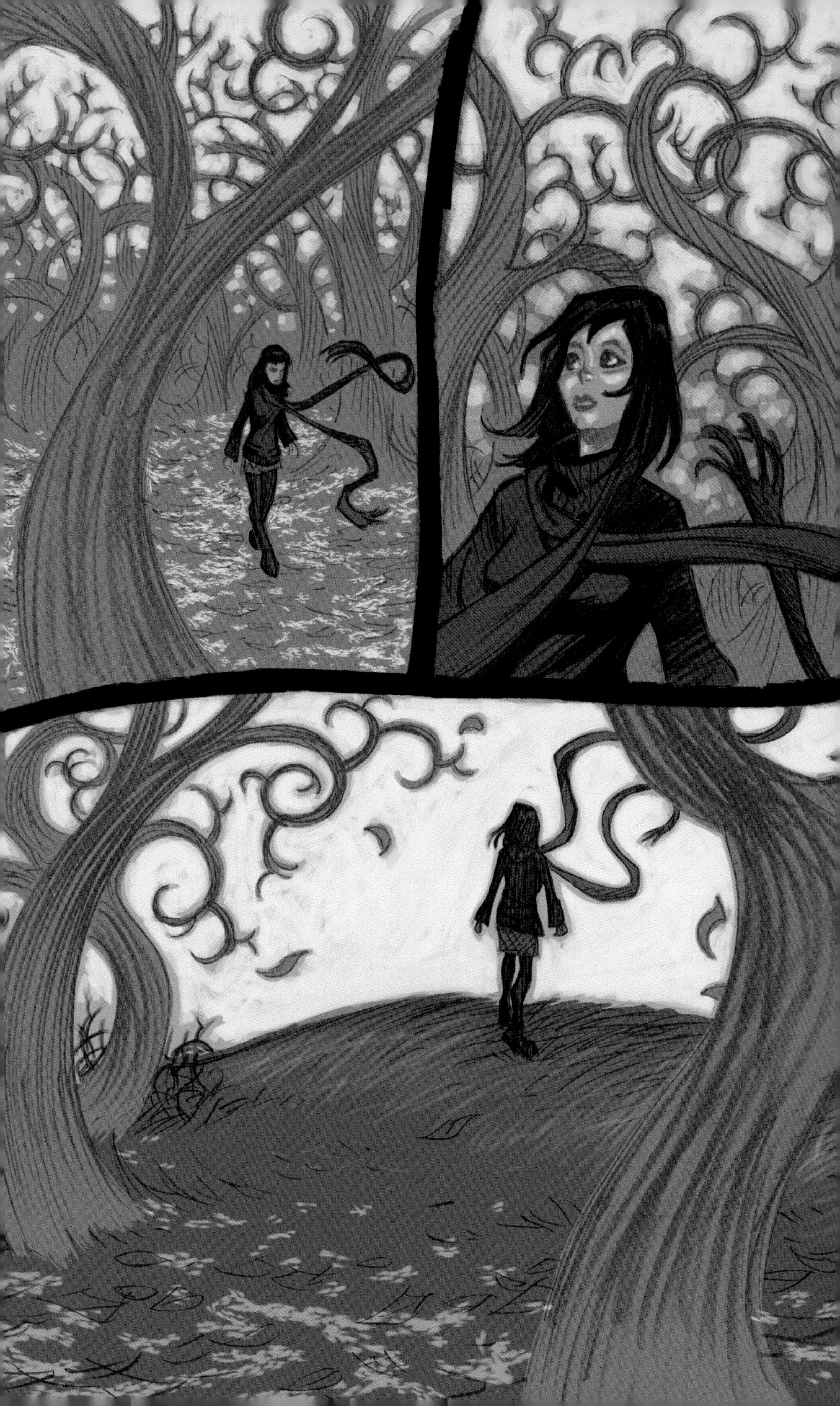

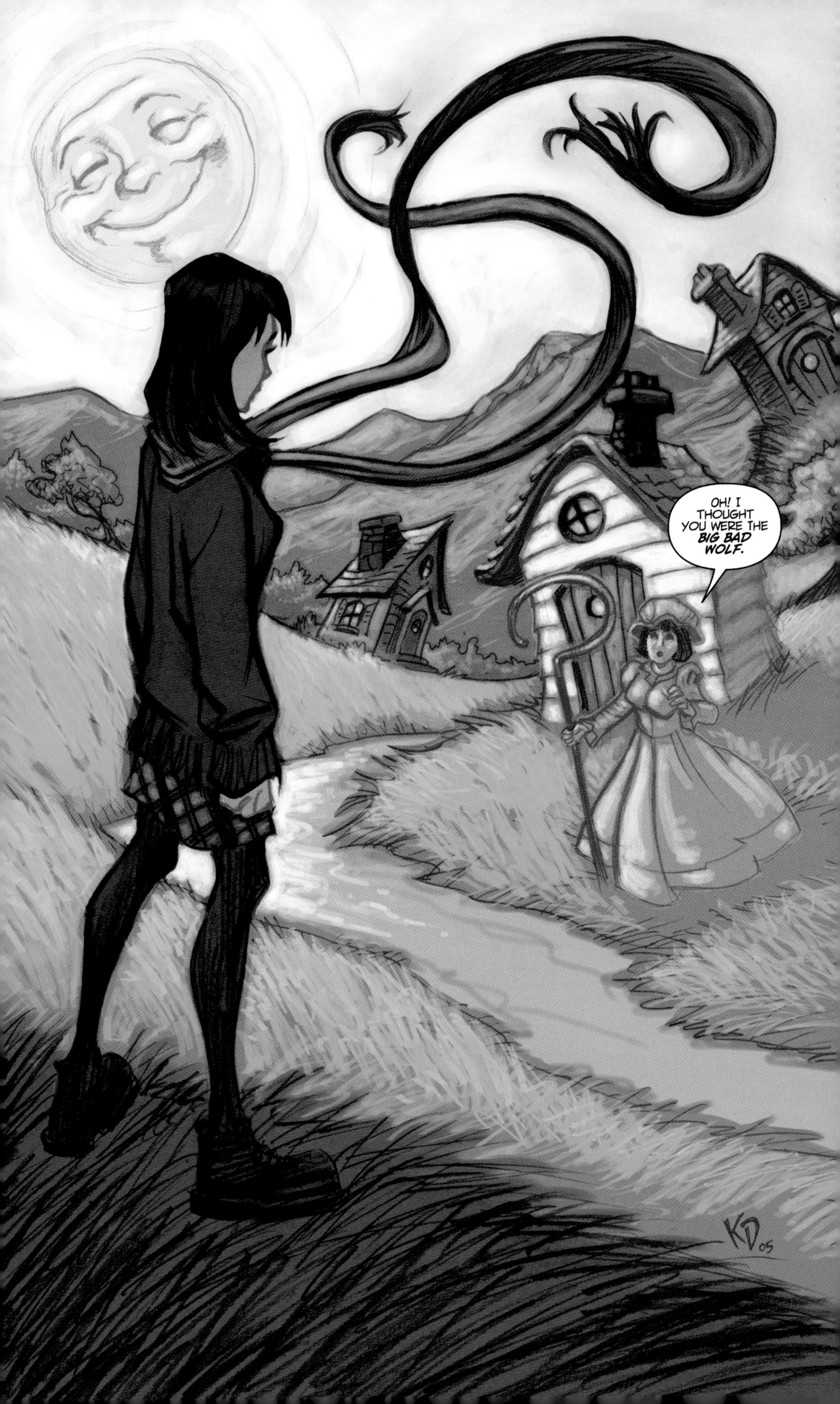
OH! I THOUGHT YOU WERE THE BIG BAD WOLF.
KD 05

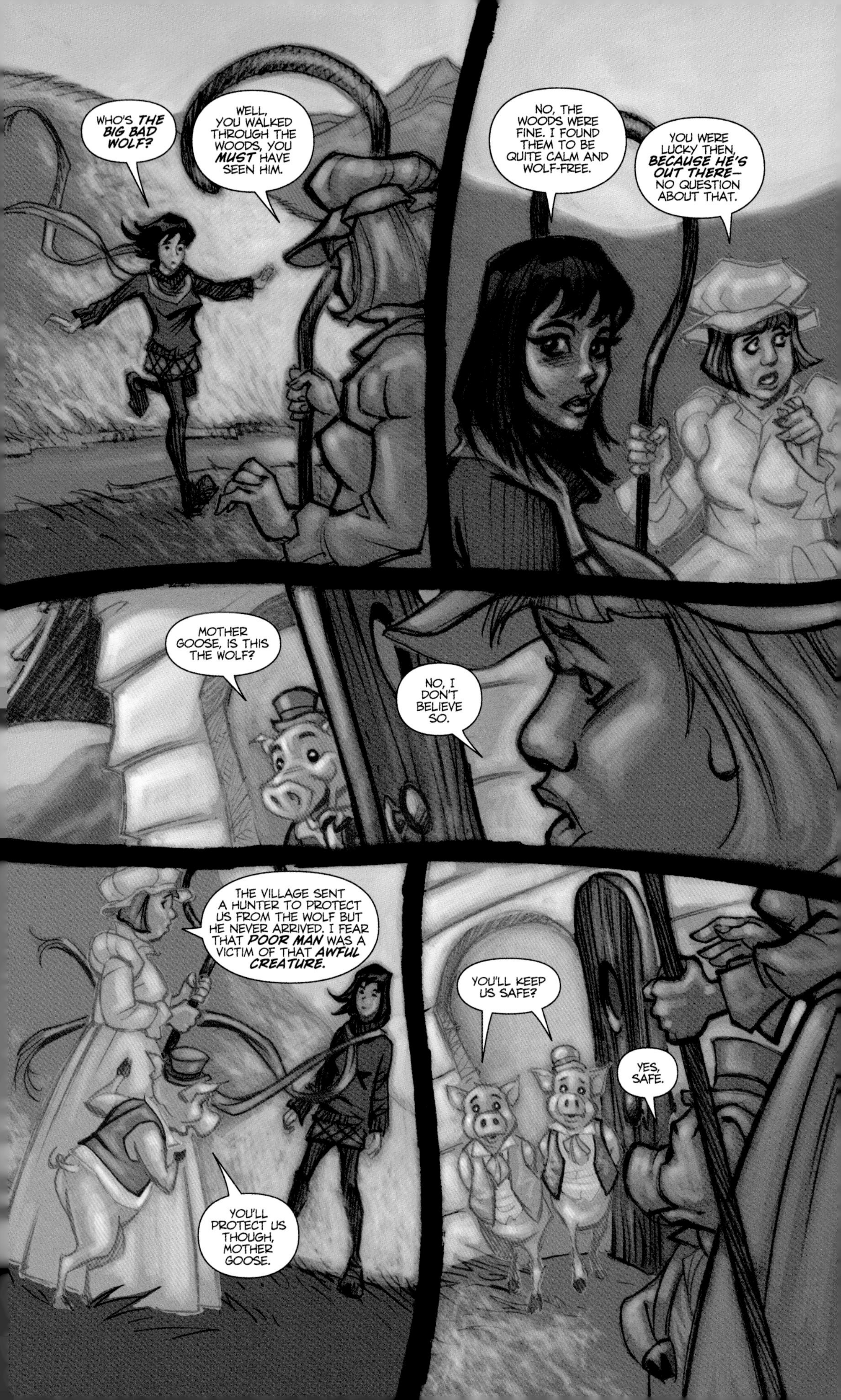
WHO'S THE BIG BAD WOLF?
WELL, YOU WALKED THROUGH THE WOODS, YOU MUST HAVE SEEN HIM.
NO, THE WOODS WERE FINE. I FOUND THEM TO BE QUITE CALM AND WOLF-FREE.
YOU WERE LUCKY THEN, BECAUSE HE'S OUT THERE— NO QUESTION ABOUT THAT.
MOTHER GOOSE, IS THIS THE WOLF?
NO, I DON'T BELIEVE SO.
THE VILLAGE SENT A HUNTER TO PROTECT US FROM THE WOLF BUT HE NEVER ARRIVED. I FEAR THAT POOR MAN WAS A VICTIM OF THAT AWFUL CREATURE.
YOU'LL PROTECT US THOUGH, MOTHER GOOSE.
YOU'LL KEEP US SAFE?
YES, SAFE.

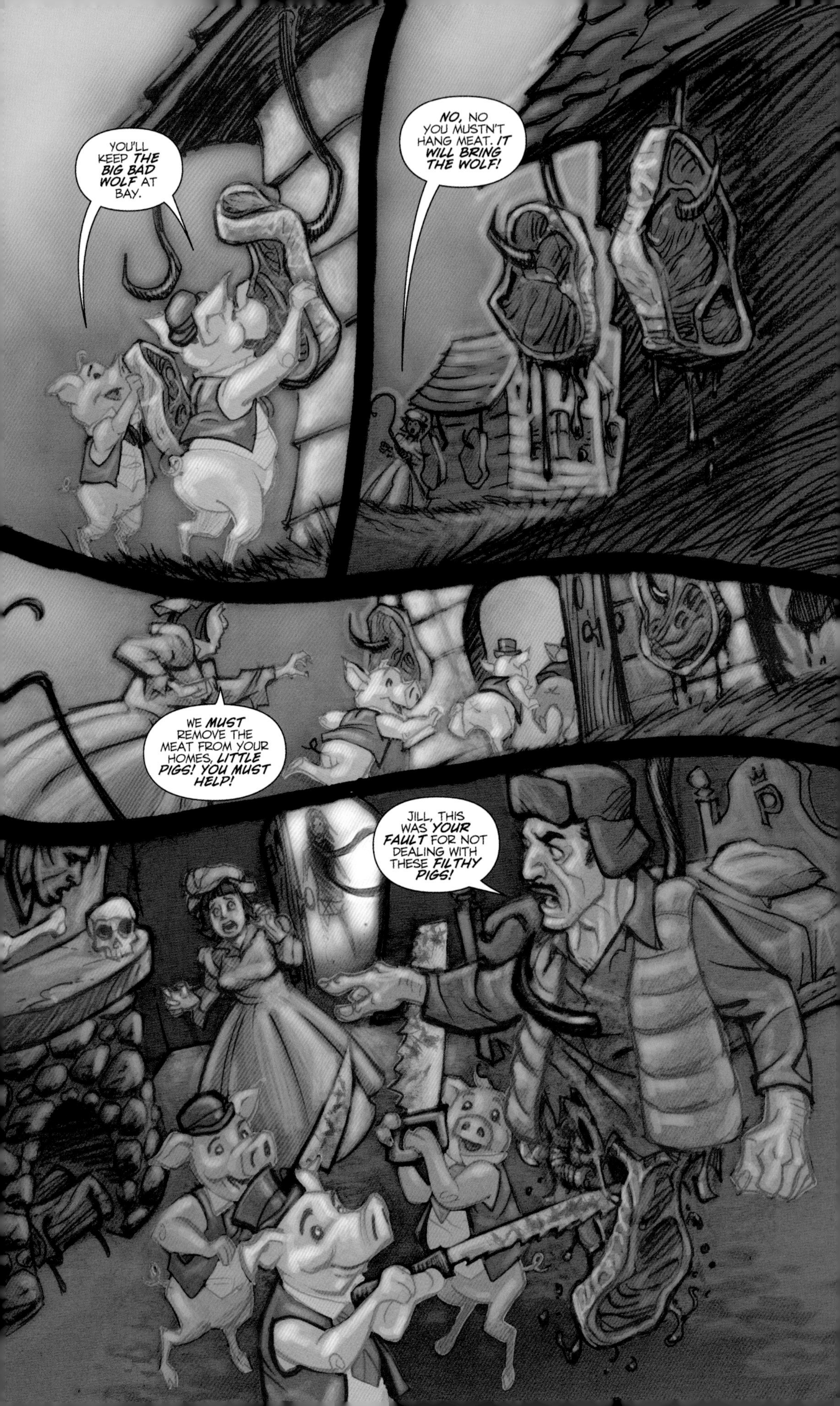
YOU'LL KEEP THE BIG BAD WOLF AT BAY.
NO, NO YOU MUSTN'T HANG MEAT. IT WILL BRING THE WOLF!
WE MUST REMOVE THE MEAT FROM YOUR HOMES, LITTLE PIGS! YOU MUST HELP!
JILL, THIS WAS YOUR FAULT FOR NOT DEALING WITH THESE FILTHY PIGS!

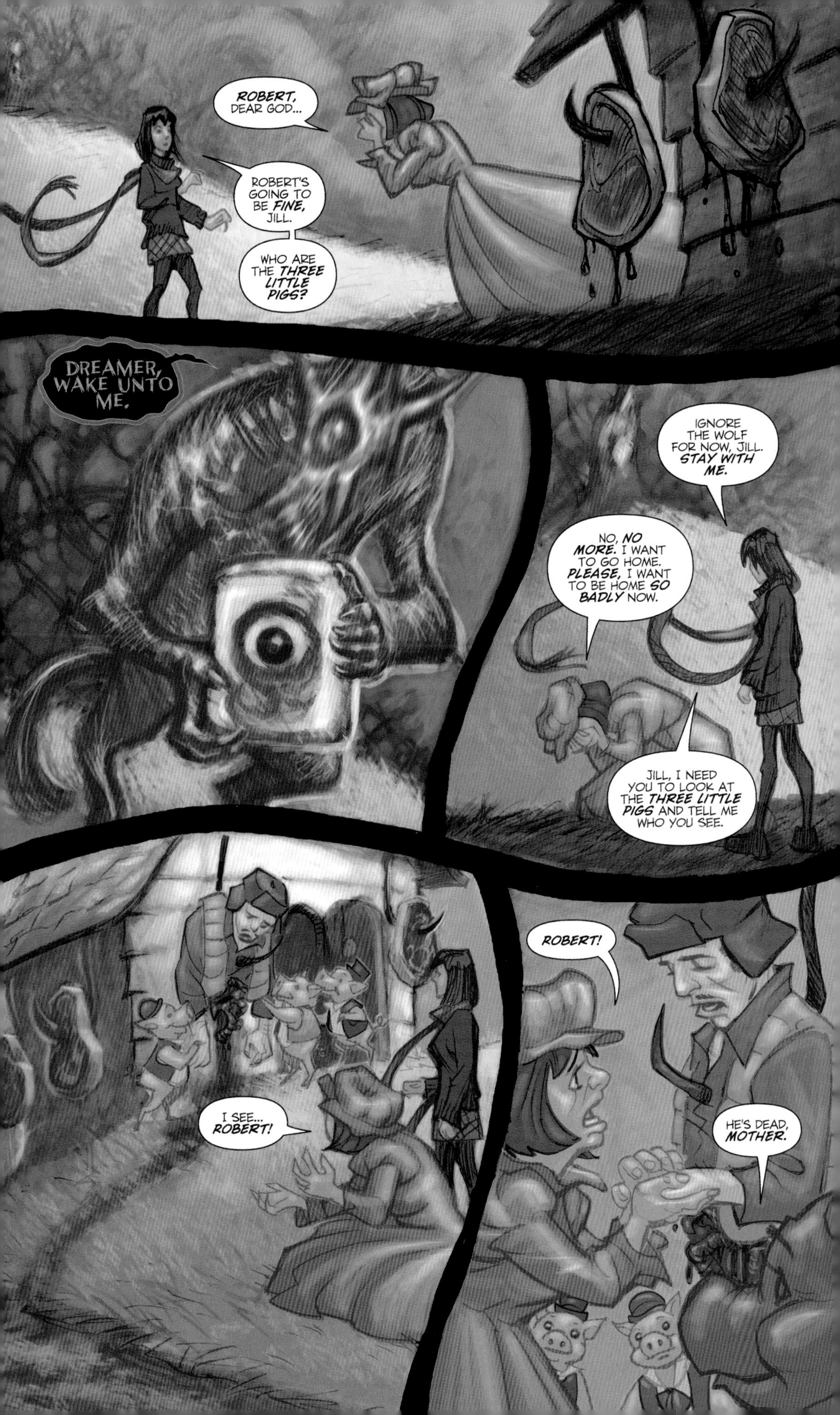
ROBERT, DEAR GOD...
ROBERT'S GOING TO BE FINE, JILL.
WHO ARE THE THREE LITTLE PIGS?
DREAMER, WAKE UNTO ME.
IGNORE THE WOLF FOR NOW, JILL. STAY WITH ME.
NO, NO MORE. I WANT TO GO HOME. PLEASE, I WANT TO BE HOME SO BADLY NOW.
JILL, I NEED YOU TO LOOK AT THE THREE LITTLE PIGS AND TELL ME WHO YOU SEE.
I SEE... ROBERT!
ROBERT!
HE'S DEAD, MOTHER.

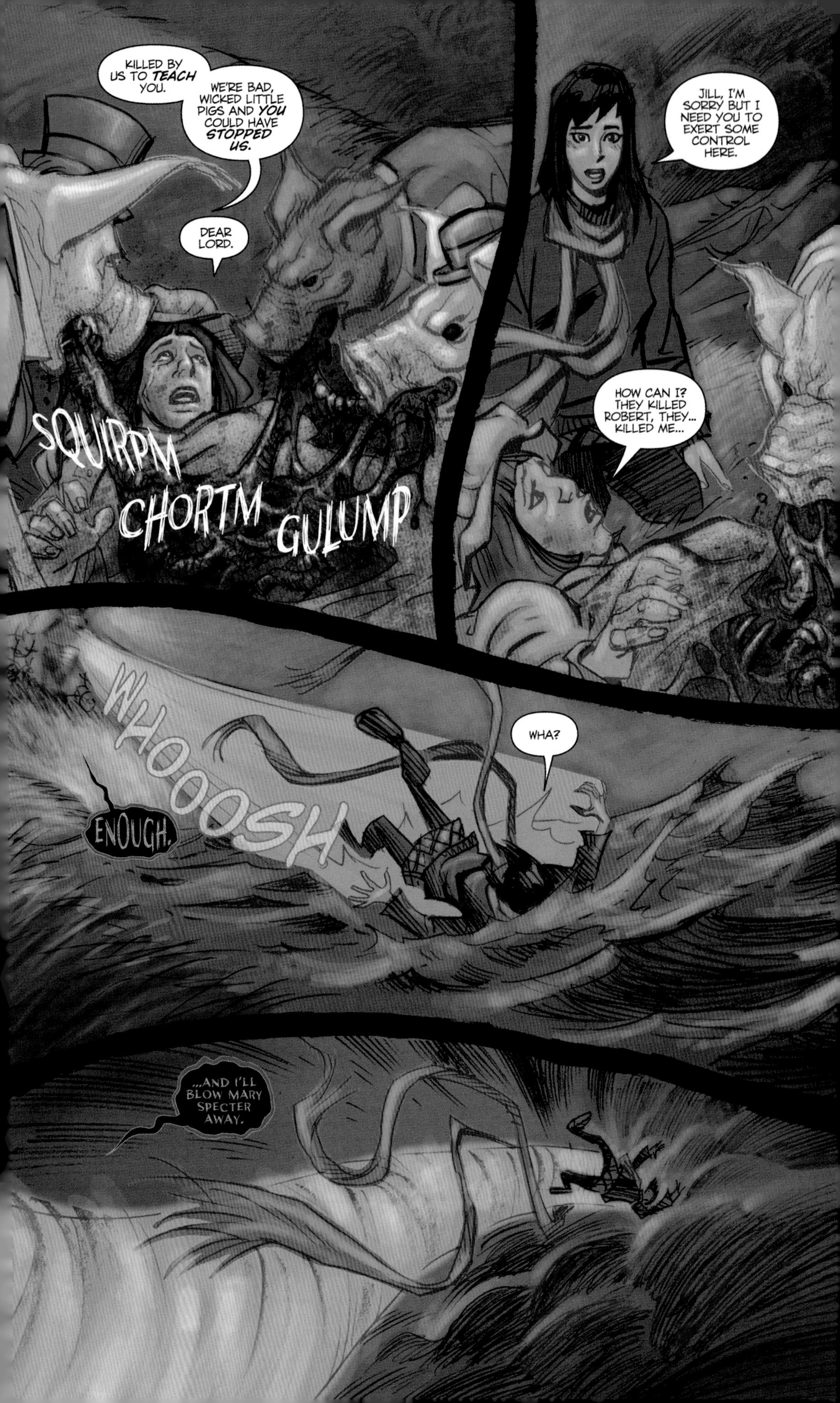
KILLED BY US TO TEACH YOU.
WE'RE BAD, WICKED LITTLE PIGS AND YOU COULD HAVE STOPPED US.
DEAR LORD.
SQUIRPM
CHORTM
GULUMP
JILL, I'M SORRY BUT I NEED YOU TO EXERT SOME CONTROL HERE.
HOW CAN I? THEY KILLED ROBERT, THEY... KILLED ME...
WHOOOOSH
WHA?
ENOUGH.
...AND I'LL BLOW MARY SPECTER AWAY.

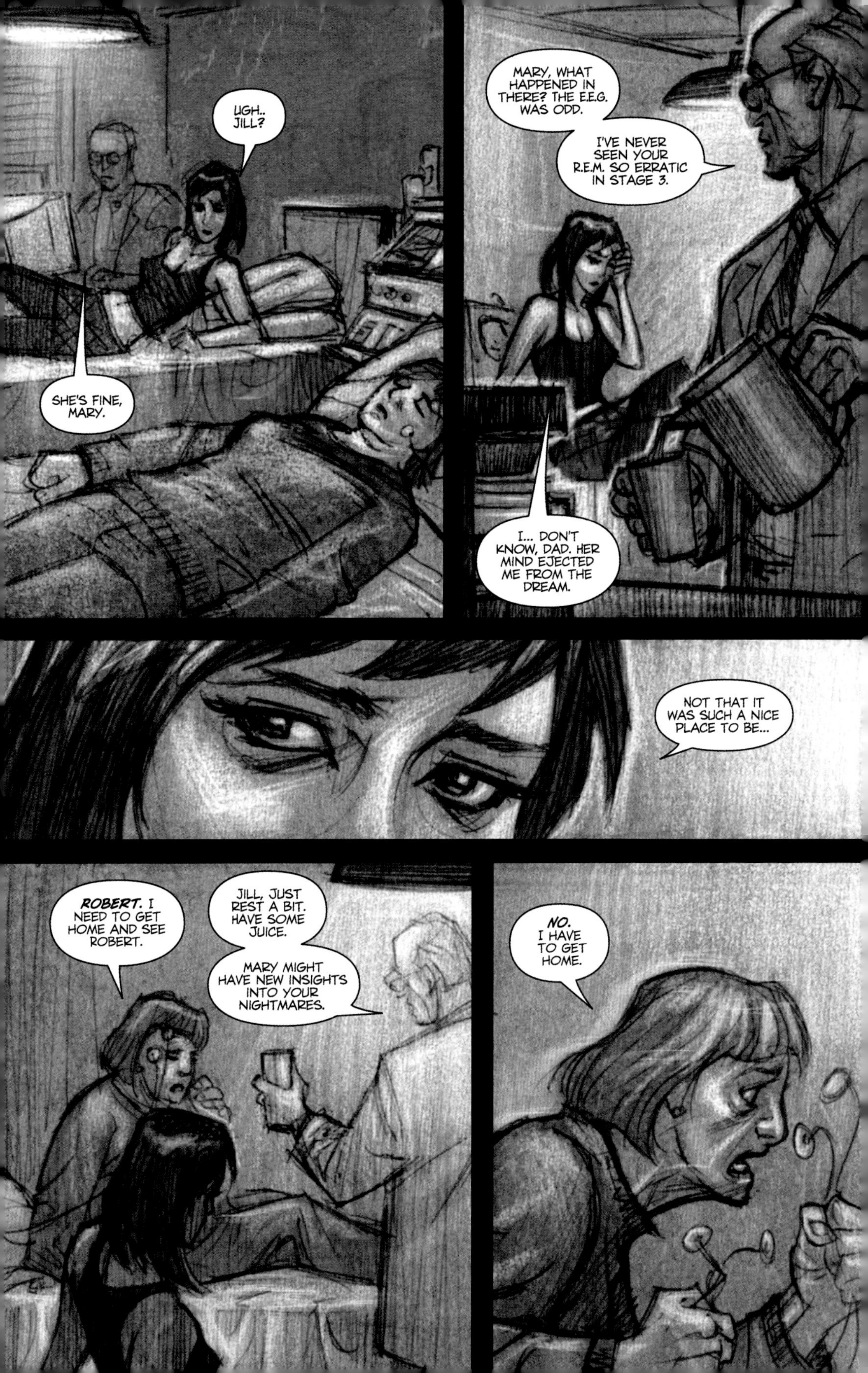
UGH.. JILL?
SHE'S FINE, MARY.
MARY, WHAT HAPPENED IN THERE? THE E.E.G. WAS ODD.
I'VE NEVER SEEN YOUR R.E.M. SO ERRATIC IN STAGE 3.
I... DON'T KNOW, DAD. HER MIND EJECTED ME FROM THE DREAM.
NOT THAT IT WAS SUCH A NICE PLACE TO BE...
ROBERT. I NEED TO GET HOME AND SEE ROBERT.
JILL, JUST REST A BIT. HAVE SOME JUICE.
MARY MIGHT HAVE NEW INSIGHTS INTO YOUR NIGHTMARES.
NO. I HAVE TO GET HOME.

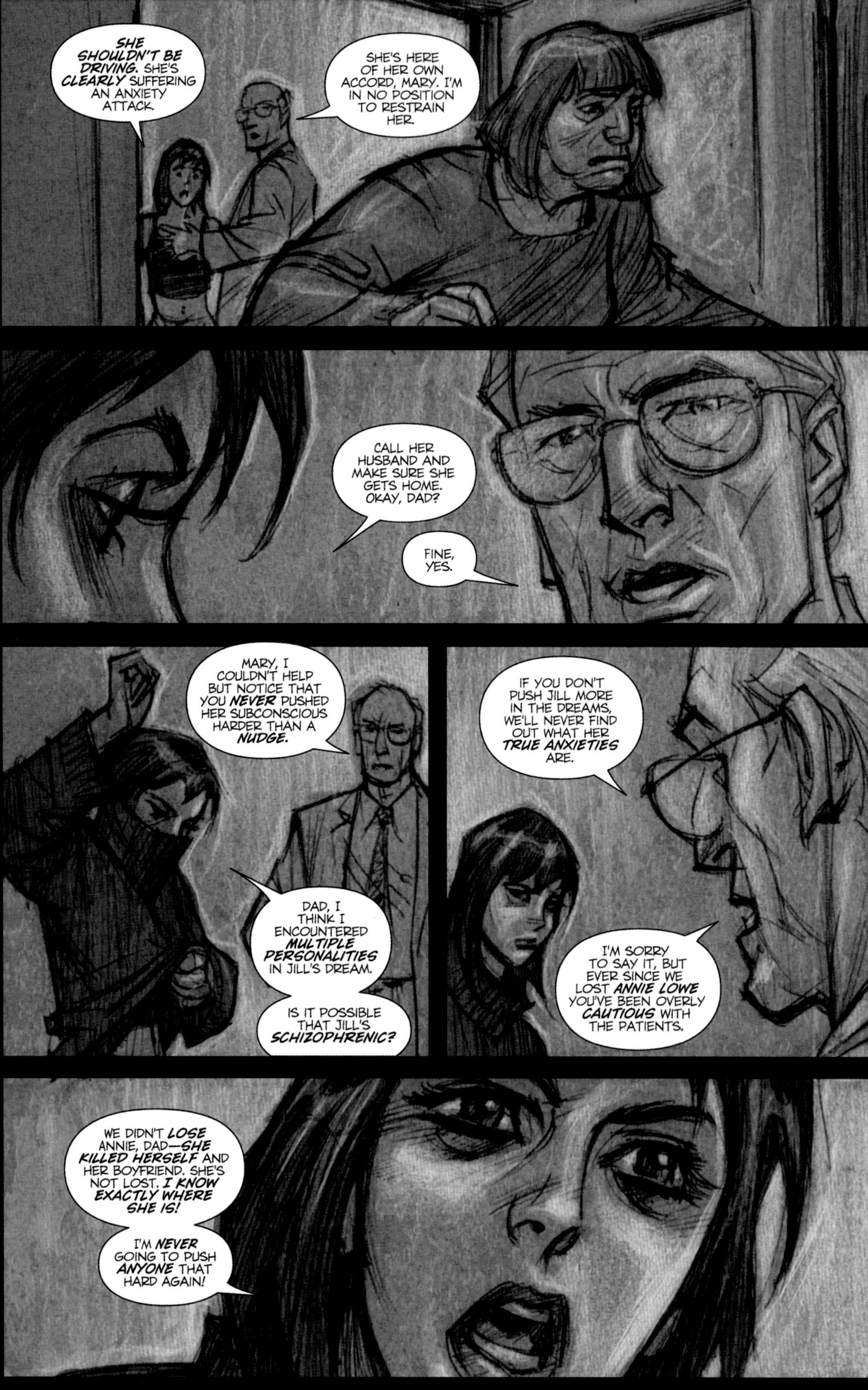
SHE SHOULDN'T BE DRIVING. SHE'S CLEARLY SUFFERING AN ANXIETY ATTACK.
SHE'S HERE OF HER OWN ACCORD, MARY. I'M IN NO POSITION TO RESTRAIN HER.
CALL HER HUSBAND AND MAKE SURE SHE GETS HOME. OKAY, DAD?
FINE, YES.
MARY, I COULDN'T HELP BUT NOTICE THAT YOU NEVER PUSHED HER SUBCONSCIOUS HARDER THAN A NUDGE.
DAD, I THINK I ENCOUNTERED MULTIPLE PERSONALITIES IN JILL'S DREAM.
IS IT POSSIBLE THAT JILL'S SCHIZOPHRENIC?
IF YOU DON'T PUSH JILL MORE IN THE DREAMS, WE'LL NEVER FIND OUT WHAT HER TRUE ANXIETIES ARE.
I'M SORRY TO SAY IT, BUT EVER SINCE WE LOST ANNIE LOWE YOU'VE BEEN OVERLY CAUTIOUS WITH THE PATIENTS.
WE DIDN'T LOSE ANNIE, DAD—SHE KILLED HERSELF AND HER BOYFRIEND. SHE'S NOT LOST. I KNOW EXACTLY WHERE SHE IS!
I'M NEVER GOING TO PUSH ANYONE THAT HARD AGAIN!

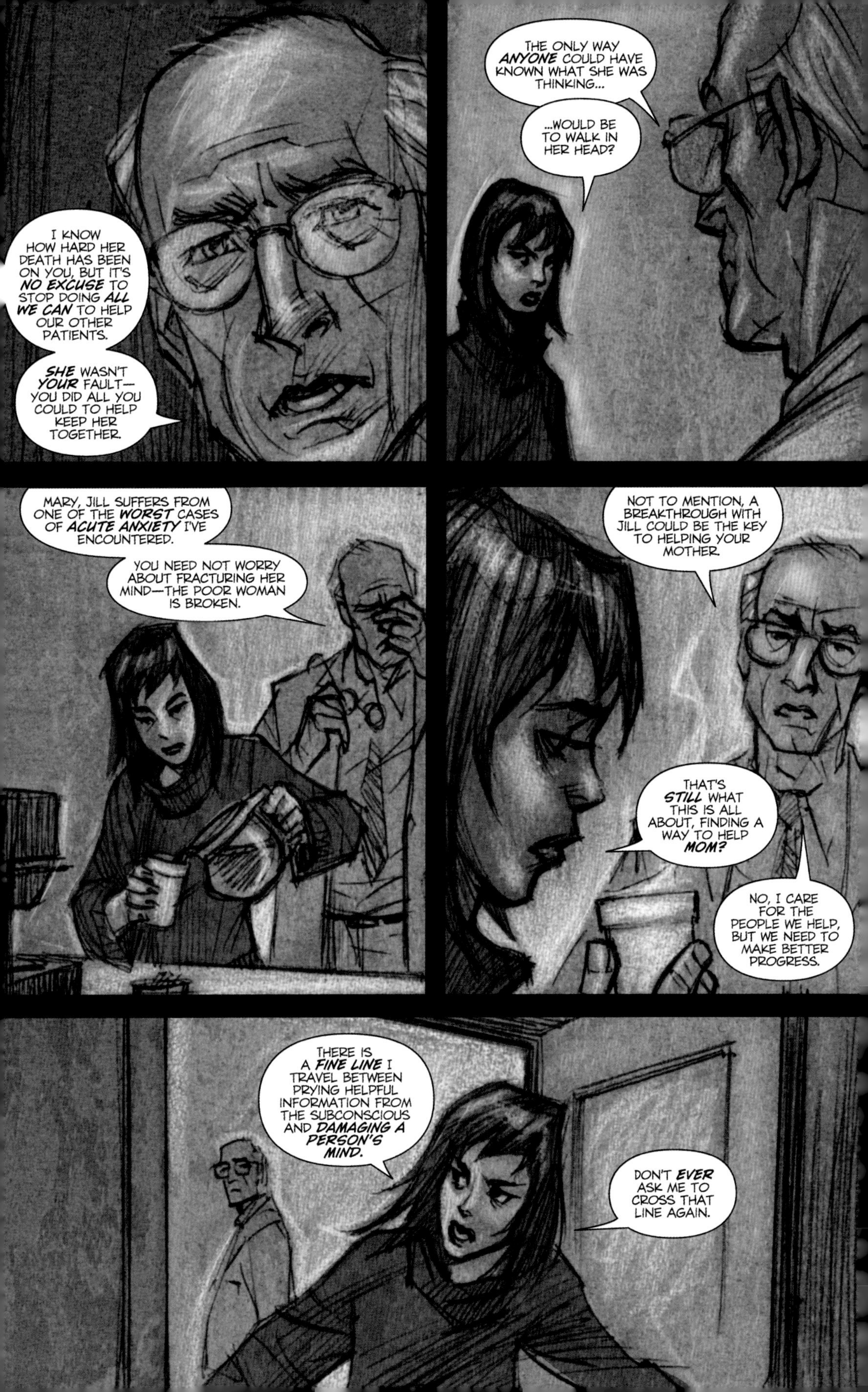
I KNOW HOW HARD HER DEATH HAS BEEN ON YOU, BUT IT'S NO EXCUSE TO STOP DOING ALL WE CAN TO HELP OUR OTHER PATIENTS.
SHE WASN'T YOUR FAULT—YOU DID ALL YOU COULD TO HELP KEEP HER TOGETHER.
THE ONLY WAY ANYONE COULD HAVE KNOWN WHAT SHE WAS THINKING...
...WOULD BE TO WALK IN HER HEAD?
MARY, JILL SUFFERS FROM ONE OF THE WORST CASES OF ACUTE ANXIETY I'VE ENCOUNTERED.
YOU NEED NOT WORRY ABOUT FRACTURING HER MIND—THE POOR WOMAN IS BROKEN.
NOT TO MENTION, A BREAKTHROUGH WITH JILL COULD BE THE KEY TO HELPING YOUR MOTHER.
THAT'S STILL WHAT THIS IS ALL ABOUT, FINDING A WAY TO HELP MOM?
NO, I CARE FOR THE PEOPLE WE HELP, BUT WE NEED TO MAKE BETTER PROGRESS.
THERE IS A FINE LINE I TRAVEL BETWEEN PRYING HELPFUL INFORMATION FROM THE SUBCONSCIOUS AND DAMAGING A PERSON'S MIND.
DON'T EVER ASK ME TO CROSS THAT LINE AGAIN.

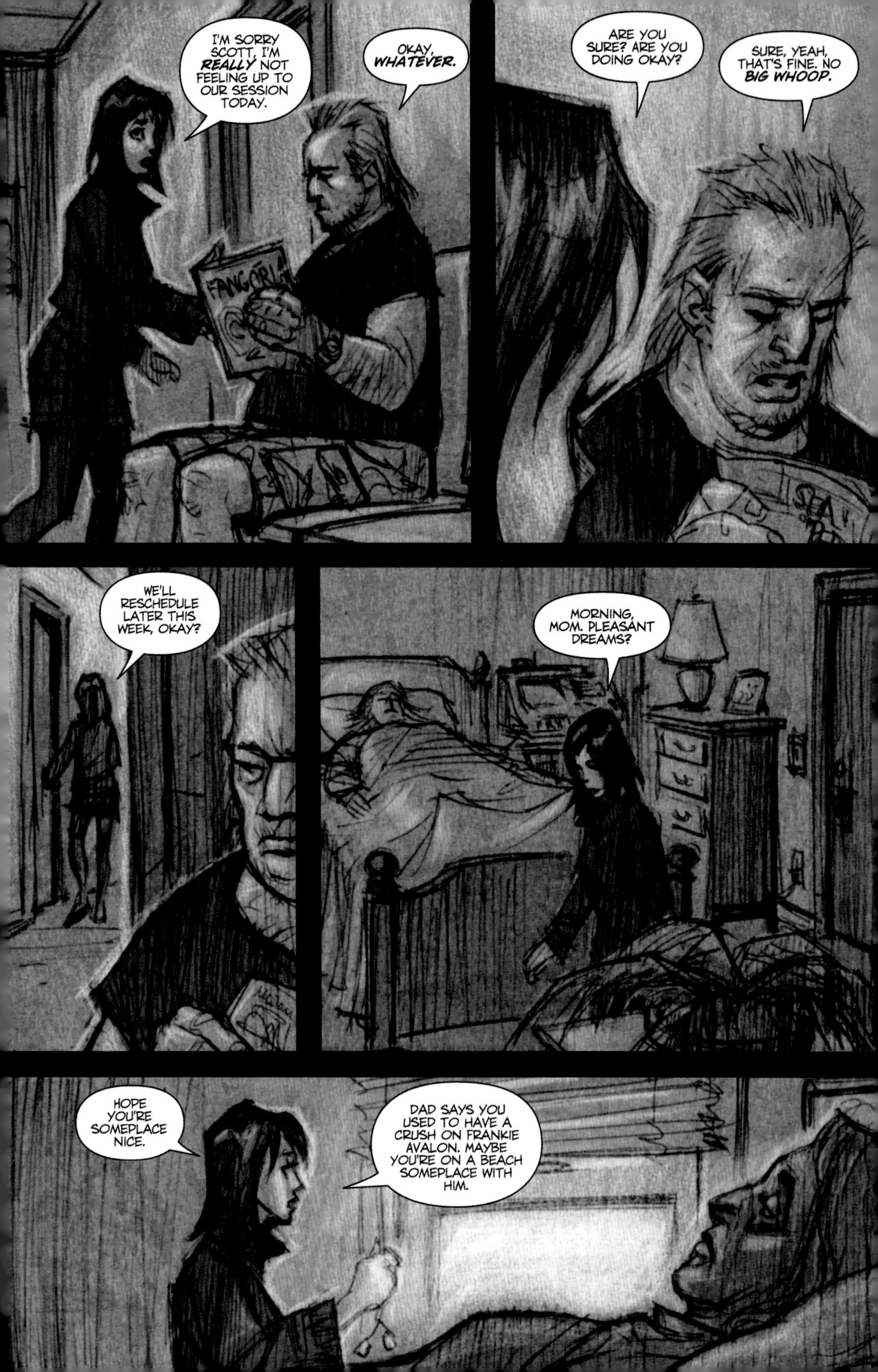
I'M SORRY SCOTT, I'M REALLY NOT FEELING UP TO OUR SESSION TODAY.
OKAY, WHATEVER.
ARE YOU SURE? ARE YOU DOING OKAY?
SURE, YEAH, THAT'S FINE. NO BIG WHOOP.
WE'LL RESCHEDULE LATER THIS WEEK, OKAY?
MORNING, MOM. PLEASANT DREAMS?
HOPE YOU'RE SOMEPLACE NICE.
DAD SAYS YOU USED TO HAVE A CRUSH ON FRANKIE AVALON. MAYBE YOU'RE ON A BEACH SOMEPLACE WITH HIM.

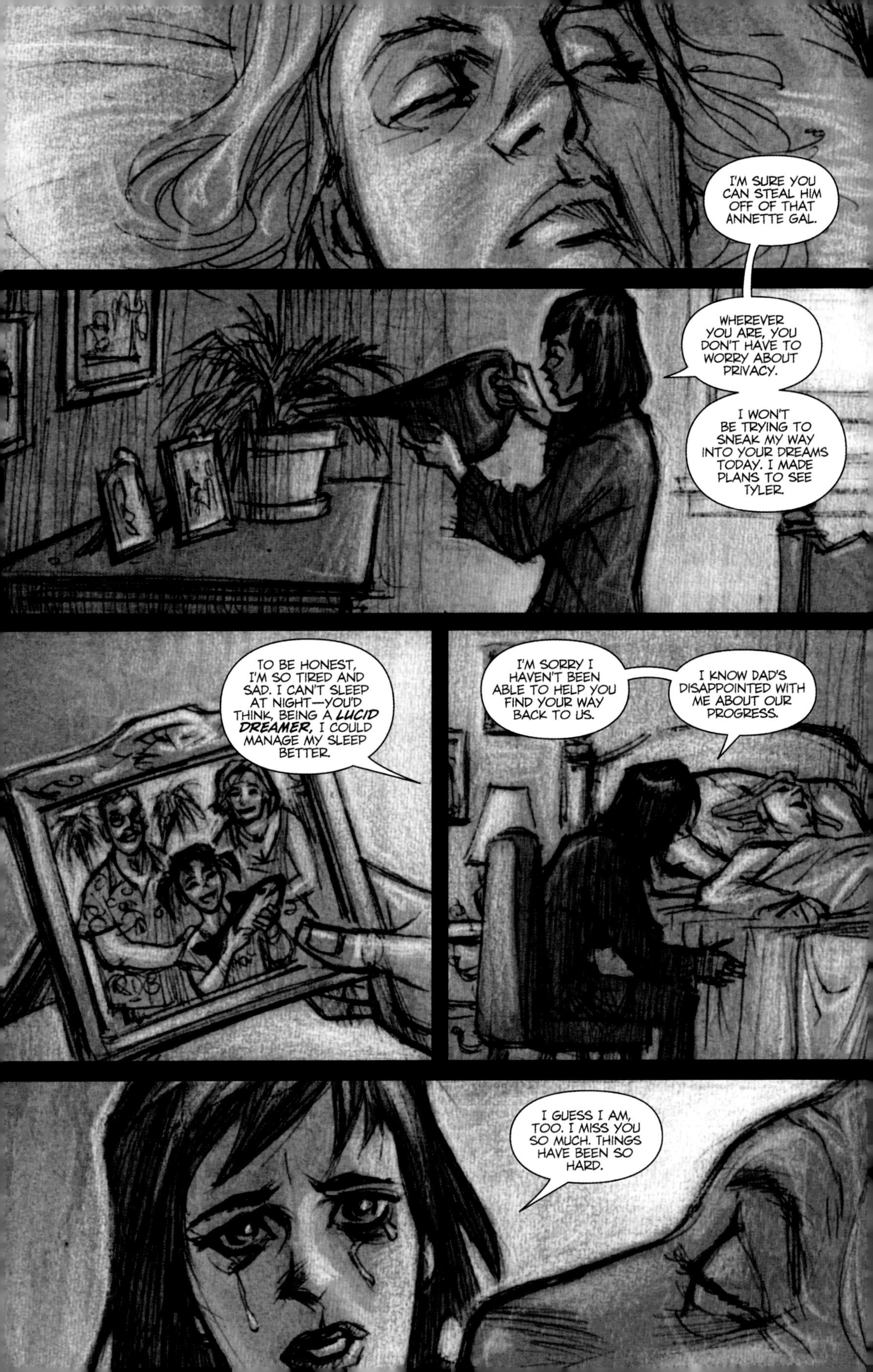

I'M SURE YOU CAN STEAL HIM OFF OF THAT ANNETTE GAL.
WHEREVER YOU ARE, YOU DON'T HAVE TO WORRY ABOUT PRIVACY.
I WON'T BE TRYING TO SNEAK MY WAY INTO YOUR DREAMS TODAY. I MADE PLANS TO SEE TYLER.
TO BE HONEST, I'M SO TIRED AND SAD. I CAN'T SLEEP AT NIGHT—YOU'D THINK, BEING A LUCID DREAMER, I COULD MANAGE MY SLEEP BETTER.
I'M SORRY I HAVEN'T BEEN ABLE TO HELP YOU FIND YOUR WAY BACK TO US.
I KNOW DAD'S DISAPPOINTED WITH ME ABOUT OUR PROGRESS.
I GUESS I AM, TOO. I MISS YOU SO MUCH. THINGS HAVE BEEN SO HARD.

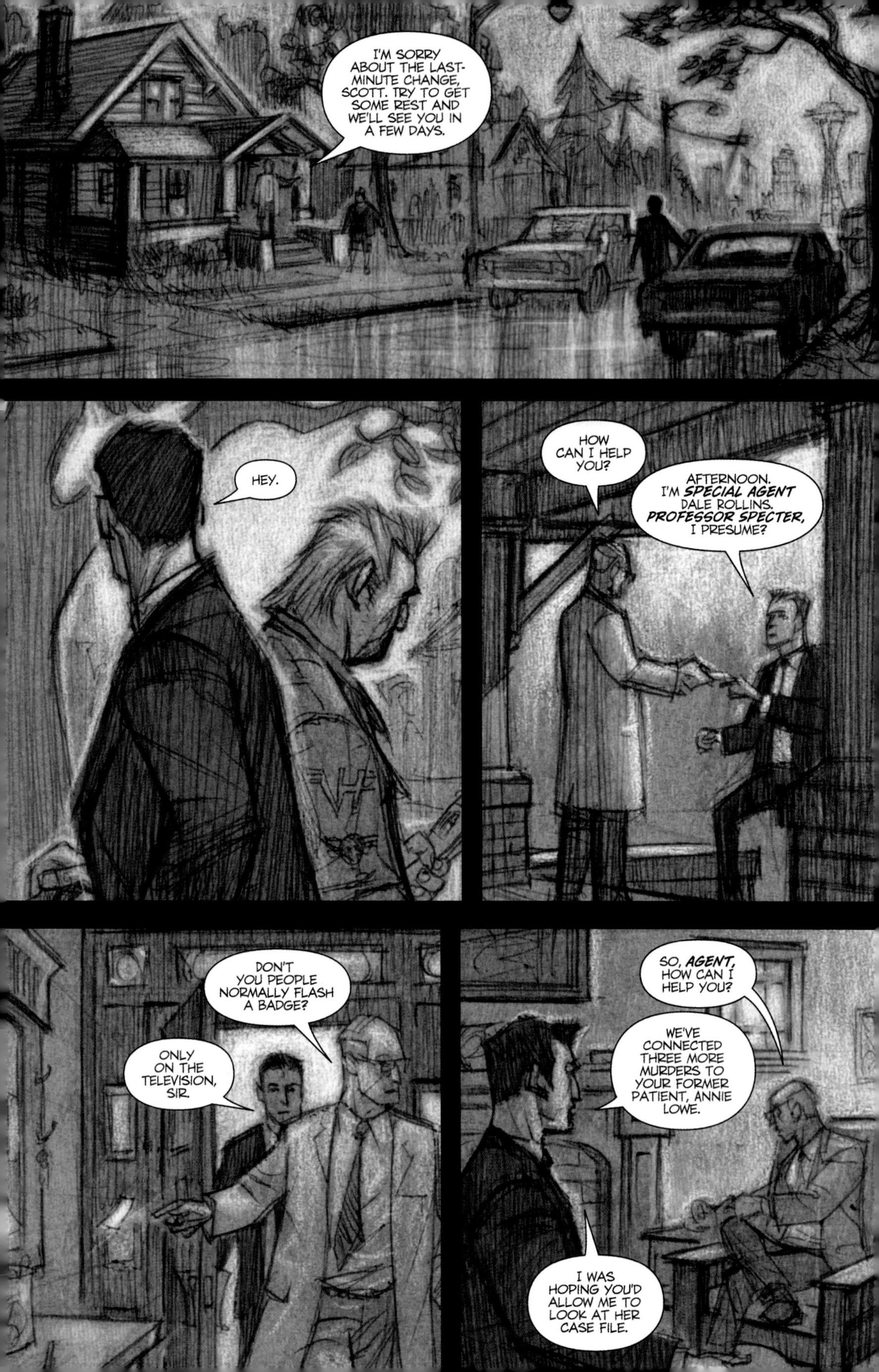
I'M SORRY ABOUT THE LAST-MINUTE CHANGE, SCOTT. TRY TO GET SOME REST AND WE'LL SEE YOU IN A FEW DAYS.
HEY.
HOW CAN I HELP YOU?
AFTERNOON. I'M SPECIAL AGENT DALE ROLLINS. PROFESSOR SPECTER, I PRESUME?
DON'T YOU PEOPLE NORMALLY FLASH A BADGE?
ONLY ON THE TELEVISION, SIR.
SO, AGENT, HOW CAN I HELP YOU?
WE'VE CONNECTED THREE MORE MURDERS TO YOUR FORMER PATIENT, ANNIE LOWE.
I WAS HOPING YOU'D ALLOW ME TO LOOK AT HER CASE FILE.

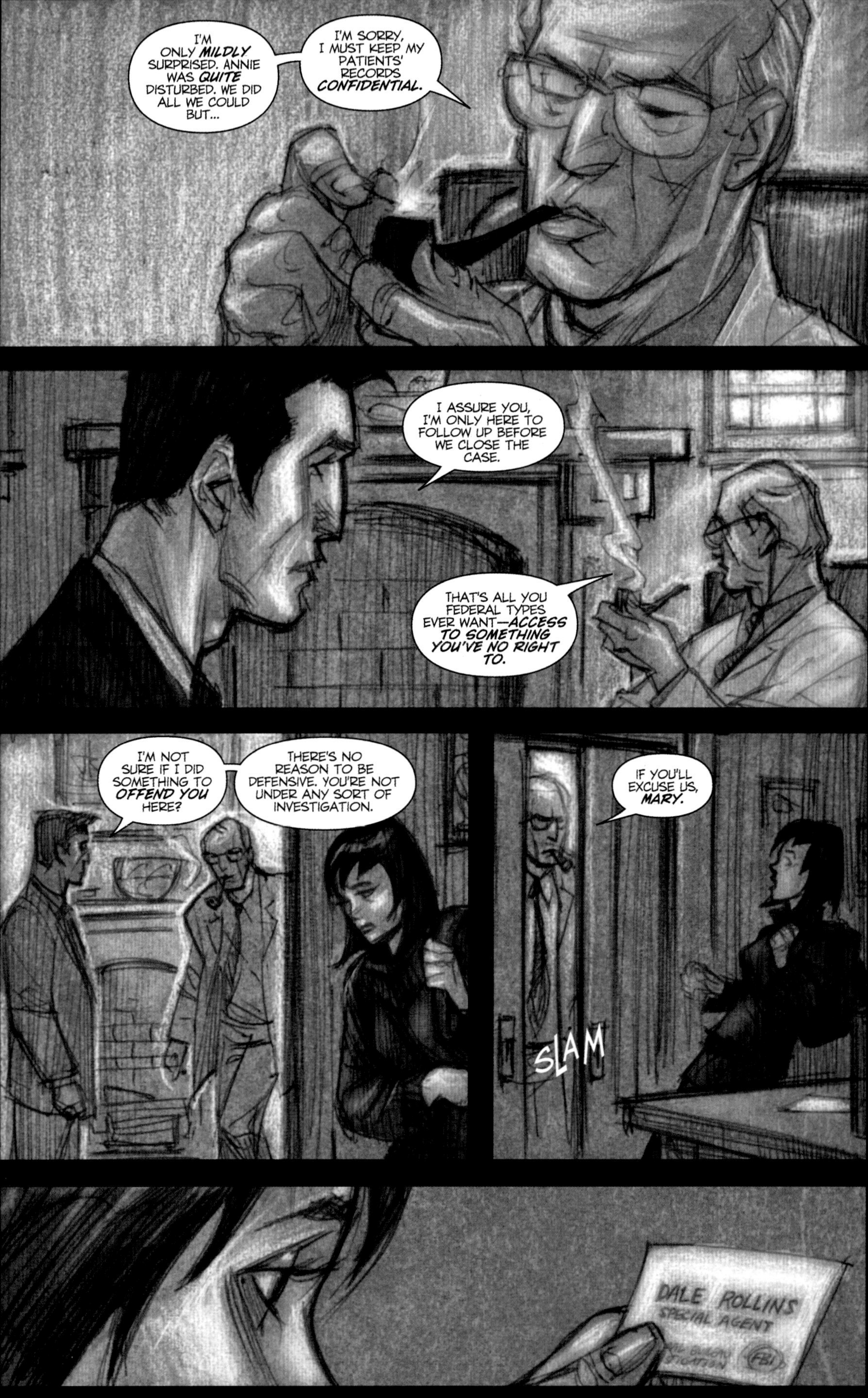

I'M ONLY *MILDLY* SURPRISED. ANNIE WAS *QUITE* DISTURBED. WE DID ALL WE COULD BUT...
I'M SORRY, I MUST KEEP MY PATIENTS' RECORDS *CONFIDENTIAL.*
I ASSURE YOU, I'M ONLY HERE TO FOLLOW UP BEFORE WE CLOSE THE CASE.
THAT'S ALL YOU FEDERAL TYPES EVER WANT—*ACCESS TO SOMETHING YOU'VE NO RIGHT TO.*
I'M NOT SURE IF I DID SOMETHING TO *OFFEND YOU* HERE?
THERE'S NO REASON TO BE DEFENSIVE. YOU'RE NOT UNDER ANY SORT OF INVESTIGATION.
IF YOU'LL EXCUSE US, *MARY.*
SLAM
DALE ROLLINS
SPECIAL AGENT
FBI

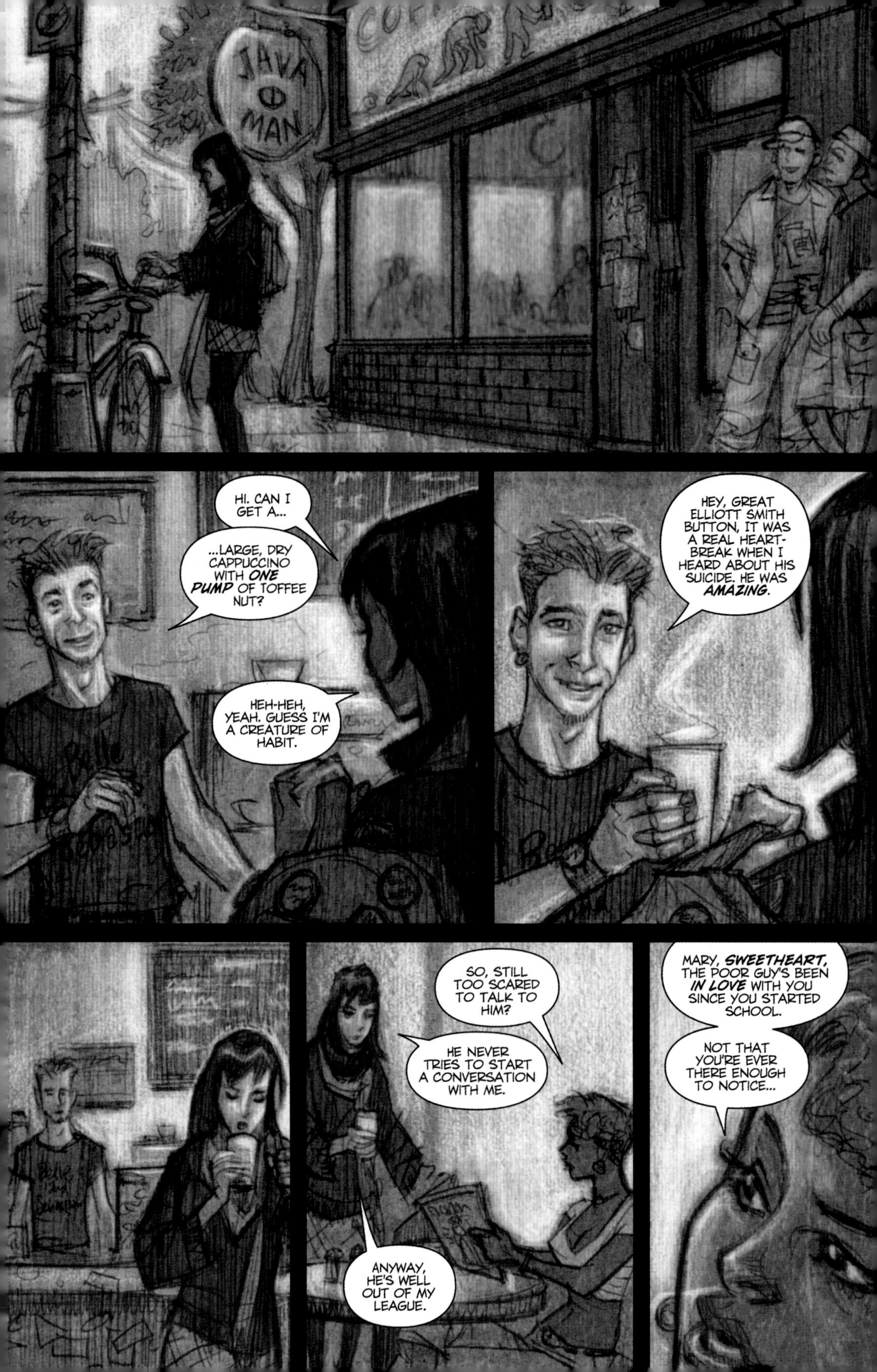

JAVA MAN
HI. CAN I GET A...
...LARGE, DRY CAPPUCCINO WITH ONE PUMP OF TOFFEE NUT?
HEH-HEH, YEAH. GUESS I'M A CREATURE OF HABIT.
HEY, GREAT ELLIOTT SMITH BUTTON, IT WAS A REAL HEART-BREAK WHEN I HEARD ABOUT HIS SUICIDE. HE WAS AMAZING.
SO, STILL TOO SCARED TO TALK TO HIM?
HE NEVER TRIES TO START A CONVERSATION WITH ME.
ANYWAY, HE'S WELL OUT OF MY LEAGUE.
MARY, SWEETHEART, THE POOR GUY'S BEEN IN LOVE WITH YOU SINCE YOU STARTED SCHOOL.
NOT THAT YOU'RE EVER THERE ENOUGH TO NOTICE...

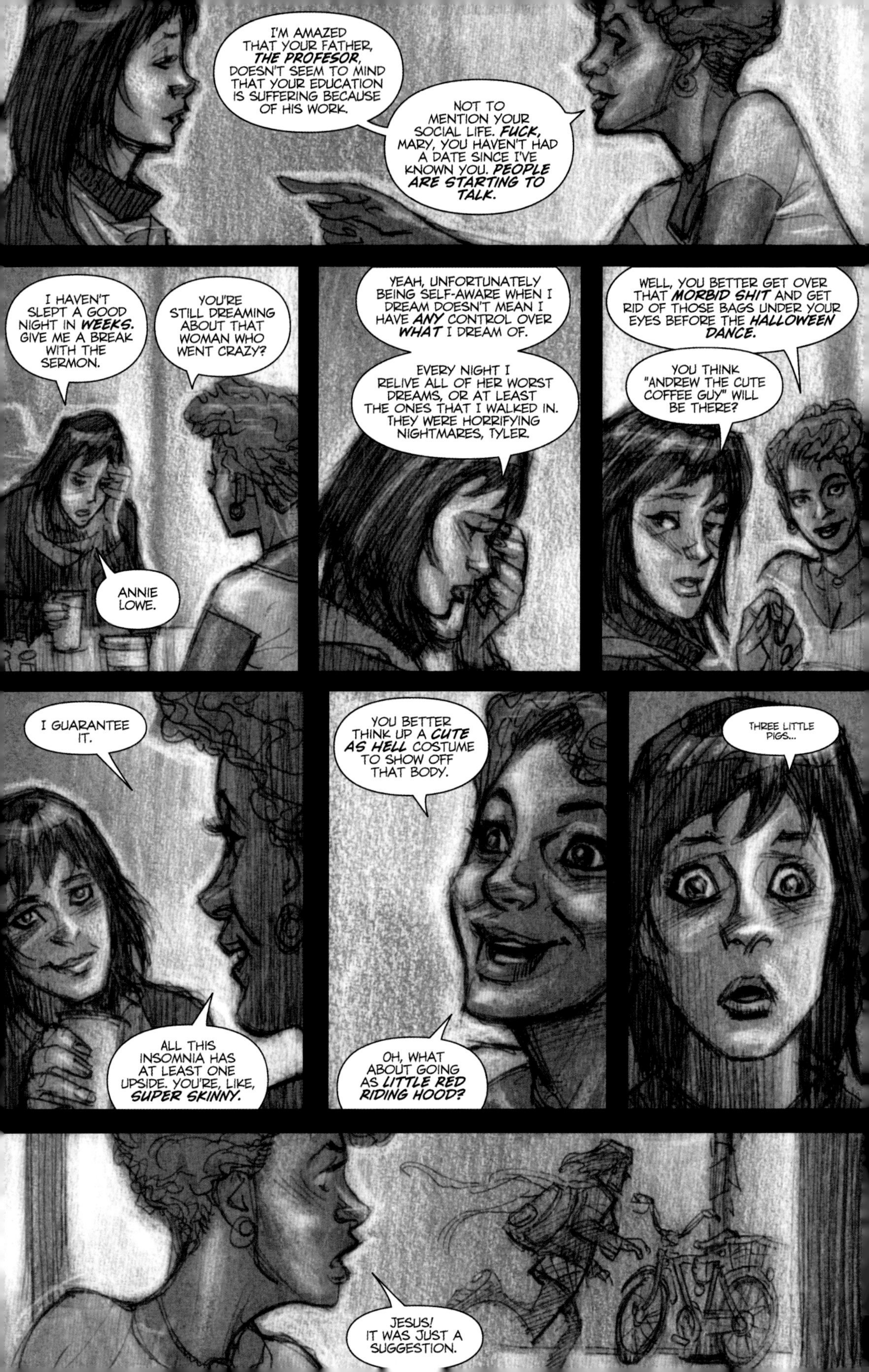
I'M AMAZED THAT YOUR FATHER, THE PROFESOR, DOESN'T SEEM TO MIND THAT YOUR EDUCATION IS SUFFERING BECAUSE OF HIS WORK.
NOT TO MENTION YOUR SOCIAL LIFE. FUCK, MARY, YOU HAVEN'T HAD A DATE SINCE I'VE KNOWN YOU. PEOPLE ARE STARTING TO TALK.
I HAVEN'T SLEPT A GOOD NIGHT IN WEEKS. GIVE ME A BREAK WITH THE SERMON.
YOU'RE STILL DREAMING ABOUT THAT WOMAN WHO WENT CRAZY?
ANNIE LOWE.
YEAH, UNFORTUNATELY BEING SELF-AWARE WHEN I DREAM DOESN'T MEAN I HAVE ANY CONTROL OVER WHAT I DREAM OF.
EVERY NIGHT I RELIVE ALL OF HER WORST DREAMS, OR AT LEAST THE ONES THAT I WALKED IN. THEY WERE HORRIFYING NIGHTMARES, TYLER.
WELL, YOU BETTER GET OVER THAT MORBID SHIT AND GET RID OF THOSE BAGS UNDER YOUR EYES BEFORE THE HALLOWEEN DANCE.
YOU THINK "ANDREW THE CUTE COFFEE GUY" WILL BE THERE?
I GUARANTEE IT.
ALL THIS INSOMNIA HAS AT LEAST ONE UPSIDE. YOU'RE, LIKE, SUPER SKINNY.
YOU BETTER THINK UP A CUTE AS HELL COSTUME TO SHOW OFF THAT BODY.
OH, WHAT ABOUT GOING AS LITTLE RED RIDING HOOD?
THREE LITTLE PIGS...
JESUS! IT WAS JUST A SUGGESTION.

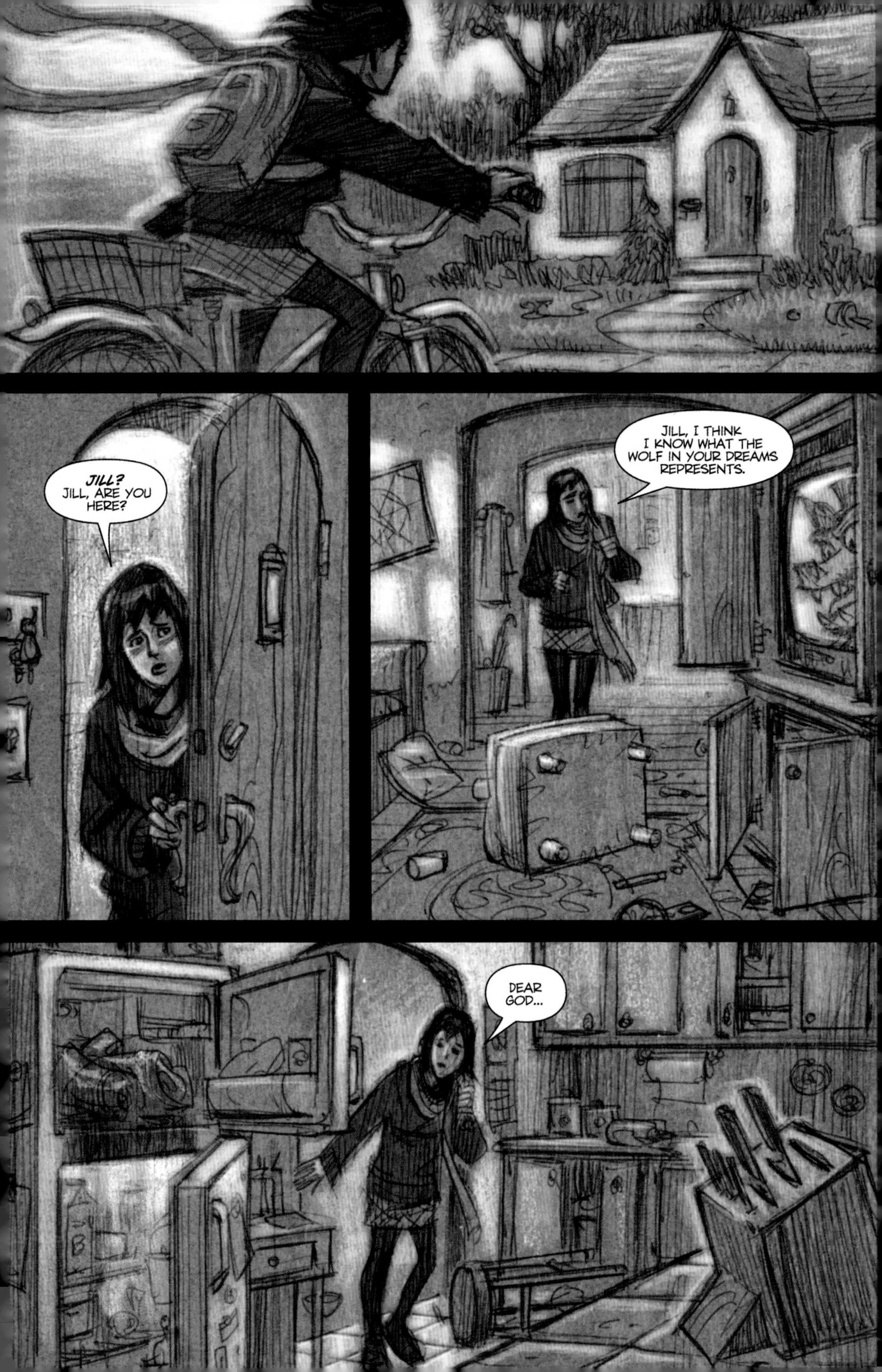
JILL?
JILL, ARE YOU HERE?
JILL, I THINK I KNOW WHAT THE WOLF IN YOUR DREAMS REPRESENTS.
DEAR GOD...

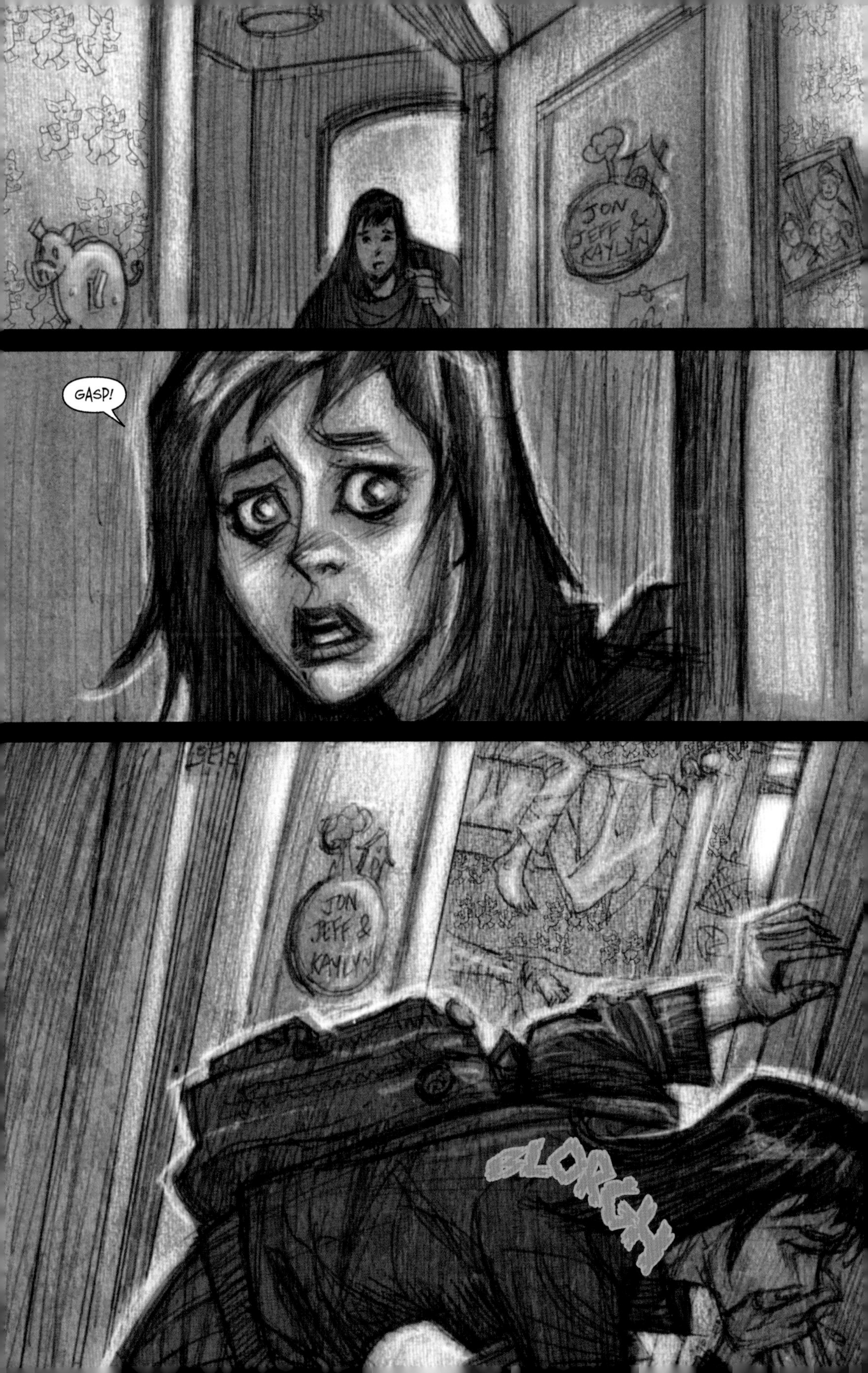
JON JEFF & KAYLYN
GASP!
JON JEFF & KAYLYN
GLORGH

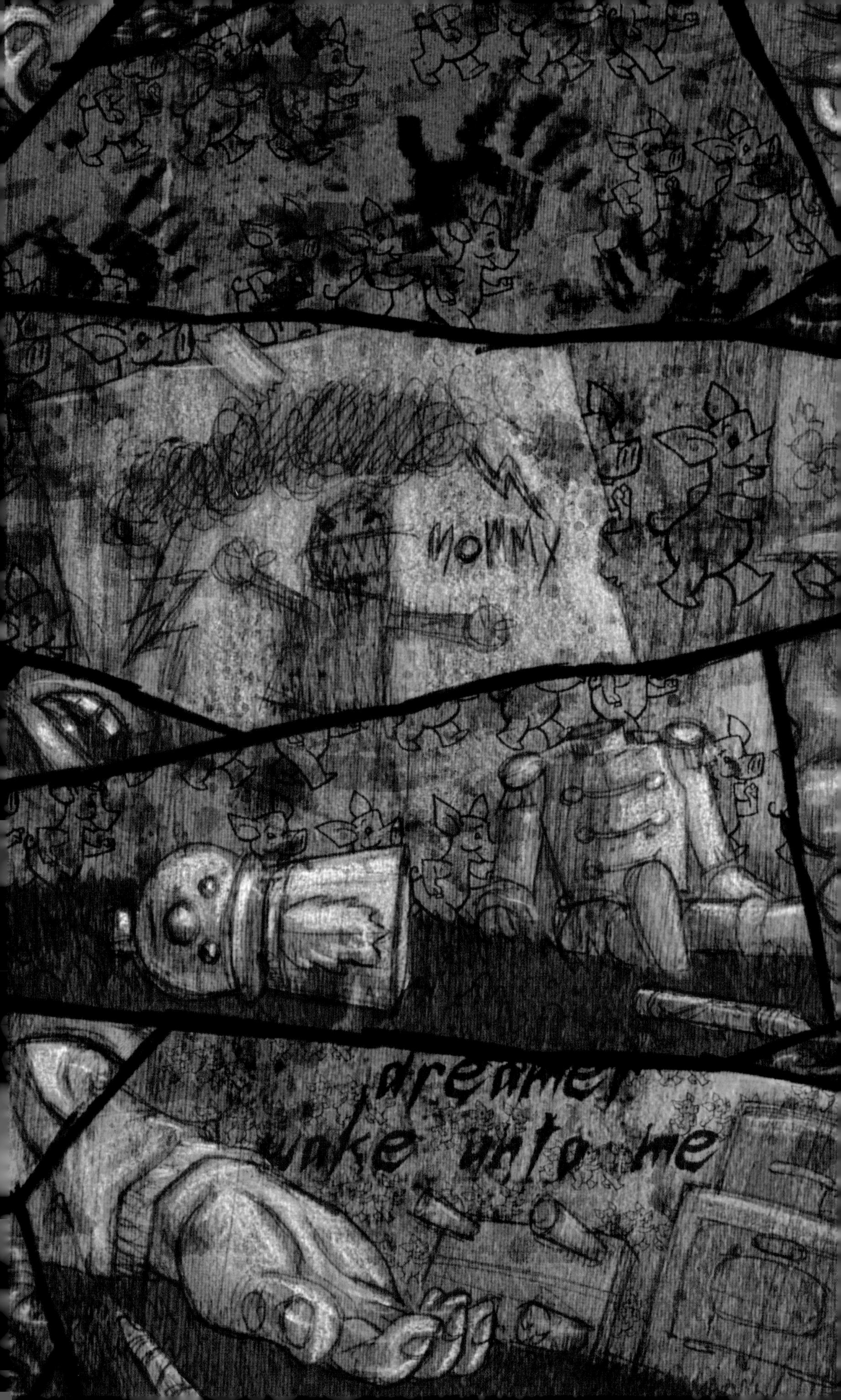
MOMMY
dreamer
wake unto me

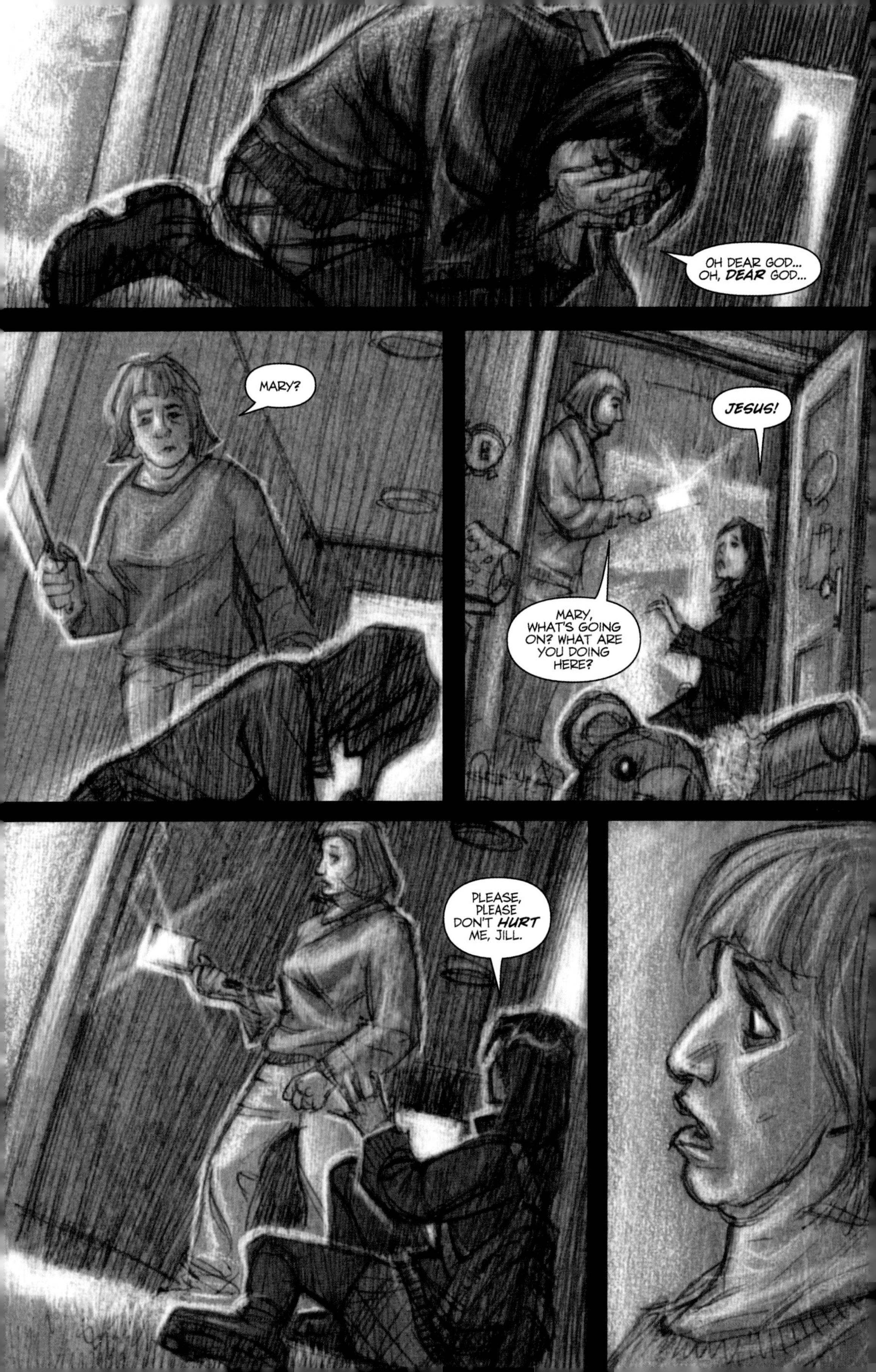
OH DEAR GOD...
OH, DEAR GOD...
MARY?
JESUS!
MARY, WHAT'S GOING ON? WHAT ARE YOU DOING HERE?
PLEASE, PLEASE DON'T HURT ME, JILL.

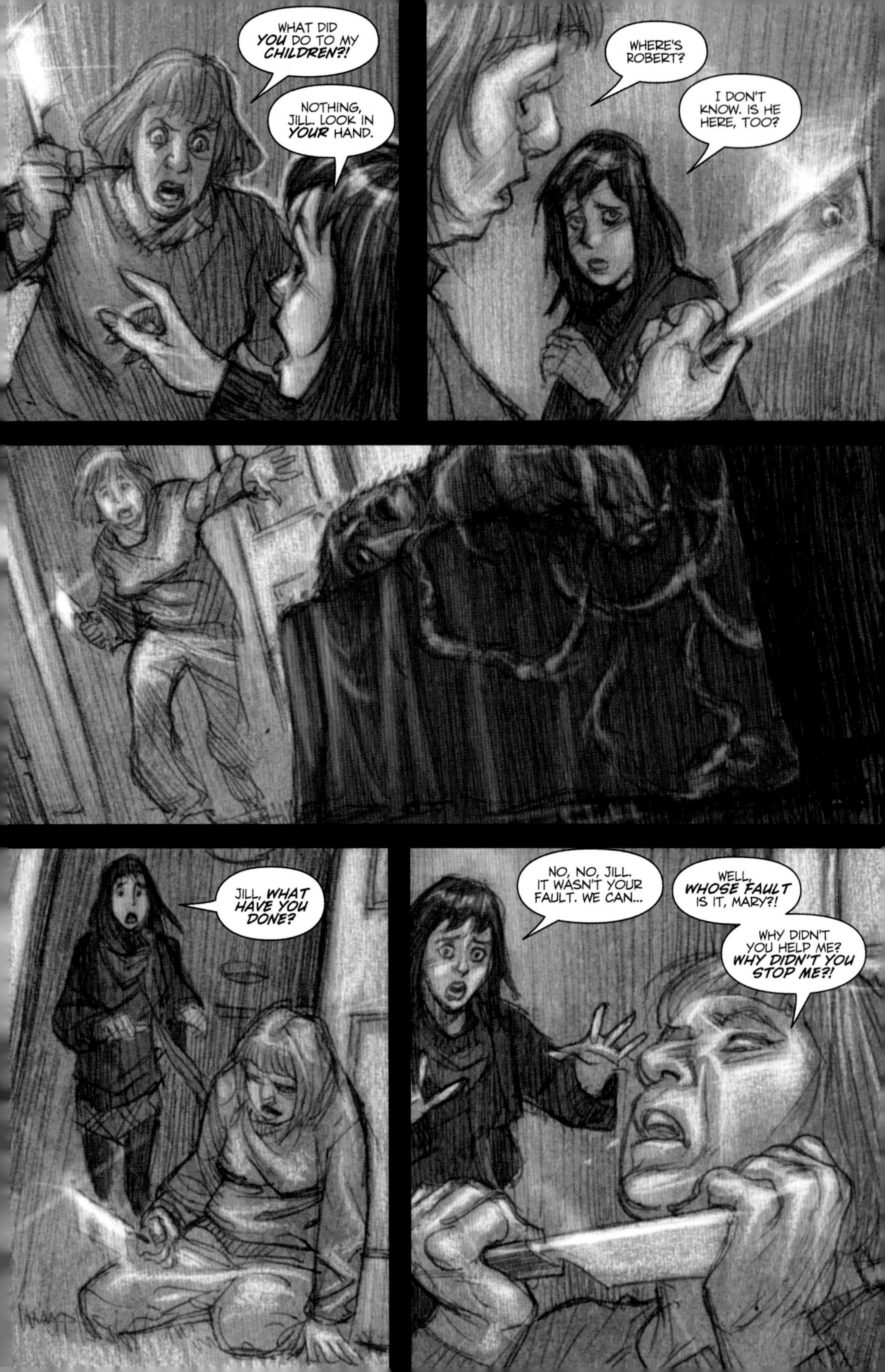
WHAT DID *YOU* DO TO MY *CHILDREN?!*
NOTHING, JILL. LOOK IN *YOUR* HAND.
WHERE'S ROBERT?
I DON'T KNOW. IS HE HERE, TOO?
JILL, *WHAT HAVE YOU DONE?*
NO, NO, JILL. IT WASN'T YOUR FAULT. WE CAN...
WELL, *WHOSE FAULT* IS IT, MARY?!
WHY DIDN'T YOU HELP ME? *WHY DIDN'T YOU STOP ME?!*

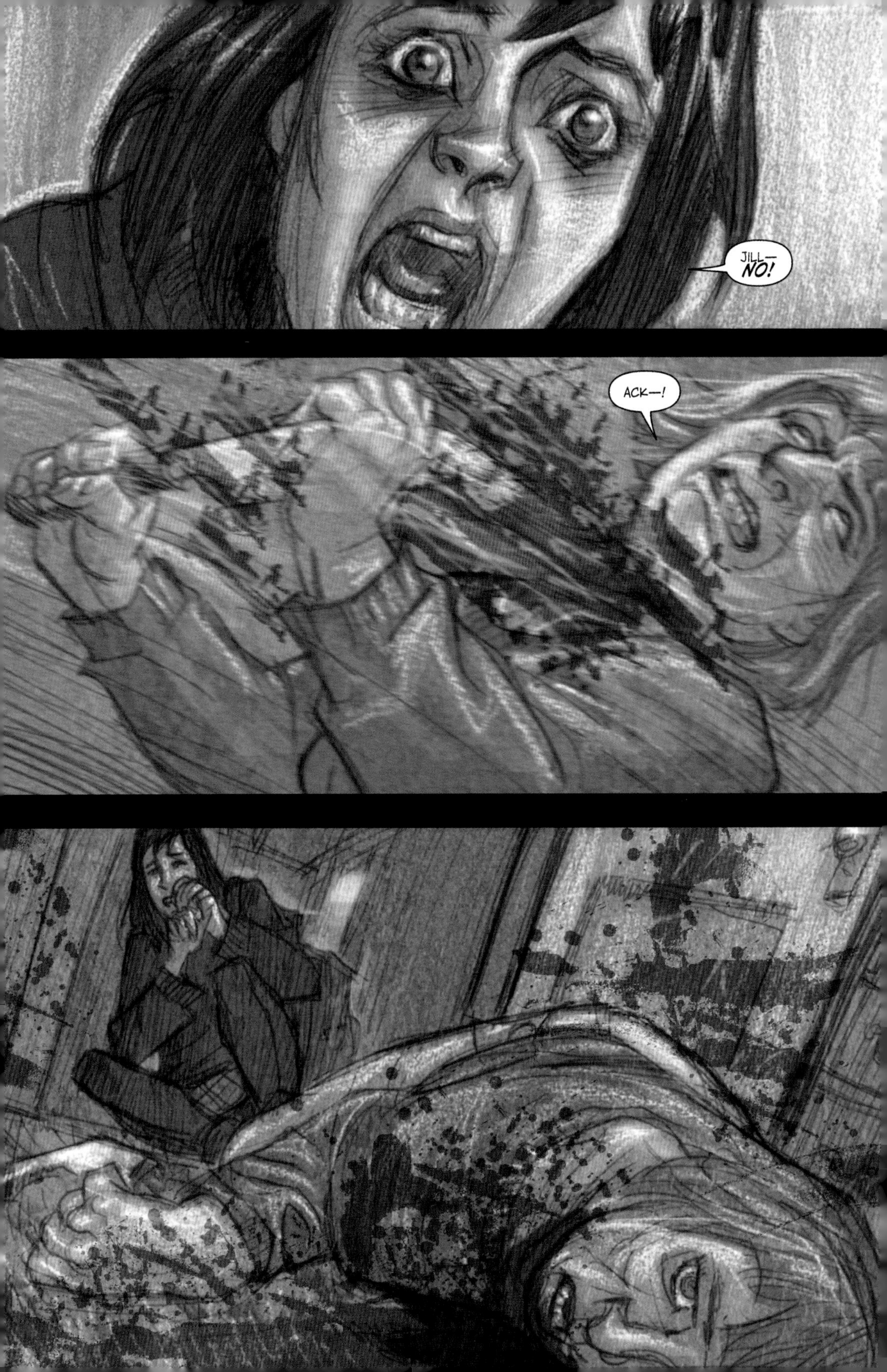
JILL—
NO!
ACK—!

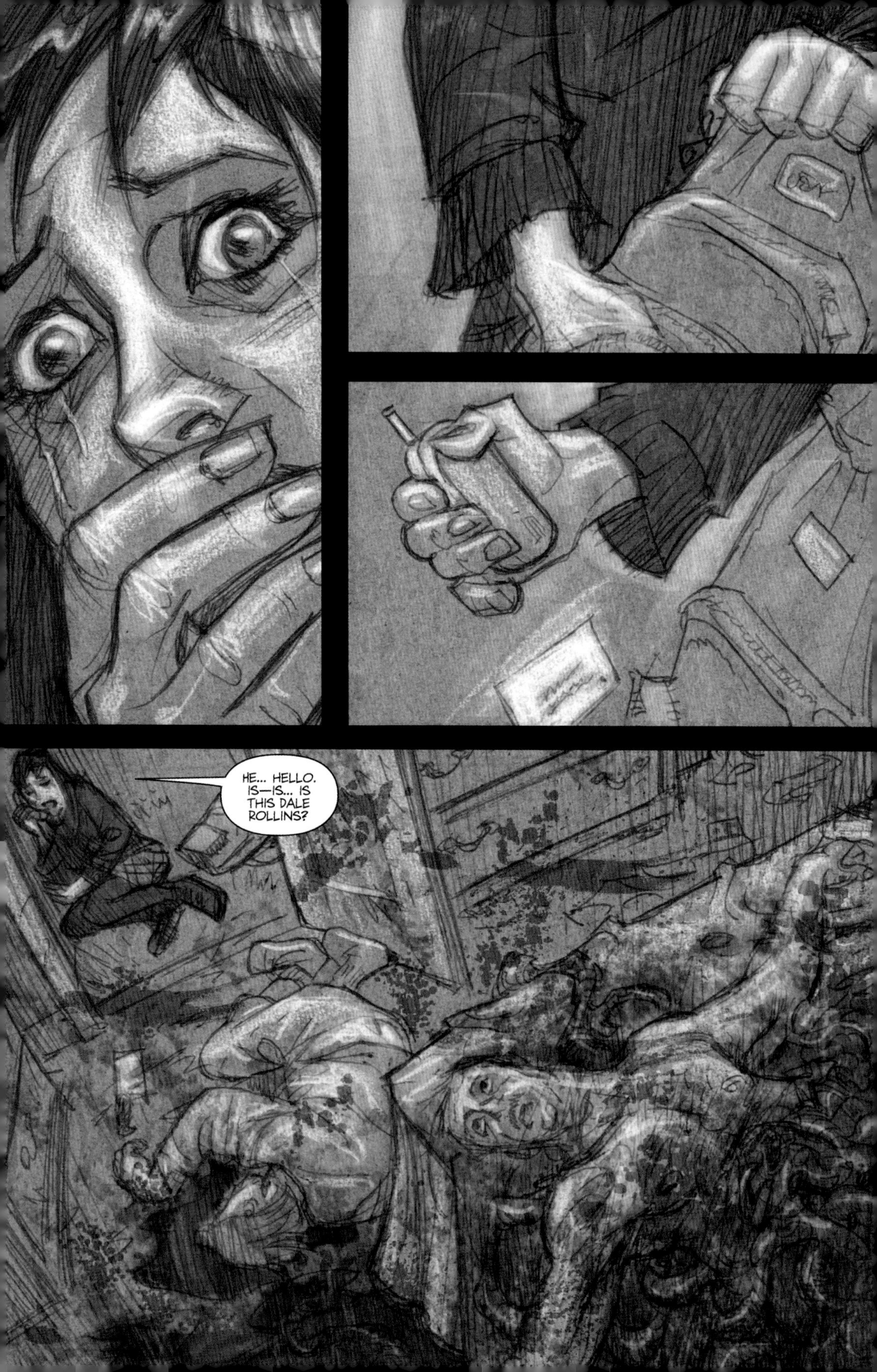
HE... HELLO. IS—IS... IS THIS DALE ROLLINS?

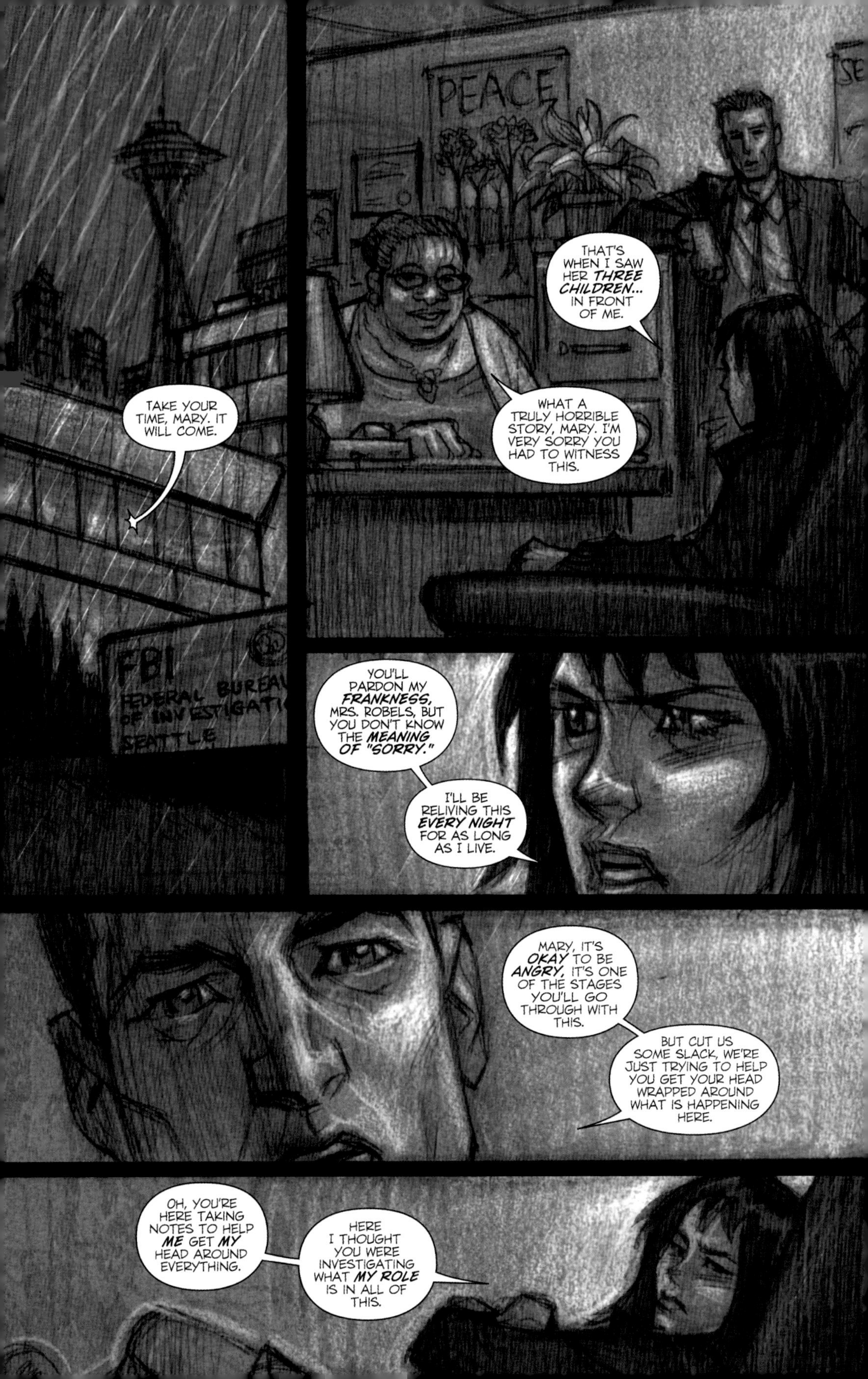
PEACE
TAKE YOUR TIME, MARY. IT WILL COME.
FBI
FEDERAL BUREAU OF INVESTIGATI
SEATTLE
THAT'S WHEN I SAW HER ***THREE CHILDREN...*** IN FRONT OF ME.
WHAT A TRULY HORRIBLE STORY, MARY. I'M VERY SORRY YOU HAD TO WITNESS THIS.
YOU'LL PARDON MY ***FRANKNESS,*** MRS. ROBELS, BUT YOU DON'T KNOW THE ***MEANING OF "SORRY."***
I'LL BE RELIVING THIS ***EVERY NIGHT*** FOR AS LONG AS I LIVE.
MARY, IT'S ***OKAY*** TO BE ***ANGRY,*** IT'S ONE OF THE STAGES YOU'LL GO THROUGH WITH THIS.
BUT CUT US SOME SLACK, WE'RE JUST TRYING TO HELP YOU GET YOUR HEAD WRAPPED AROUND WHAT IS HAPPENING HERE.
OH, YOU'RE HERE TAKING NOTES TO HELP ***ME*** GET ***MY*** HEAD AROUND EVERYTHING.
HERE I THOUGHT YOU WERE INVESTIGATING WHAT ***MY ROLE*** IS IN ALL OF THIS.

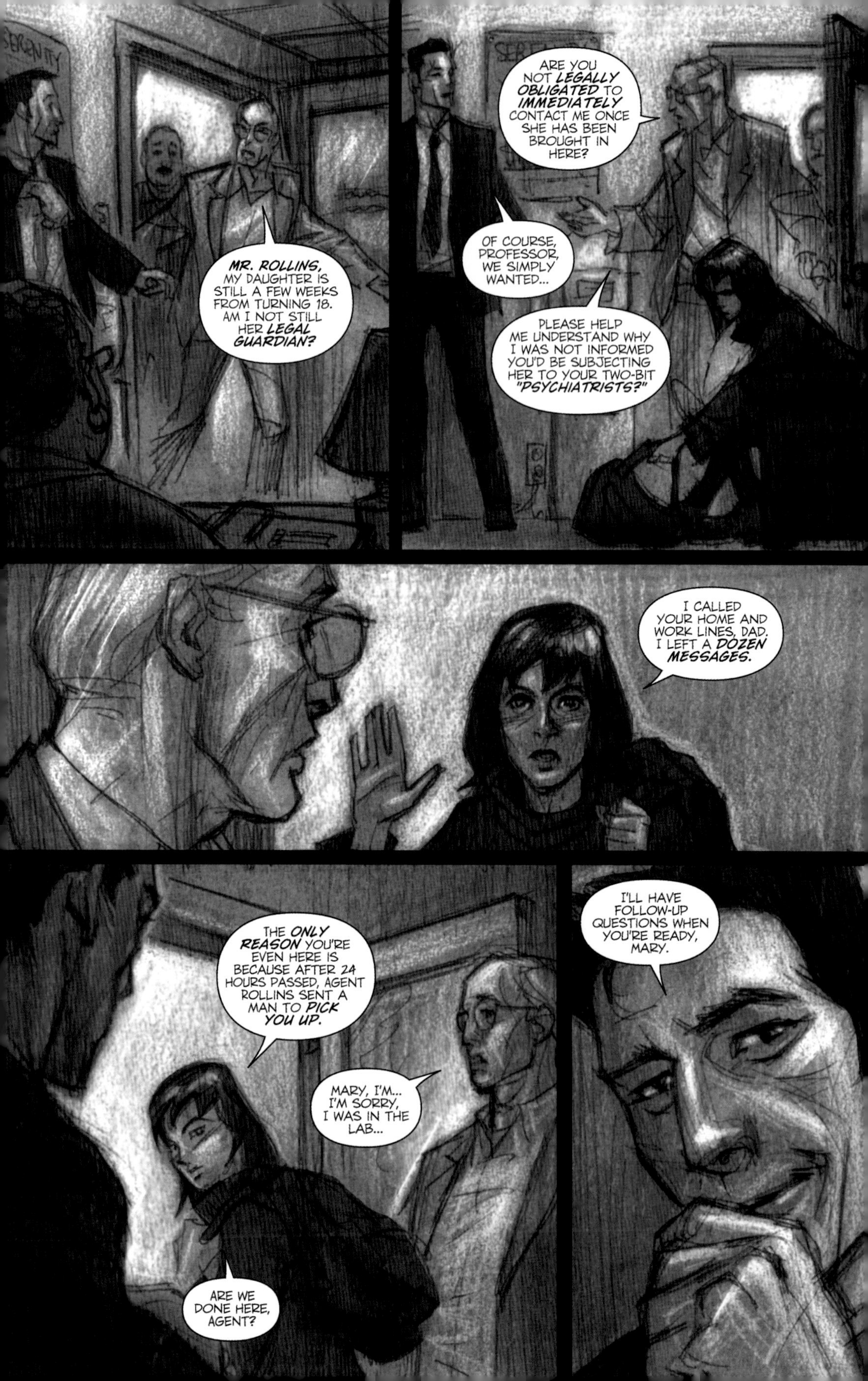
MR. ROLLINS, MY DAUGHTER IS STILL A FEW WEEKS FROM TURNING 18. AM I NOT STILL HER LEGAL GUARDIAN?
ARE YOU NOT LEGALLY OBLIGATED TO IMMEDIATELY CONTACT ME ONCE SHE HAS BEEN BROUGHT IN HERE?
OF COURSE, PROFESSOR, WE SIMPLY WANTED...
PLEASE HELP ME UNDERSTAND WHY I WAS NOT INFORMED YOU'D BE SUBJECTING HER TO YOUR TWO-BIT "PSYCHIATRISTS?"
I CALLED YOUR HOME AND WORK LINES, DAD. I LEFT A DOZEN MESSAGES.
THE ONLY REASON YOU'RE EVEN HERE IS BECAUSE AFTER 24 HOURS PASSED, AGENT ROLLINS SENT A MAN TO PICK YOU UP.
MARY, I'M... I'M SORRY, I WAS IN THE LAB...
ARE WE DONE HERE, AGENT?
I'LL HAVE FOLLOW-UP QUESTIONS WHEN YOU'RE READY, MARY.

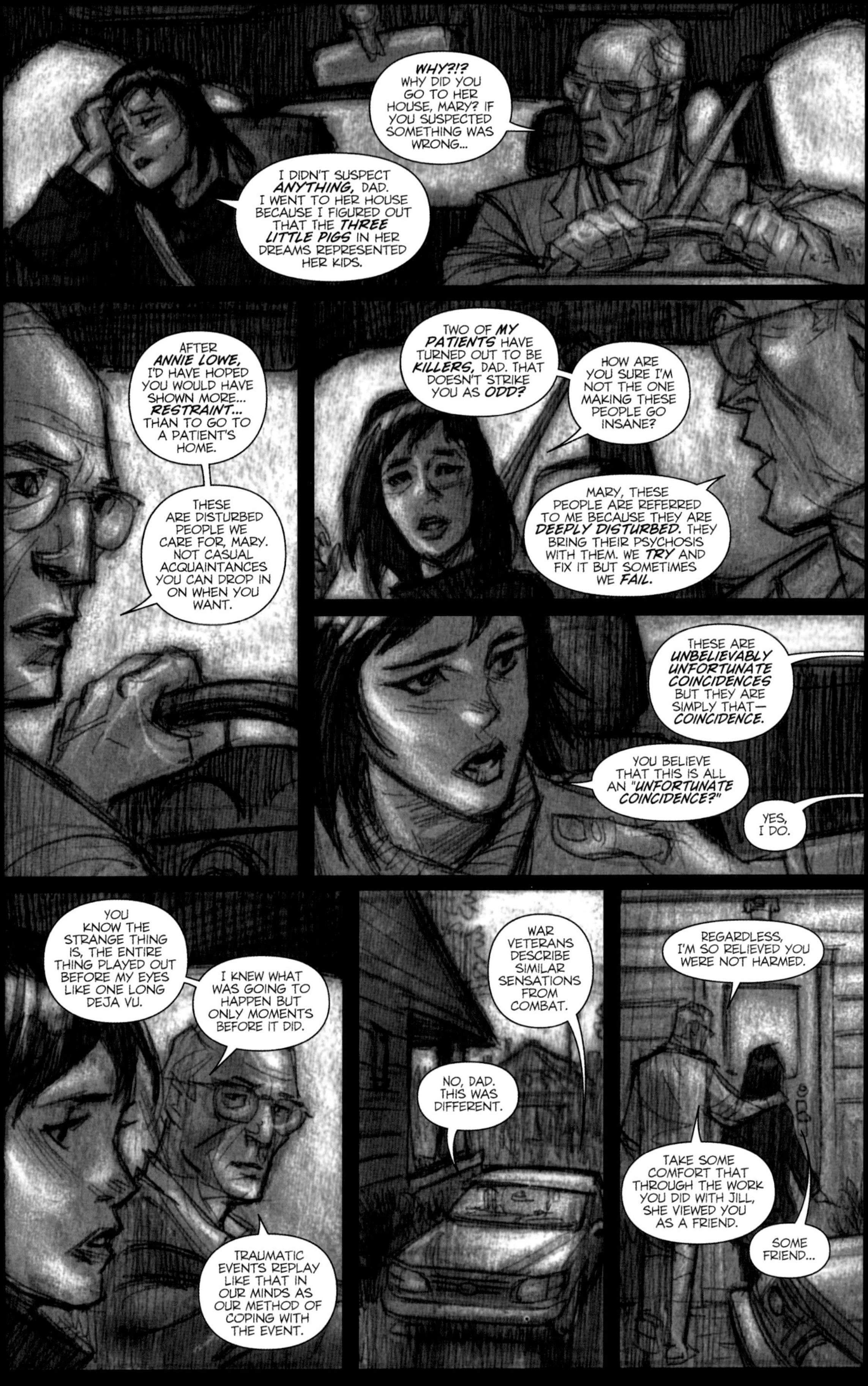
WHY?!? WHY DID YOU GO TO HER HOUSE, MARY? IF YOU SUSPECTED SOMETHING WAS WRONG...
I DIDN'T SUSPECT ANYTHING, DAD. I WENT TO HER HOUSE BECAUSE I FIGURED OUT THAT THE THREE LITTLE PIGS IN HER DREAMS REPRESENTED HER KIDS.
AFTER ANNIE LOWE, I'D HAVE HOPED YOU WOULD HAVE SHOWN MORE... RESTRAINT... THAN TO GO TO A PATIENT'S HOME.
THESE ARE DISTURBED PEOPLE WE CARE FOR, MARY. NOT CASUAL ACQUAINTANCES YOU CAN DROP IN ON WHEN YOU WANT.
TWO OF MY PATIENTS HAVE TURNED OUT TO BE KILLERS, DAD. THAT DOESN'T STRIKE YOU AS ODD?
HOW ARE YOU SURE I'M NOT THE ONE MAKING THESE PEOPLE GO INSANE?
MARY, THESE PEOPLE ARE REFERRED TO ME BECAUSE THEY ARE DEEPLY DISTURBED. THEY BRING THEIR PSYCHOSIS WITH THEM. WE TRY AND FIX IT BUT SOMETIMES WE FAIL.
THESE ARE UNBELIEVABLY UNFORTUNATE COINCIDENCES BUT THEY ARE SIMPLY THAT—COINCIDENCE.
YOU BELIEVE THAT THIS IS ALL AN "UNFORTUNATE COINCIDENCE?"
YES, I DO.
YOU KNOW THE STRANGE THING IS, THE ENTIRE THING PLAYED OUT BEFORE MY EYES LIKE ONE LONG DEJA VU.
I KNEW WHAT WAS GOING TO HAPPEN BUT ONLY MOMENTS BEFORE IT DID.
TRAUMATIC EVENTS REPLAY LIKE THAT IN OUR MINDS AS OUR METHOD OF COPING WITH THE EVENT.
WAR VETERANS DESCRIBE SIMILAR SENSATIONS FROM COMBAT.
NO, DAD. THIS WAS DIFFERENT.
REGARDLESS, I'M SO RELIEVED YOU WERE NOT HARMED.
TAKE SOME COMFORT THAT THROUGH THE WORK YOU DID WITH JILL, SHE VIEWED YOU AS A FRIEND.
SOME FRIEND...

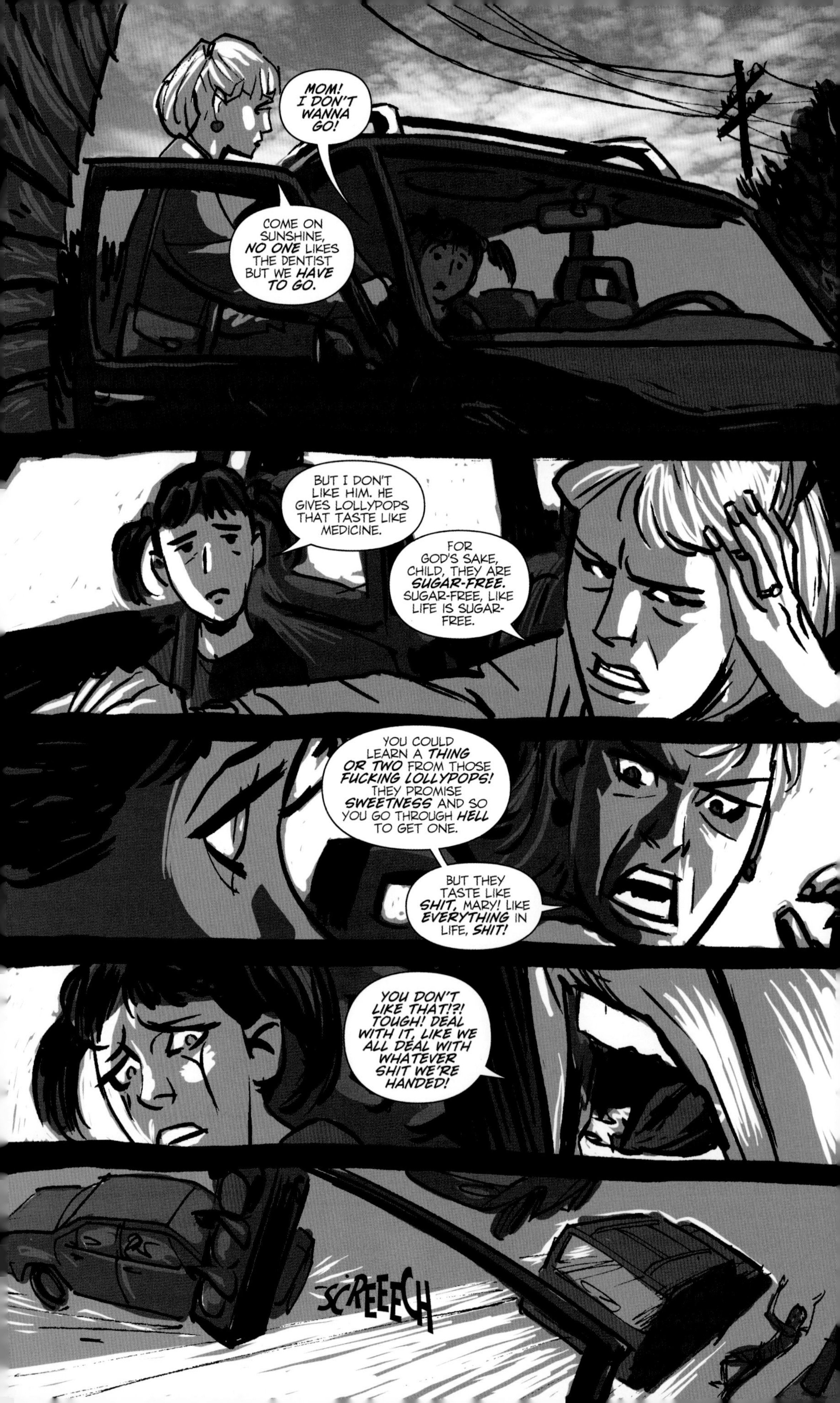

MOM! I DON'T WANNA GO!
COME ON SUNSHINE, NO ONE LIKES THE DENTIST BUT WE HAVE TO GO.
BUT I DON'T LIKE HIM. HE GIVES LOLLYPOPS THAT TASTE LIKE MEDICINE.
FOR GOD'S SAKE, CHILD, THEY ARE SUGAR-FREE. SUGAR-FREE, LIKE LIFE IS SUGAR-FREE.
YOU COULD LEARN A THING OR TWO FROM THOSE FUCKING LOLLYPOPS! THEY PROMISE SWEETNESS AND SO YOU GO THROUGH HELL TO GET ONE.
BUT THEY TASTE LIKE SHIT, MARY! LIKE EVERYTHING IN LIFE, SHIT!
YOU DON'T LIKE THAT!?! TOUGH! DEAL WITH IT, LIKE WE ALL DEAL WITH WHATEVER SHIT WE'RE HANDED!
SCREEECH

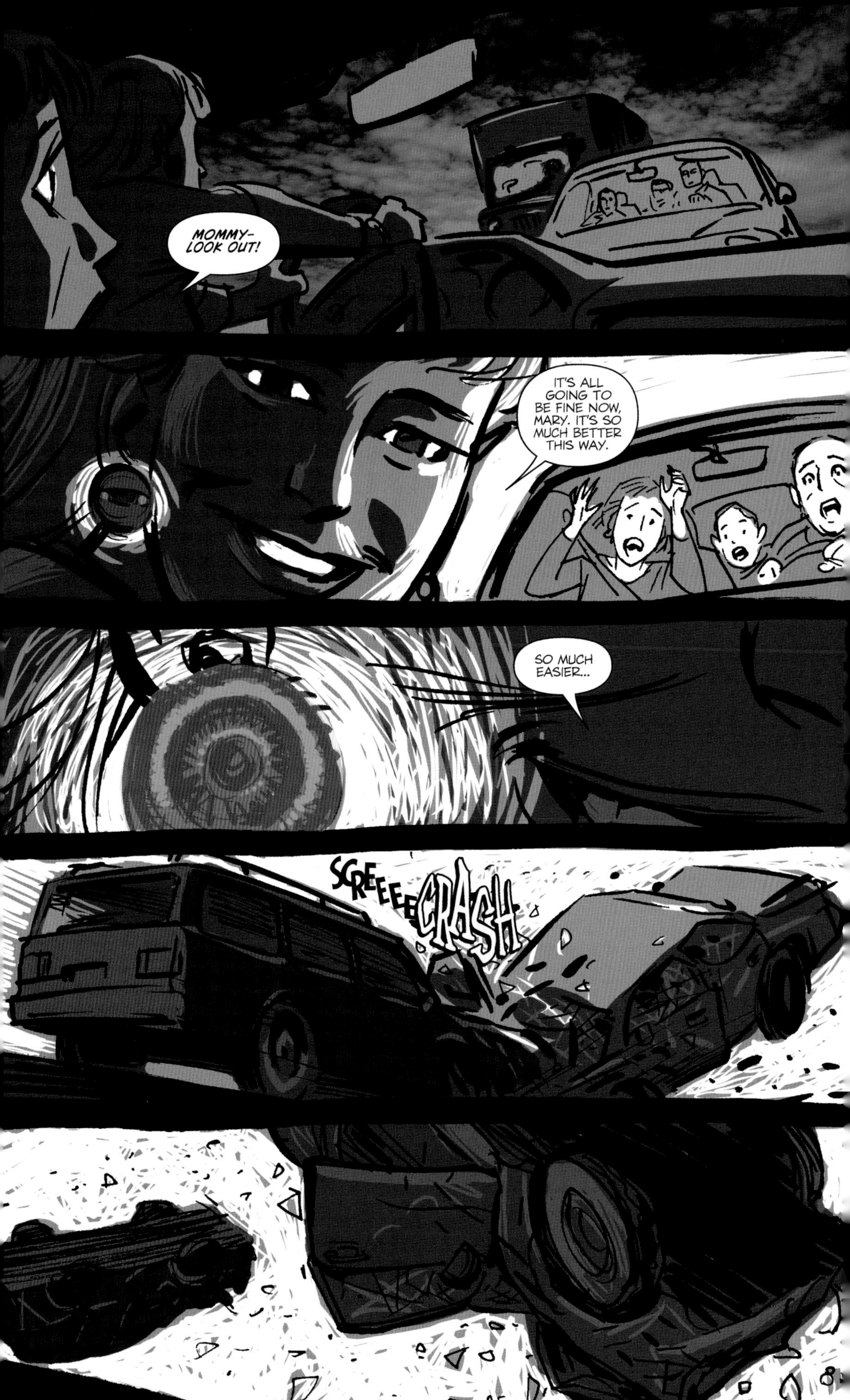
MOMMY-
LOOK OUT!
IT'S ALL GOING TO BE FINE NOW, MARY. IT'S SO MUCH BETTER THIS WAY.
SO MUCH EASIER...
SCREEEEE CRASH

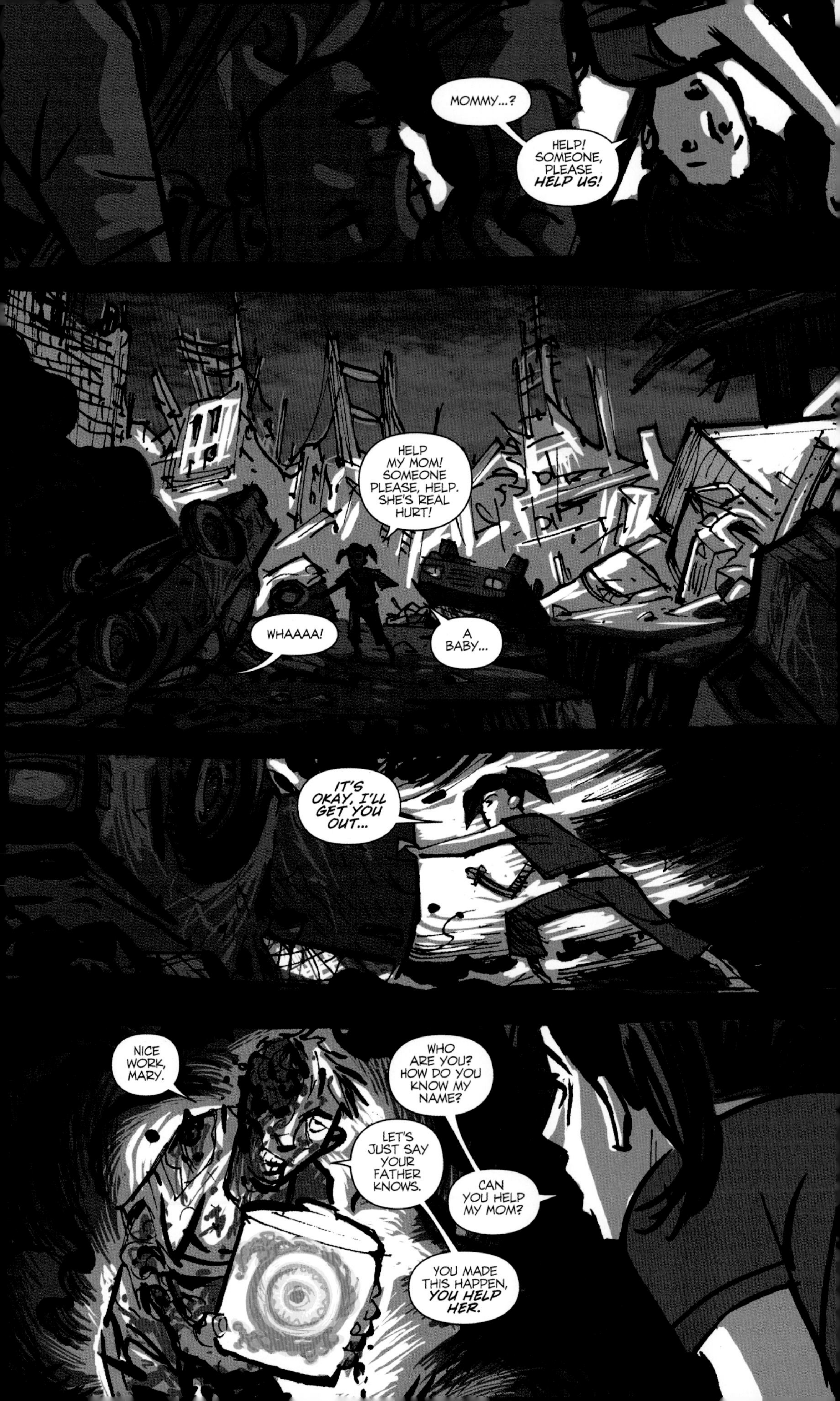
MOMMY...?
HELP! SOMEONE, PLEASE HELP US!
HELP MY MOM! SOMEONE PLEASE, HELP. SHE'S REAL HURT!
WHAAAA!
A BABY...
IT'S OKAY, I'LL GET YOU OUT...
NICE WORK, MARY.
WHO ARE YOU? HOW DO YOU KNOW MY NAME?
LET'S JUST SAY YOUR FATHER KNOWS.
CAN YOU HELP MY MOM?
YOU MADE THIS HAPPEN, YOU HELP HER.

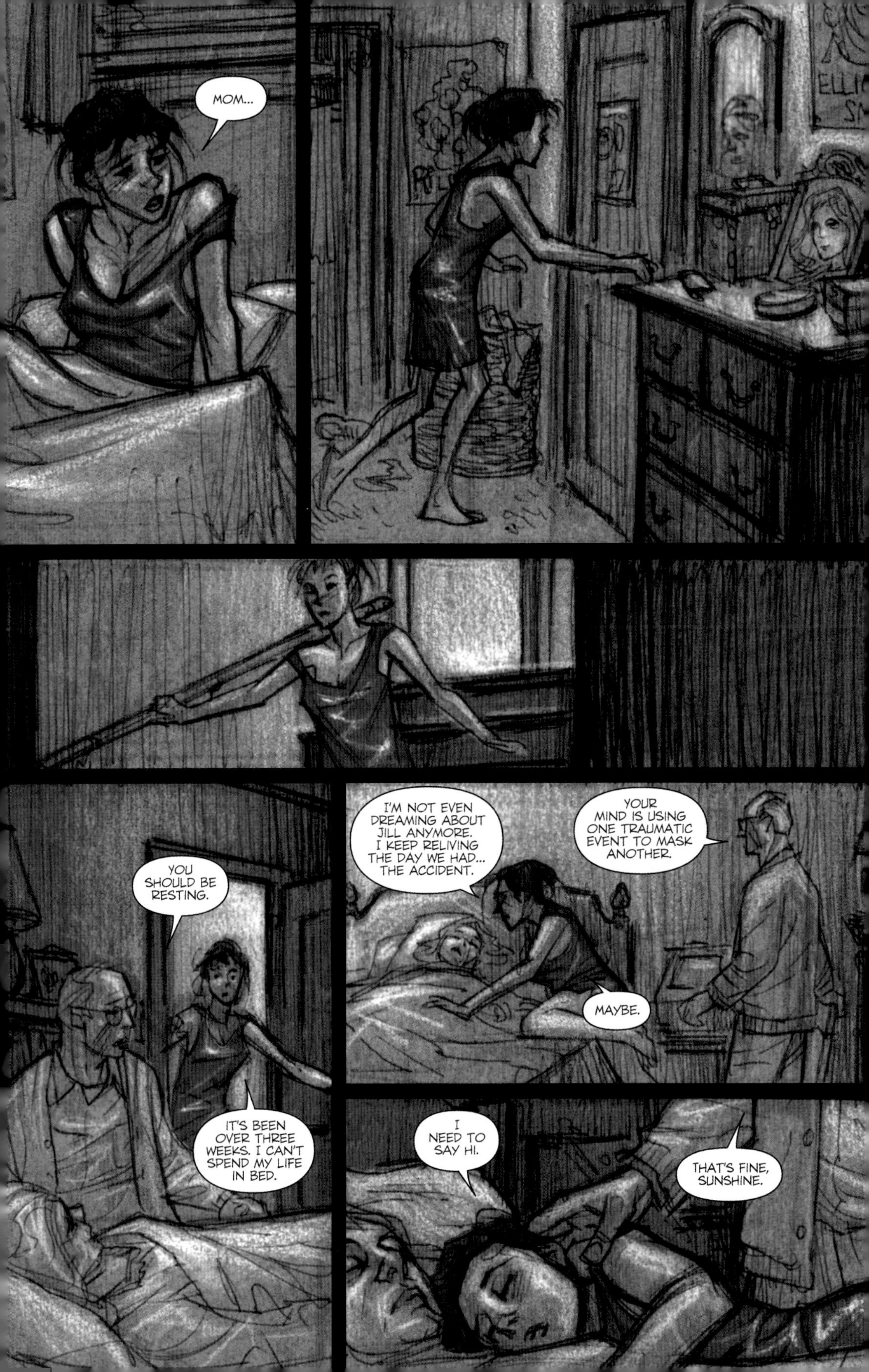
MOM...
YOU SHOULD BE RESTING.
IT'S BEEN OVER THREE WEEKS. I CAN'T SPEND MY LIFE IN BED.
I'M NOT EVEN DREAMING ABOUT JILL ANYMORE. I KEEP RELIVING THE DAY WE HAD... THE ACCIDENT.
YOUR MIND IS USING ONE TRAUMATIC EVENT TO MASK ANOTHER.
MAYBE.
I NEED TO SAY HI.
THAT'S FINE, SUNSHINE.

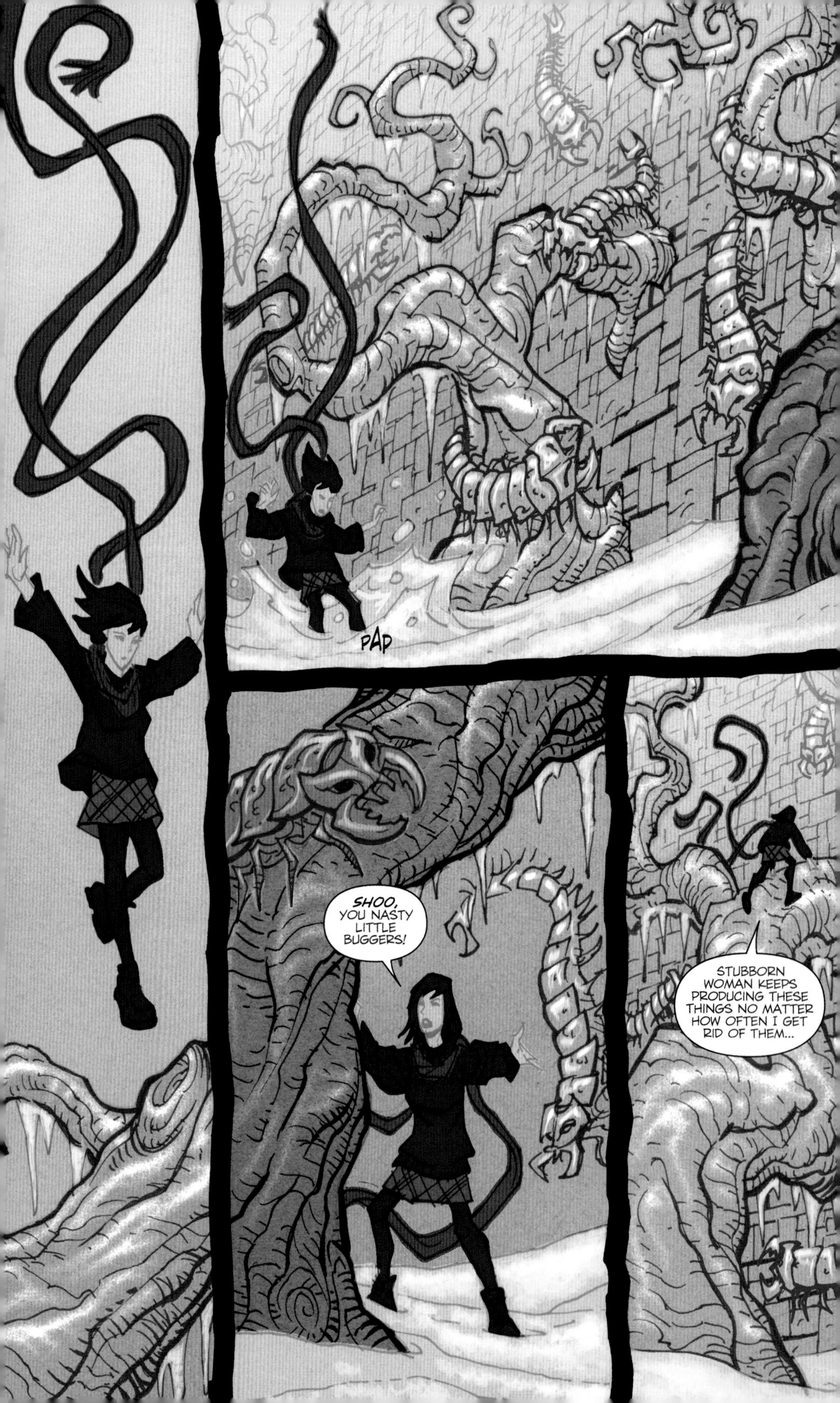
PAP
SHOO, YOU NASTY LITTLE BUGGERS!
STUBBORN WOMAN KEEPS PRODUCING THESE THINGS NO MATTER HOW OFTEN I GET RID OF THEM...

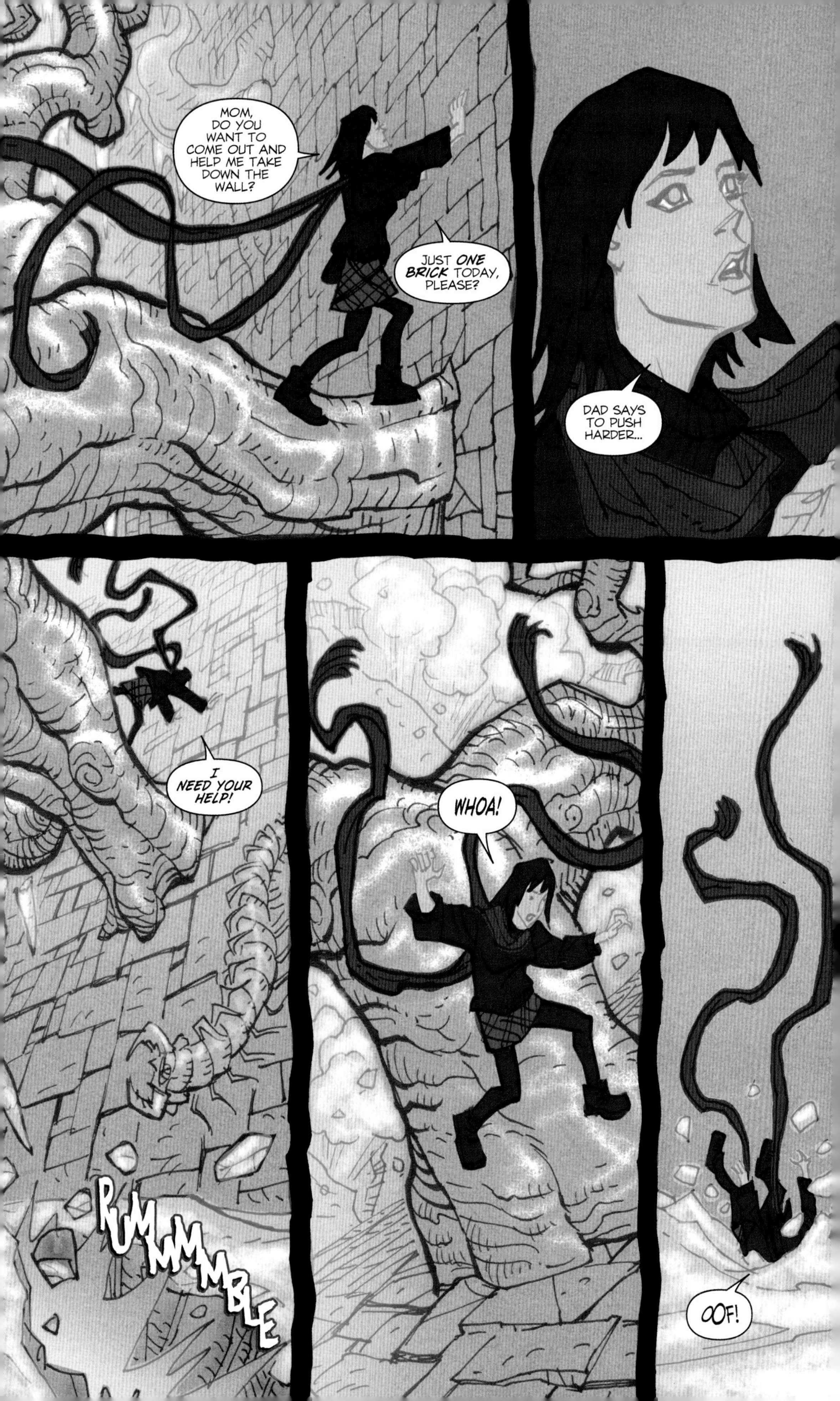
MOM, DO YOU WANT TO COME OUT AND HELP ME TAKE DOWN THE WALL?
JUST ONE BRICK TODAY, PLEASE?
DAD SAYS TO PUSH HARDER...
I NEED YOUR HELP!
RUMMMMBLE
WHOA!
OOF!

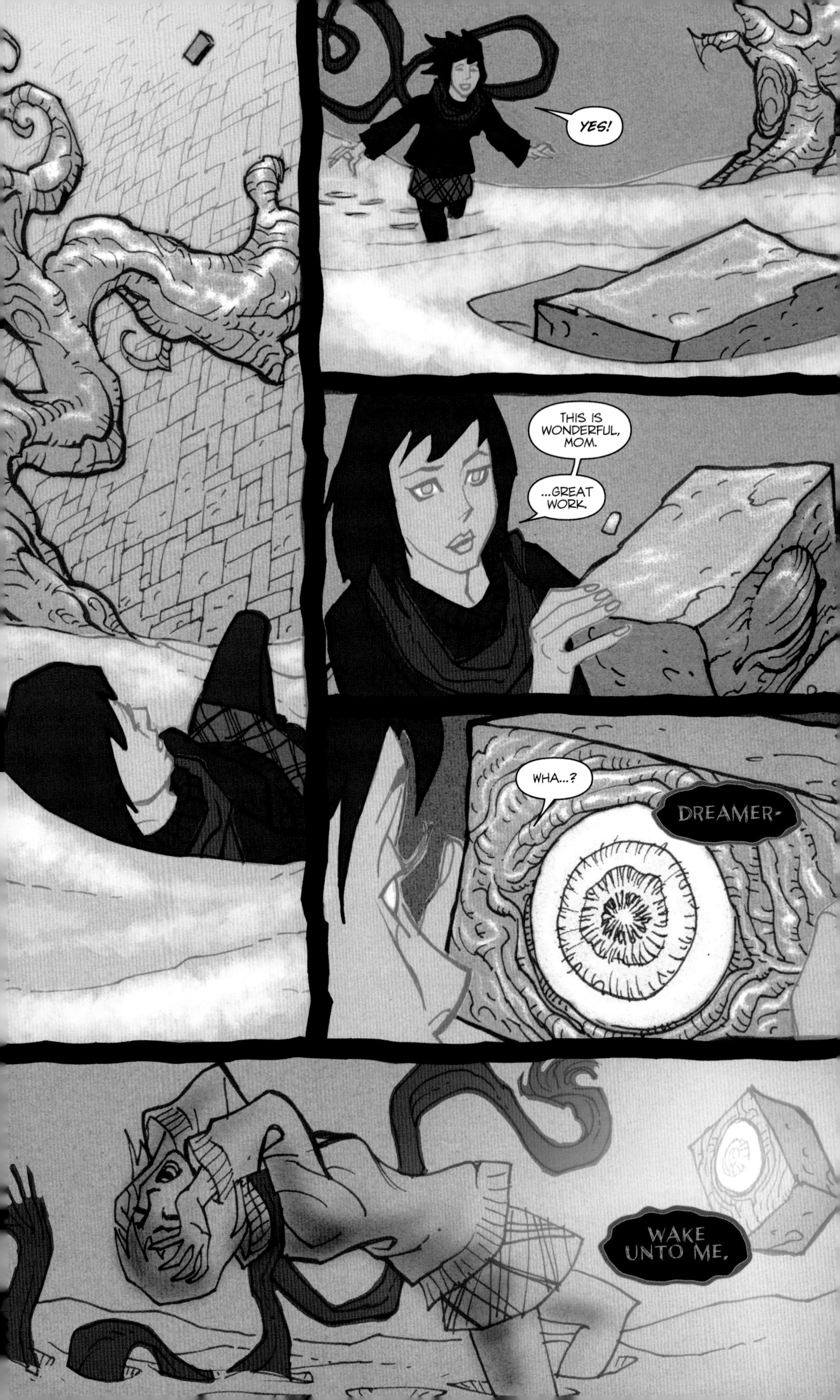
YES!
THIS IS WONDERFUL, MOM.
...GREAT WORK.
WHA...?
DREAMER-
WAKE UNTO ME.

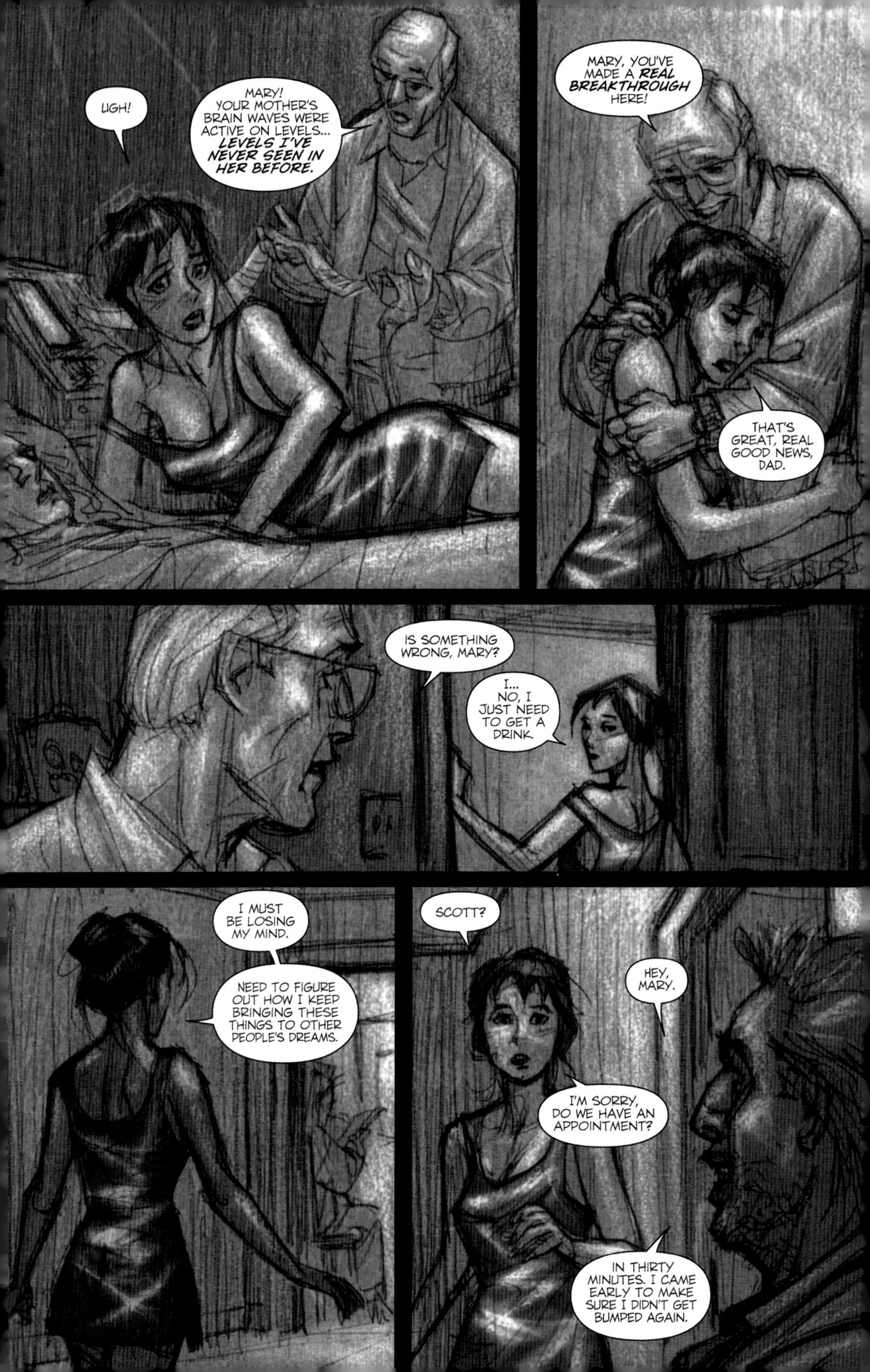
UGH!
MARY! YOUR MOTHER'S BRAIN WAVES WERE ACTIVE ON LEVELS... ***LEVELS I'VE NEVER SEEN IN HER BEFORE.***
MARY, YOU'VE MADE A ***REAL BREAKTHROUGH*** HERE!
THAT'S GREAT, REAL GOOD NEWS, DAD.
IS SOMETHING WRONG, MARY?
I... NO, I JUST NEED TO GET A DRINK.
I MUST BE LOSING MY MIND.
NEED TO FIGURE OUT HOW I KEEP BRINGING THESE THINGS TO OTHER PEOPLE'S DREAMS.
SCOTT?
HEY, MARY.
I'M SORRY, DO WE HAVE AN APPOINTMENT?
IN THIRTY MINUTES. I CAME EARLY TO MAKE SURE I DIDN'T GET BUMPED AGAIN.

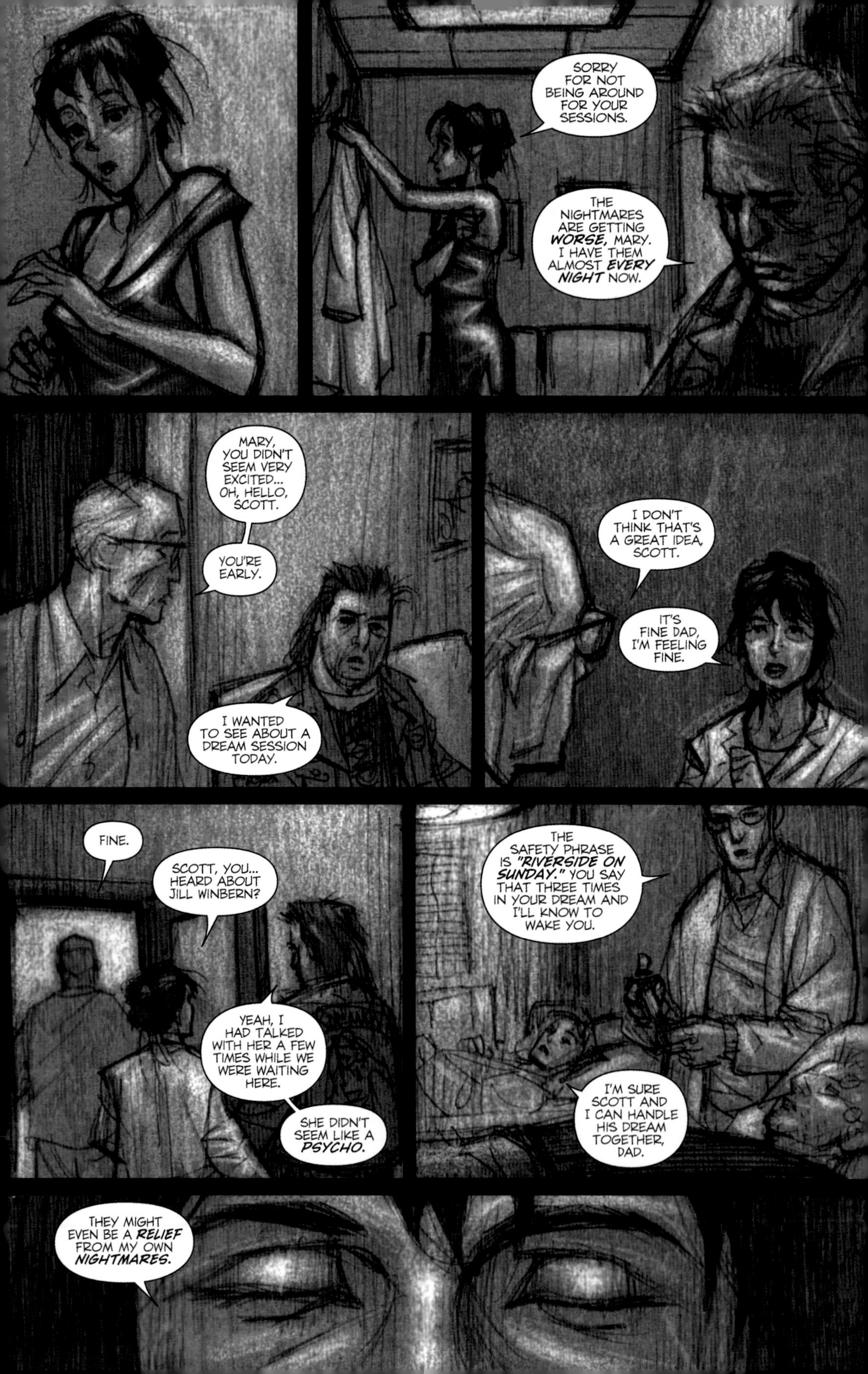
SORRY FOR NOT BEING AROUND FOR YOUR SESSIONS.
THE NIGHTMARES ARE GETTING *WORSE,* MARY. I HAVE THEM ALMOST *EVERY NIGHT* NOW.
MARY, YOU DIDN'T SEEM VERY EXCITED... OH, HELLO, SCOTT.
YOU'RE EARLY.
I WANTED TO SEE ABOUT A DREAM SESSION TODAY.
I DON'T THINK THAT'S A GREAT IDEA, SCOTT.
IT'S FINE DAD, I'M FEELING FINE.
FINE.
SCOTT, YOU... HEARD ABOUT JILL WINBERN?
YEAH, I HAD TALKED WITH HER A FEW TIMES WHILE WE WERE WAITING HERE.
SHE DIDN'T SEEM LIKE A *PSYCHO.*
THE SAFETY PHRASE IS *"RIVERSIDE ON SUNDAY."* YOU SAY THAT THREE TIMES IN YOUR DREAM AND I'LL KNOW TO WAKE YOU.
I'M SURE SCOTT AND I CAN HANDLE HIS DREAM TOGETHER, DAD.
THEY MIGHT EVEN BE A *RELIEF* FROM MY OWN *NIGHTMARES.*

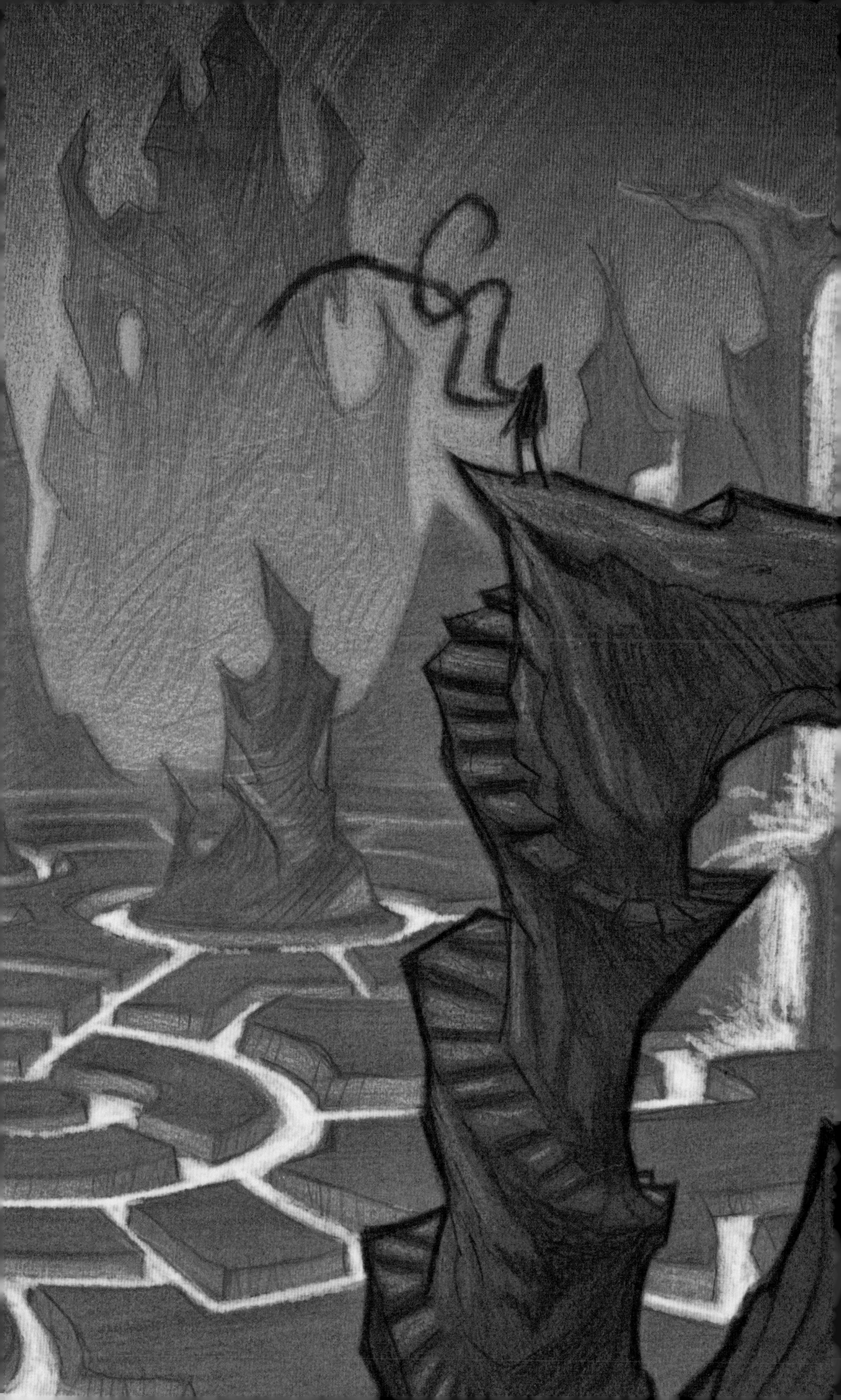

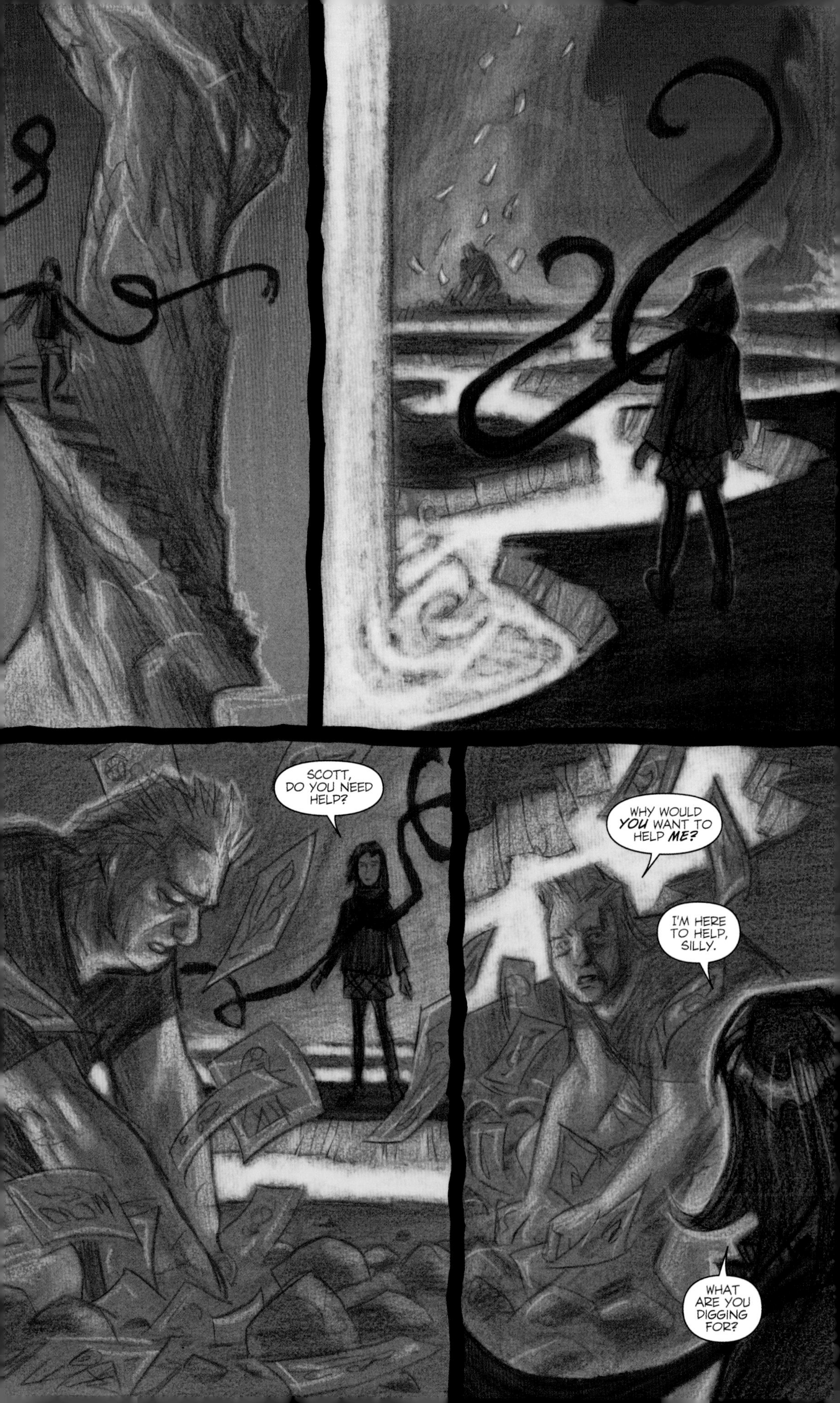
SCOTT, DO YOU NEED HELP?
WHY WOULD YOU WANT TO HELP ME?
I'M HERE TO HELP, SILLY.
WHAT ARE YOU DIGGING FOR?

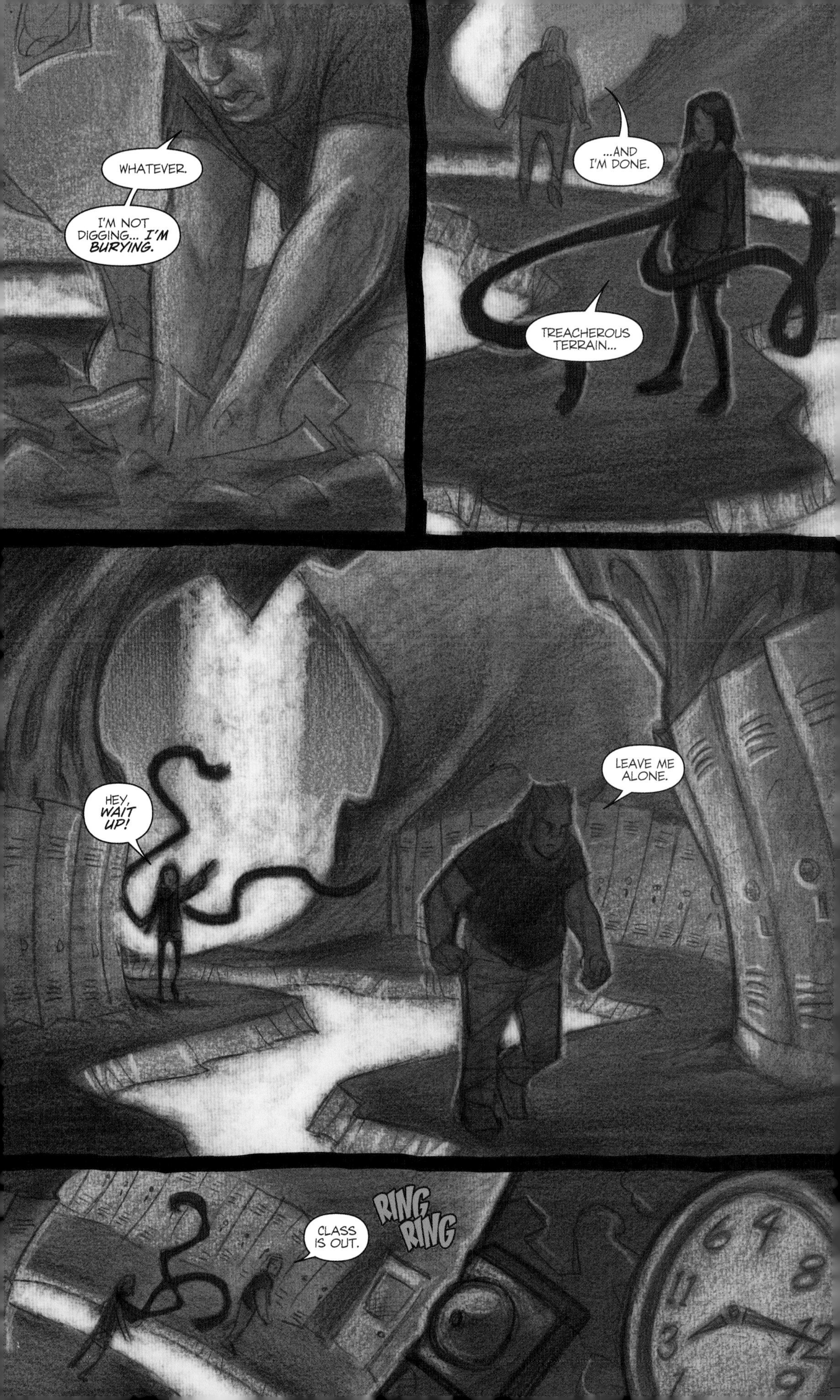
WHATEVER.
I'M NOT DIGGING... I'M BURYING.
...AND I'M DONE.
TREACHEROUS TERRAIN...
HEY, WAIT UP!
LEAVE ME ALONE.
CLASS IS OUT.
RING RING

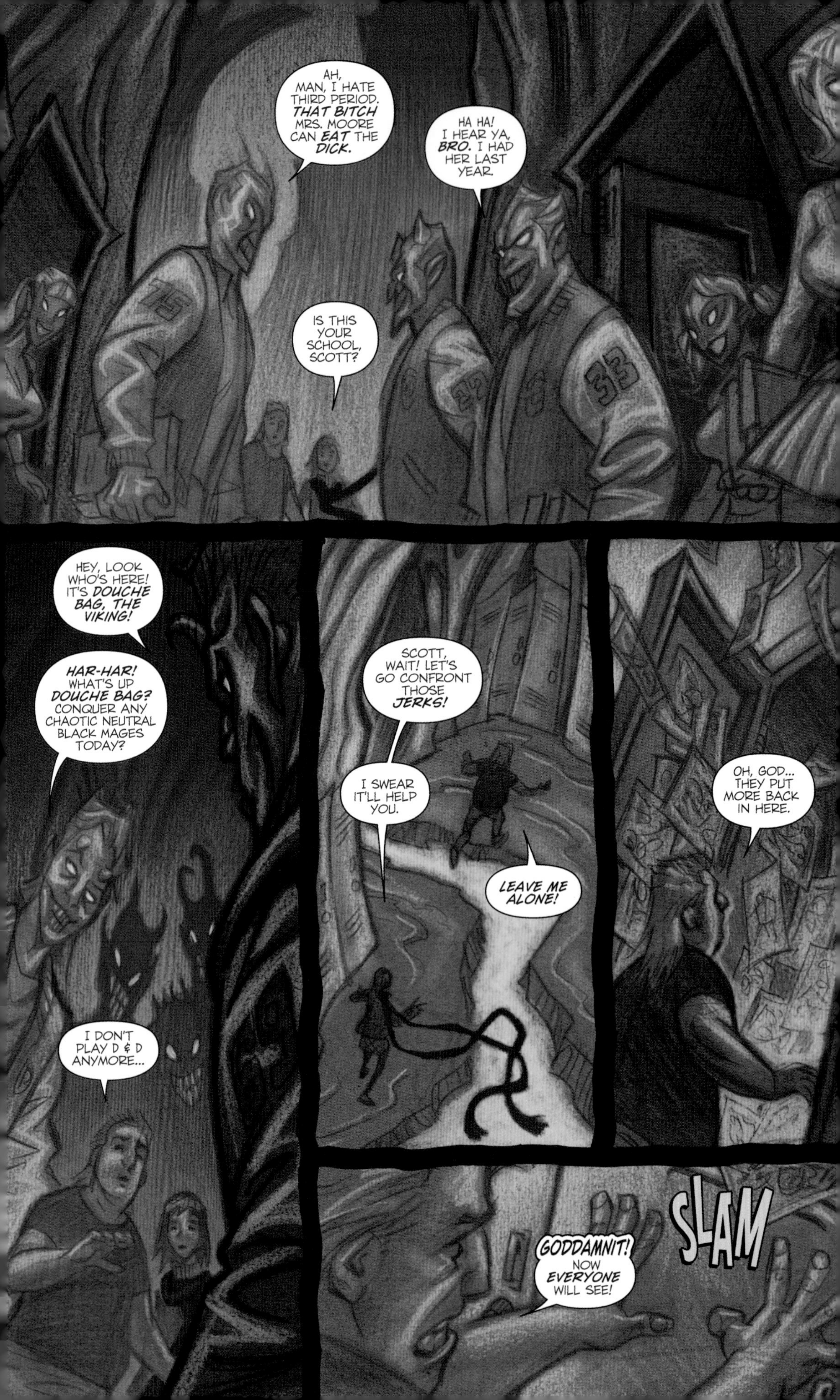

AH, MAN, I HATE THIRD PERIOD. THAT BITCH MRS. MOORE CAN EAT THE DICK.
HA HA! I HEAR YA, BRO. I HAD HER LAST YEAR.
IS THIS YOUR SCHOOL, SCOTT?
HEY, LOOK WHO'S HERE! IT'S DOUCHE BAG, THE VIKING!
HAR-HAR! WHAT'S UP DOUCHE BAG? CONQUER ANY CHAOTIC NEUTRAL BLACK MAGES TODAY?
I DON'T PLAY D & D ANYMORE...
SCOTT, WAIT! LET'S GO CONFRONT THOSE JERKS!
I SWEAR IT'LL HELP YOU.
LEAVE ME ALONE!
OH, GOD... THEY PUT MORE BACK IN HERE.
SLAM
GODDAMNIT! NOW EVERYONE WILL SEE!

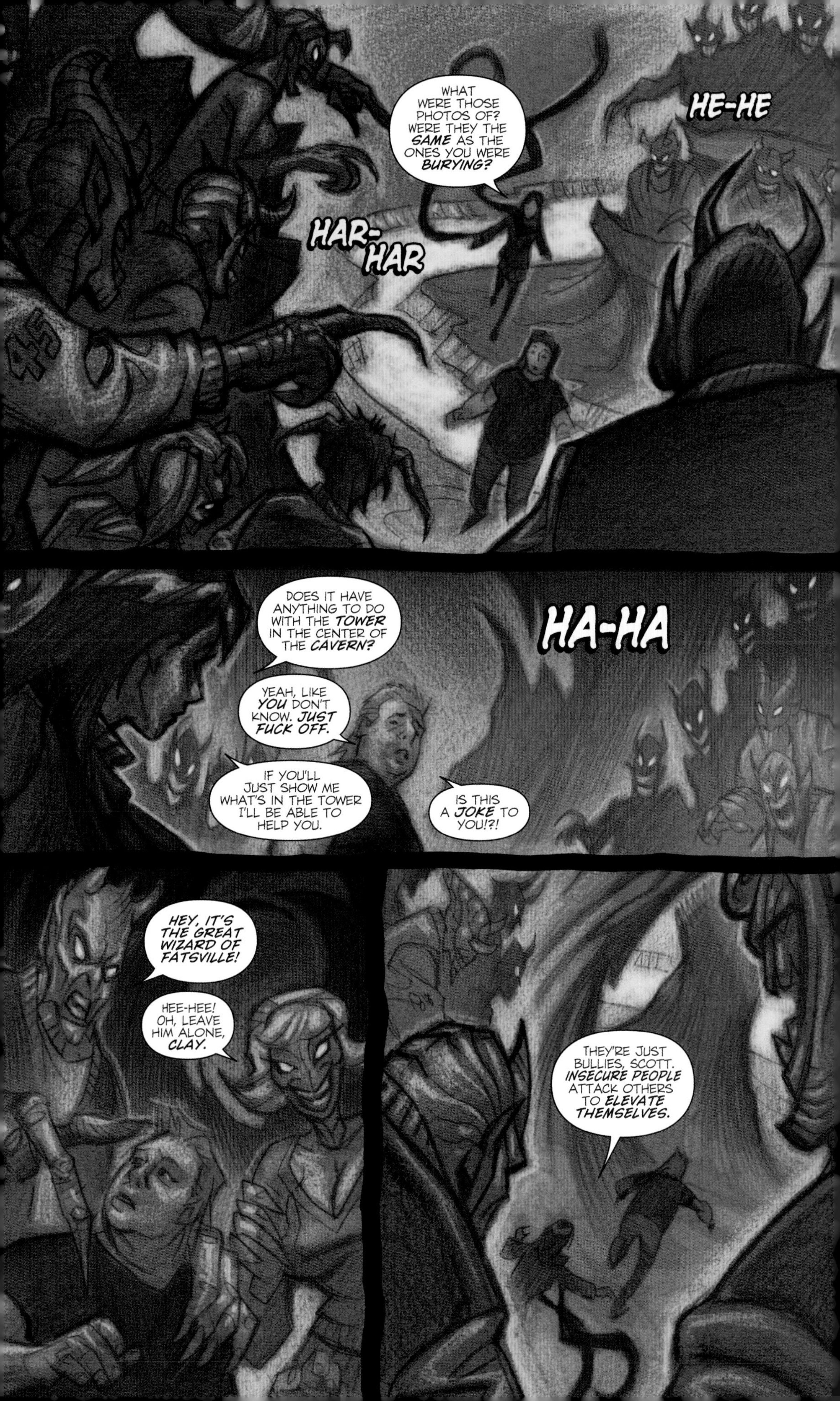
WHAT WERE THOSE PHOTOS OF? WERE THEY THE SAME AS THE ONES YOU WERE BURYING?
HE-HE
HAR-HAR
DOES IT HAVE ANYTHING TO DO WITH THE TOWER IN THE CENTER OF THE CAVERN?
HA-HA
YEAH, LIKE YOU DON'T KNOW. JUST FUCK OFF.
IF YOU'LL JUST SHOW ME WHAT'S IN THE TOWER I'LL BE ABLE TO HELP YOU.
IS THIS A JOKE TO YOU!?!
HEY, IT'S THE GREAT WIZARD OF FATSVILLE!
HEE-HEE! OH, LEAVE HIM ALONE, CLAY.
THEY'RE JUST BULLIES, SCOTT. INSECURE PEOPLE ATTACK OTHERS TO ELEVATE THEMSELVES.

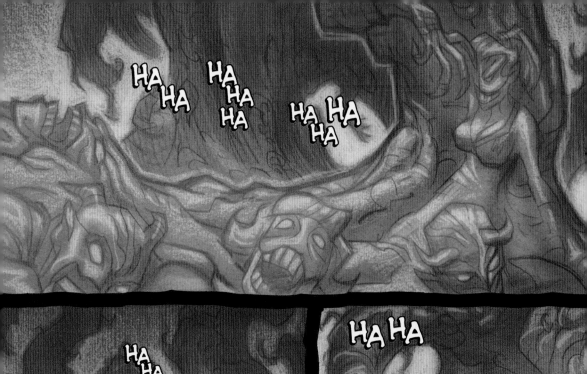

HA HA HA HA HA HA HA HA

HA HA HA HA HA HA HA

HA HA

WHERE DO YOU THINK YOU'RE GOING, DOUCHE BAG!?

WE DON'T HAVE TO RUN, SCOTT.

ROLL THE TWENTY-SIDED DICE TO FLEE, DOUCHE BAG! HAR-HAR!

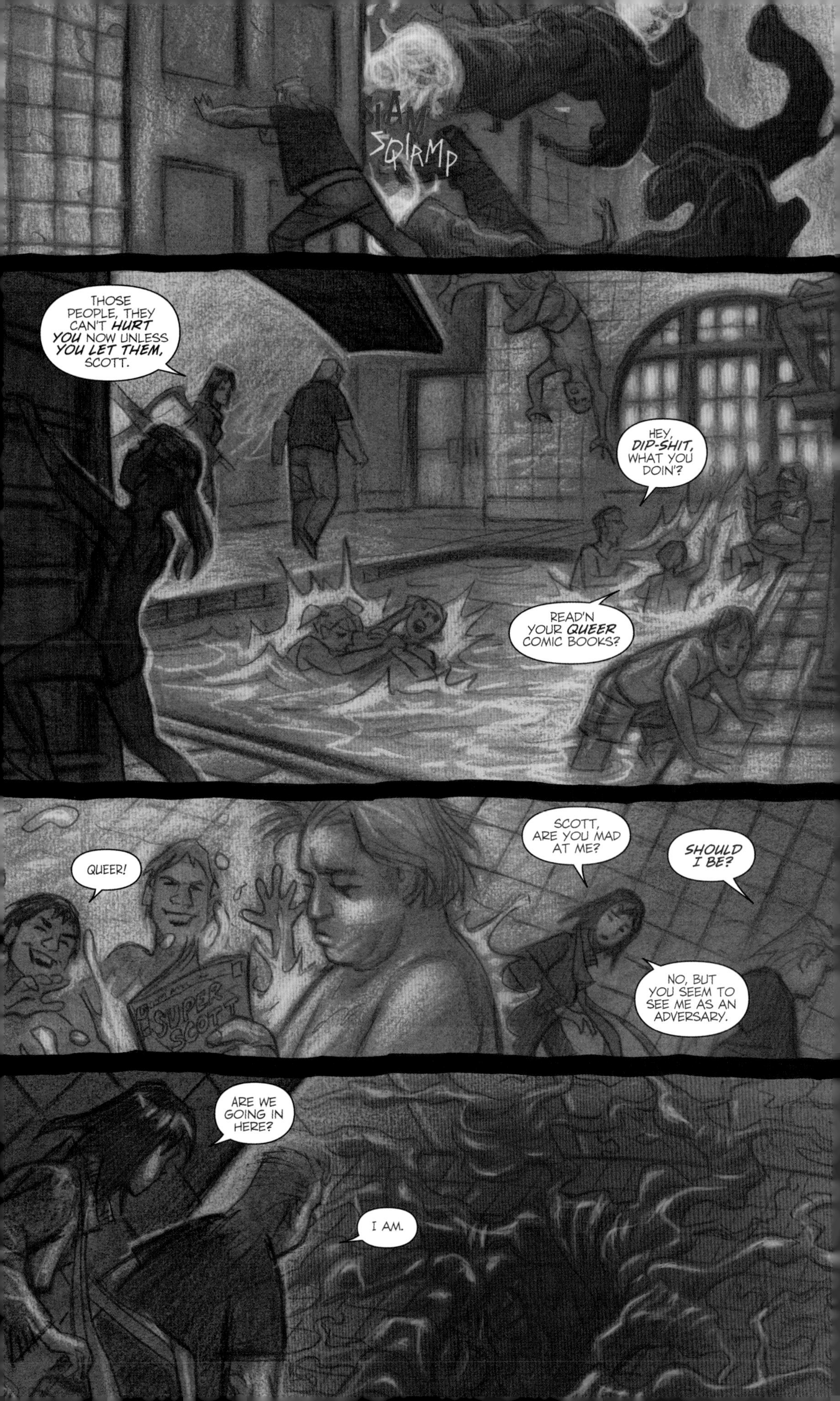
SLAM
SQIRMP
THOSE PEOPLE, THEY CAN'T **HURT YOU** NOW UNLESS **YOU LET THEM,** SCOTT.
HEY, **DIP-SHIT,** WHAT YOU DOIN'?
READ'N YOUR **QUEER** COMIC BOOKS?
QUEER!
SUPER SCOTT
SCOTT, ARE YOU MAD AT ME?
SHOULD I BE?
NO, BUT YOU SEEM TO SEE ME AS AN ADVERSARY.
ARE WE GOING IN HERE?
I AM.

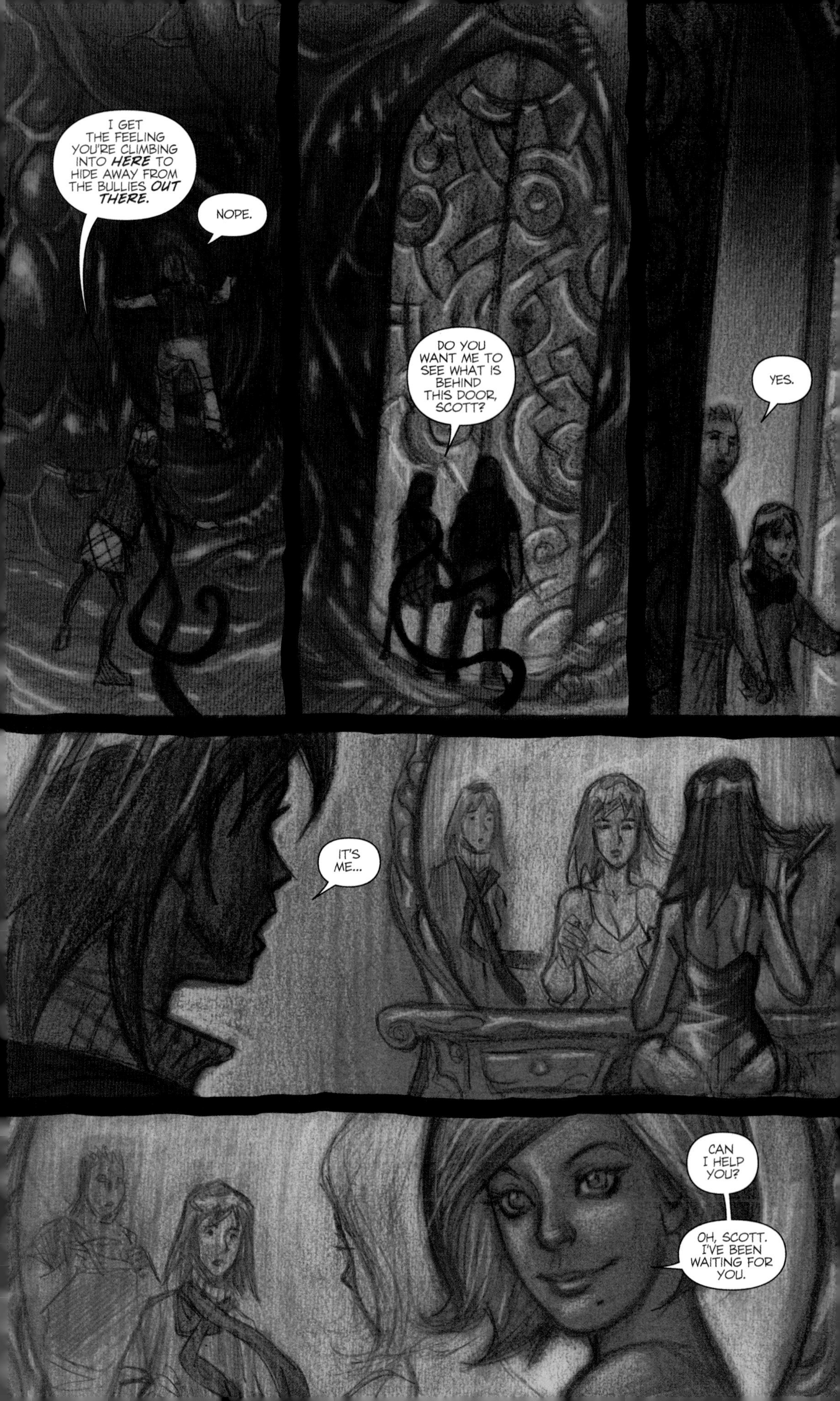
I GET THE FEELING YOU'RE CLIMBING INTO HERE TO HIDE AWAY FROM THE BULLIES OUT THERE.
NOPE.
DO YOU WANT ME TO SEE WHAT IS BEHIND THIS DOOR, SCOTT?
YES.
IT'S ME...
CAN I HELP YOU?
OH, SCOTT. I'VE BEEN WAITING FOR YOU.

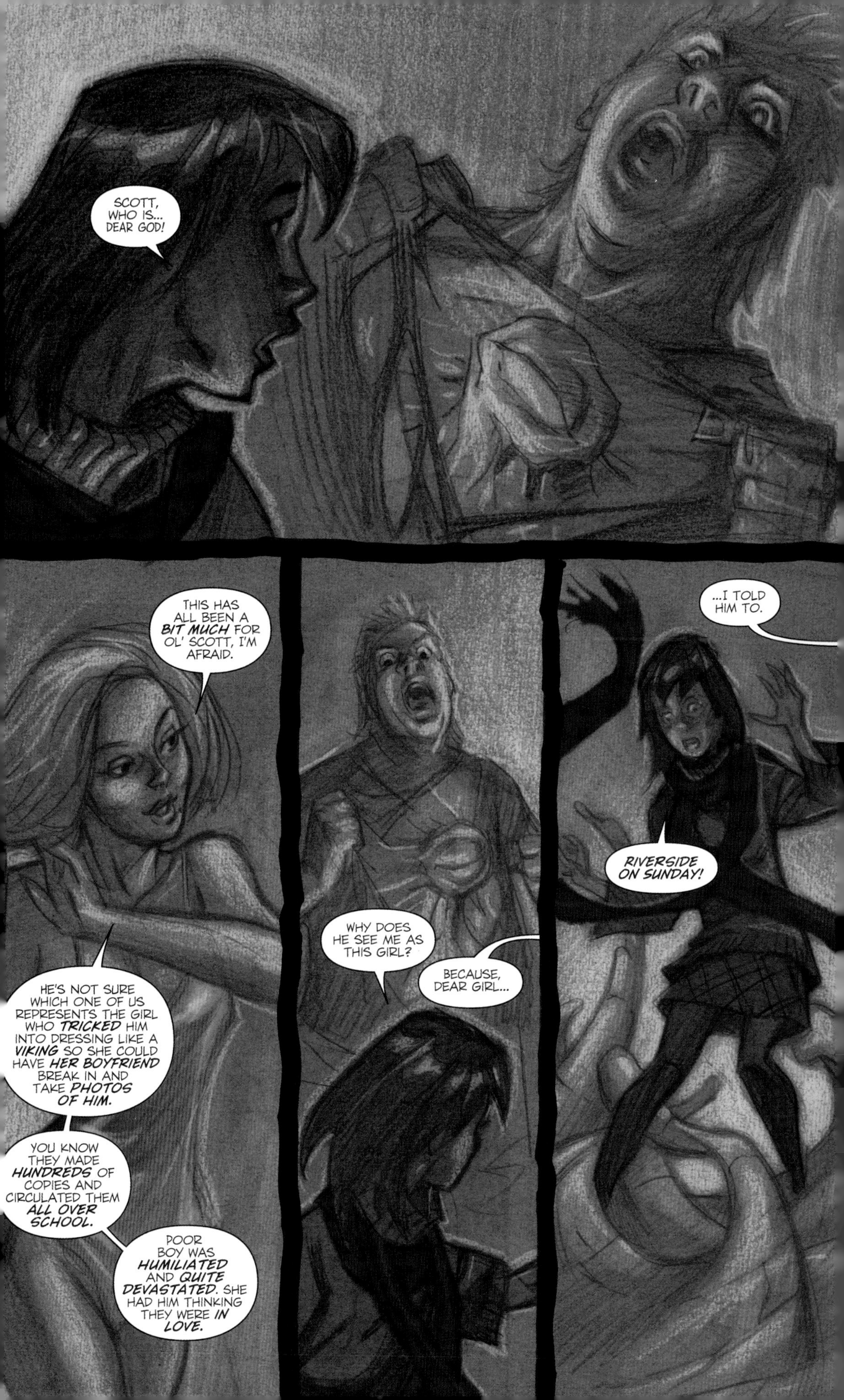
SCOTT, WHO IS... DEAR GOD!
THIS HAS ALL BEEN A BIT MUCH FOR OL' SCOTT, I'M AFRAID.
HE'S NOT SURE WHICH ONE OF US REPRESENTS THE GIRL WHO TRICKED HIM INTO DRESSING LIKE A VIKING SO SHE COULD HAVE HER BOYFRIEND BREAK IN AND TAKE PHOTOS OF HIM.
YOU KNOW THEY MADE HUNDREDS OF COPIES AND CIRCULATED THEM ALL OVER SCHOOL.
POOR BOY WAS HUMILIATED AND QUITE DEVASTATED. SHE HAD HIM THINKING THEY WERE IN LOVE.
WHY DOES HE SEE ME AS THIS GIRL?
BECAUSE, DEAR GIRL...
...I TOLD HIM TO.
RIVERSIDE ON SUNDAY!

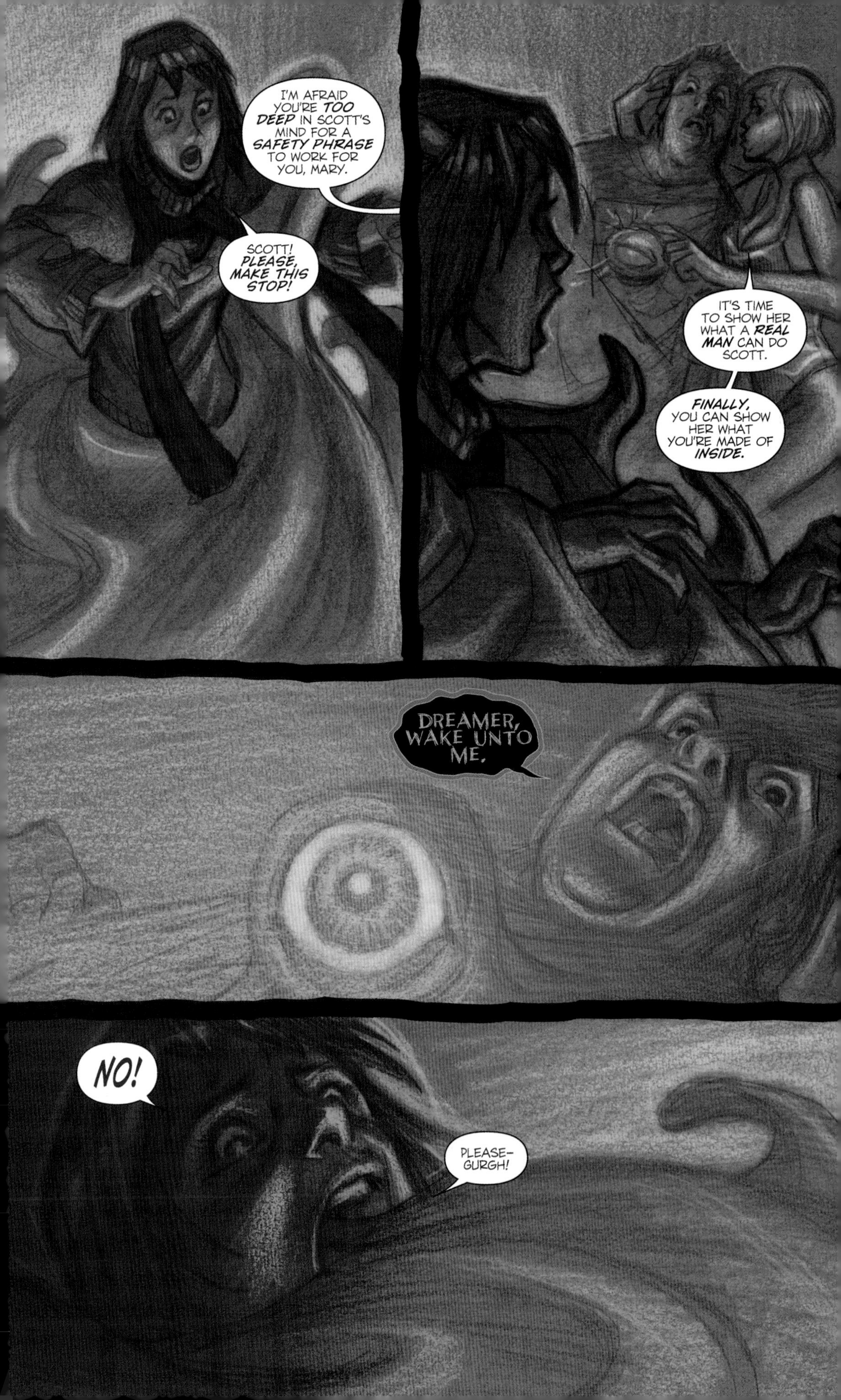
I'M AFRAID YOU'RE TOO DEEP IN SCOTT'S MIND FOR A SAFETY PHRASE TO WORK FOR YOU, MARY.
SCOTT! PLEASE, MAKE THIS STOP!
IT'S TIME TO SHOW HER WHAT A REAL MAN CAN DO SCOTT.
FINALLY, YOU CAN SHOW HER WHAT YOU'RE MADE OF INSIDE.
DREAMER, WAKE UNTO ME.
NO!
PLEASE-GURGH!

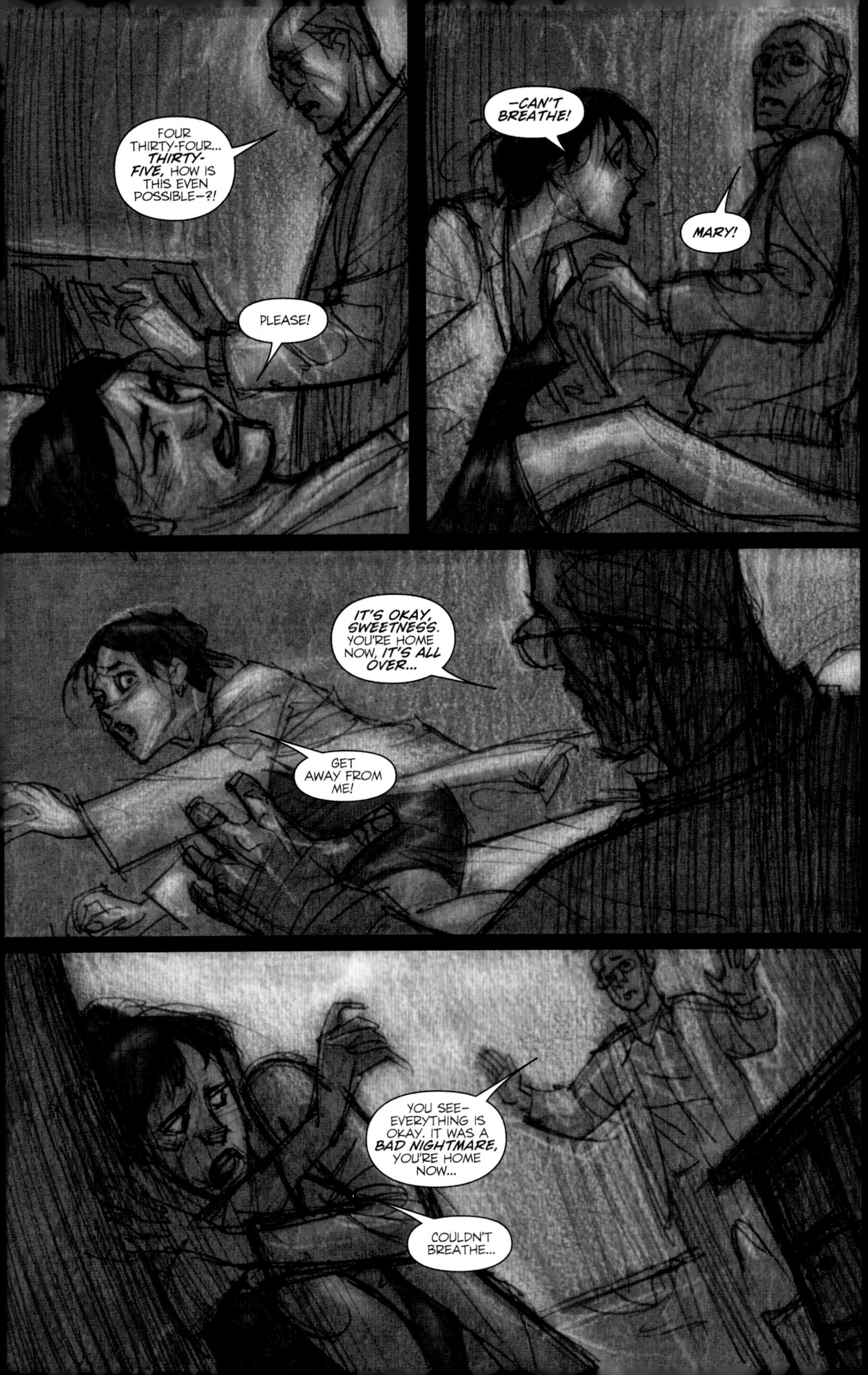
FOUR THIRTY-FOUR... THIRTY-FIVE, HOW IS THIS EVEN POSSIBLE--?!
PLEASE!
--CAN'T BREATHE!
MARY!
IT'S OKAY, SWEETNESS. YOU'RE HOME NOW, IT'S ALL OVER...
GET AWAY FROM ME!
YOU SEE-- EVERYTHING IS OKAY. IT WAS A BAD NIGHTMARE, YOU'RE HOME NOW...
COULDN'T BREATHE...

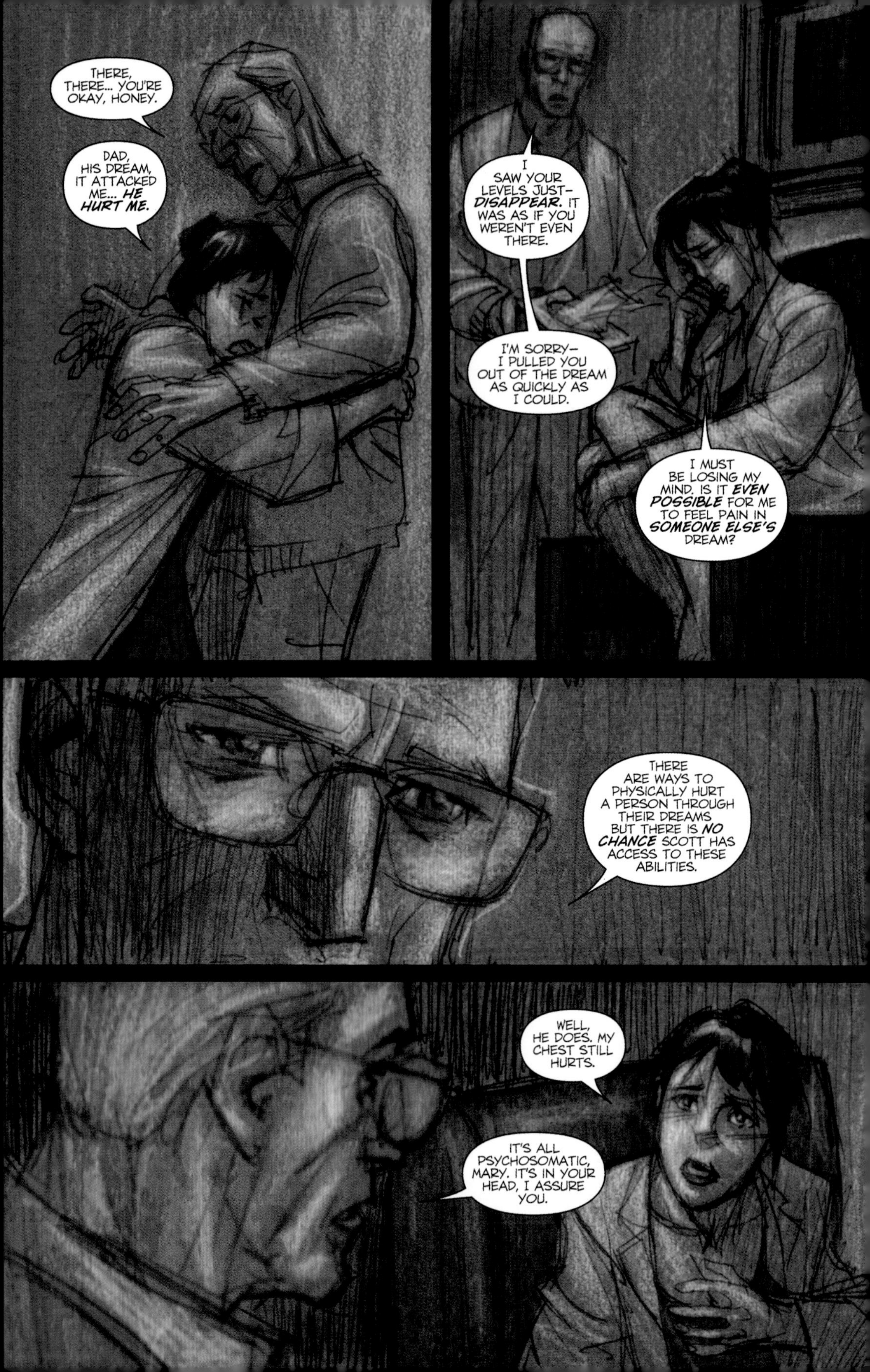

THERE, THERE... YOU'RE OKAY, HONEY.
DAD, HIS DREAM, IT ATTACKED ME... ***HE HURT ME.***
I SAW YOUR LEVELS JUST-***DISAPPEAR.*** IT WAS AS IF YOU WEREN'T EVEN THERE.
I'M SORRY—I PULLED YOU OUT OF THE DREAM AS QUICKLY AS I COULD.
I MUST BE LOSING MY MIND. IS IT ***EVEN POSSIBLE*** FOR ME TO FEEL PAIN IN ***SOMEONE ELSE'S*** DREAM?
THERE ARE WAYS TO PHYSICALLY HURT A PERSON THROUGH THEIR DREAMS BUT THERE IS ***NO CHANCE*** SCOTT HAS ACCESS TO THESE ABILITIES.
WELL, HE DOES. MY CHEST STILL HURTS.
IT'S ALL PSYCHOSOMATIC, MARY. IT'S IN YOUR HEAD, I ASSURE YOU.

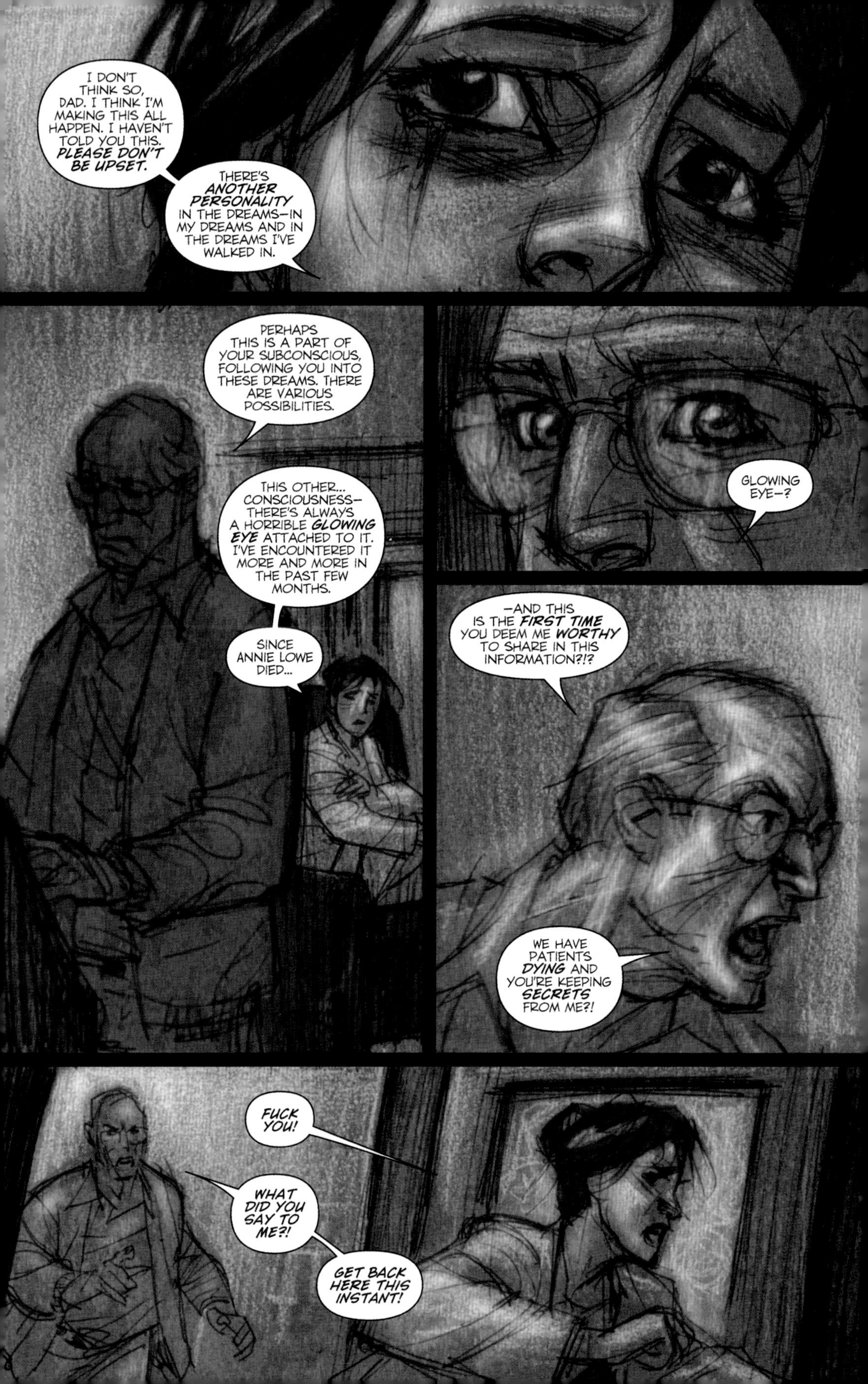
I DON'T THINK SO, DAD. I THINK I'M MAKING THIS ALL HAPPEN. I HAVEN'T TOLD YOU THIS. PLEASE DON'T BE UPSET.
THERE'S ANOTHER PERSONALITY IN THE DREAMS—IN MY DREAMS AND IN THE DREAMS I'VE WALKED IN.
PERHAPS THIS IS A PART OF YOUR SUBCONSCIOUS, FOLLOWING YOU INTO THESE DREAMS. THERE ARE VARIOUS POSSIBILITIES.
THIS OTHER... CONSCIOUSNESS—THERE'S ALWAYS A HORRIBLE GLOWING EYE ATTACHED TO IT. I'VE ENCOUNTERED IT MORE AND MORE IN THE PAST FEW MONTHS.
SINCE ANNIE LOWE DIED...
GLOWING EYE—?
—AND THIS IS THE FIRST TIME YOU DEEM ME WORTHY TO SHARE IN THIS INFORMATION?!?
WE HAVE PATIENTS DYING AND YOU'RE KEEPING SECRETS FROM ME?!
FUCK YOU!
WHAT DID YOU SAY TO ME?!
GET BACK HERE THIS INSTANT!

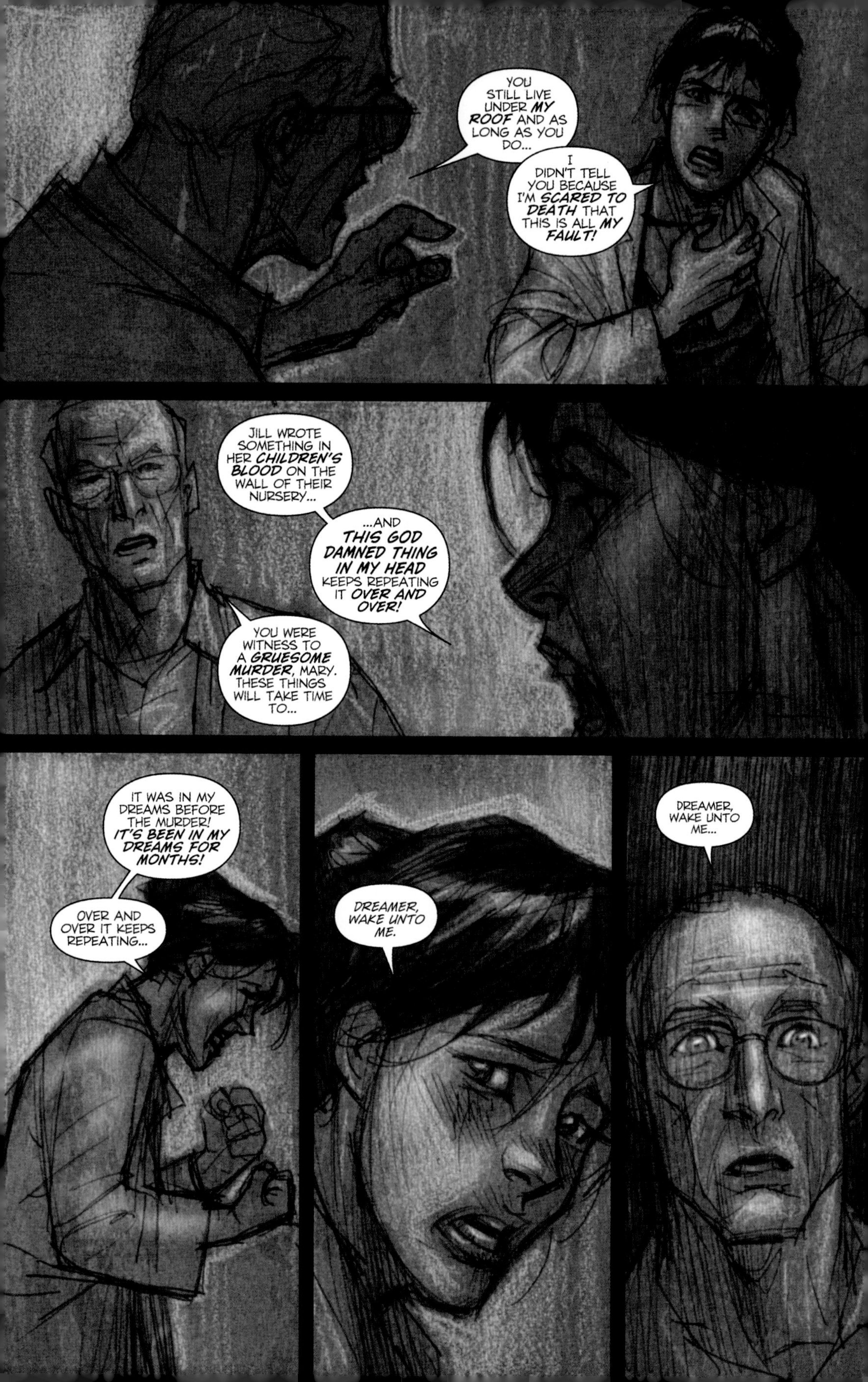
YOU STILL LIVE UNDER MY ROOF AND AS LONG AS YOU DO...
I DIDN'T TELL YOU BECAUSE I'M SCARED TO DEATH THAT THIS IS ALL MY FAULT!
JILL WROTE SOMETHING IN HER CHILDREN'S BLOOD ON THE WALL OF THEIR NURSERY...
...AND THIS GOD DAMNED THING IN MY HEAD KEEPS REPEATING IT OVER AND OVER!
YOU WERE WITNESS TO A GRUESOME MURDER, MARY. THESE THINGS WILL TAKE TIME TO...
IT WAS IN MY DREAMS BEFORE THE MURDER! IT'S BEEN IN MY DREAMS FOR MONTHS!
OVER AND OVER IT KEEPS REPEATING...
DREAMER, WAKE UNTO ME.
DREAMER, WAKE UNTO ME...

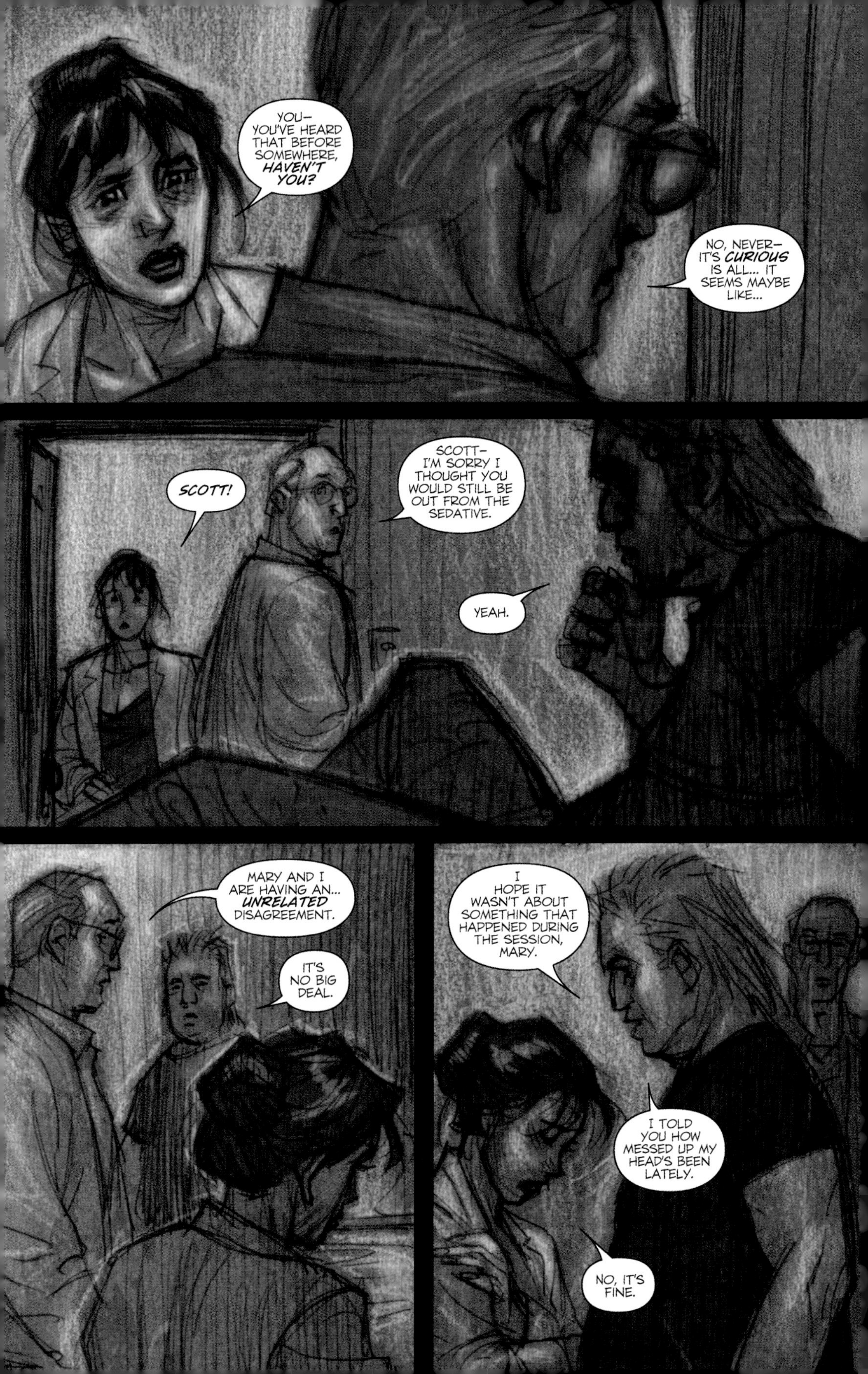

YOU— YOU'VE HEARD THAT BEFORE SOMEWHERE, ***HAVEN'T YOU?***
NO, NEVER— IT'S ***CURIOUS*** IS ALL... IT SEEMS MAYBE LIKE...
SCOTT!
SCOTT— I'M SORRY I THOUGHT YOU WOULD STILL BE OUT FROM THE SEDATIVE.
YEAH.
MARY AND I ARE HAVING AN... ***UNRELATED*** DISAGREEMENT.
IT'S NO BIG DEAL.
I HOPE IT WASN'T ABOUT SOMETHING THAT HAPPENED DURING THE SESSION, MARY.
I TOLD YOU HOW MESSED UP MY HEAD'S BEEN LATELY.
NO, IT'S FINE.

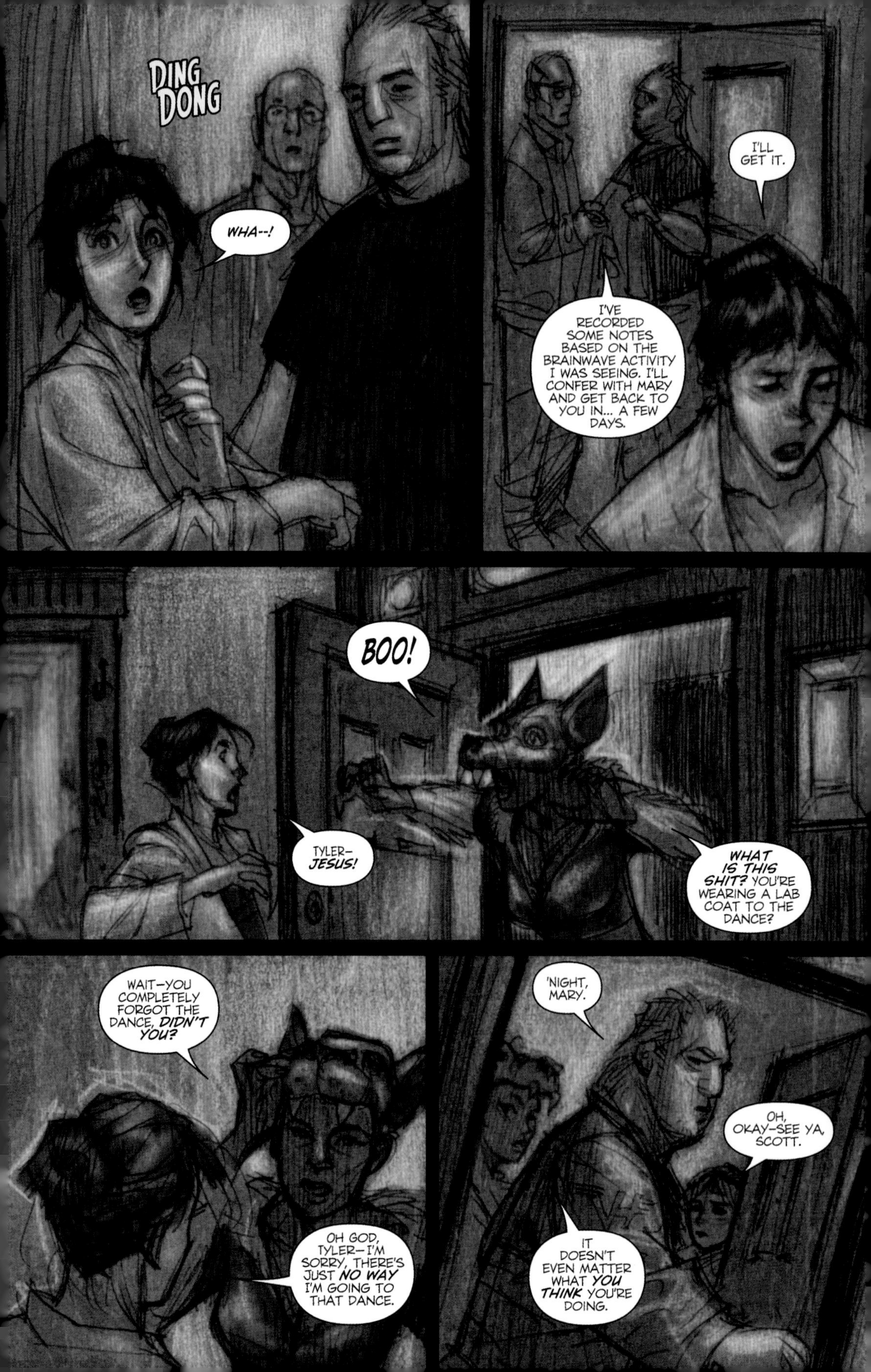
DING DONG
WHA--!
I'LL GET IT.
I'VE RECORDED SOME NOTES BASED ON THE BRAINWAVE ACTIVITY I WAS SEEING. I'LL CONFER WITH MARY AND GET BACK TO YOU IN... A FEW DAYS.
BOO!
TYLER—JESUS!
WHAT IS THIS SHIT? YOU'RE WEARING A LAB COAT TO THE DANCE?
WAIT—YOU COMPLETELY FORGOT THE DANCE, DIDN'T YOU?
OH GOD, TYLER—I'M SORRY, THERE'S JUST NO WAY I'M GOING TO THAT DANCE.
'NIGHT, MARY.
OH, OKAY—SEE YA, SCOTT.
IT DOESN'T EVEN MATTER WHAT YOU THINK YOU'RE DOING.

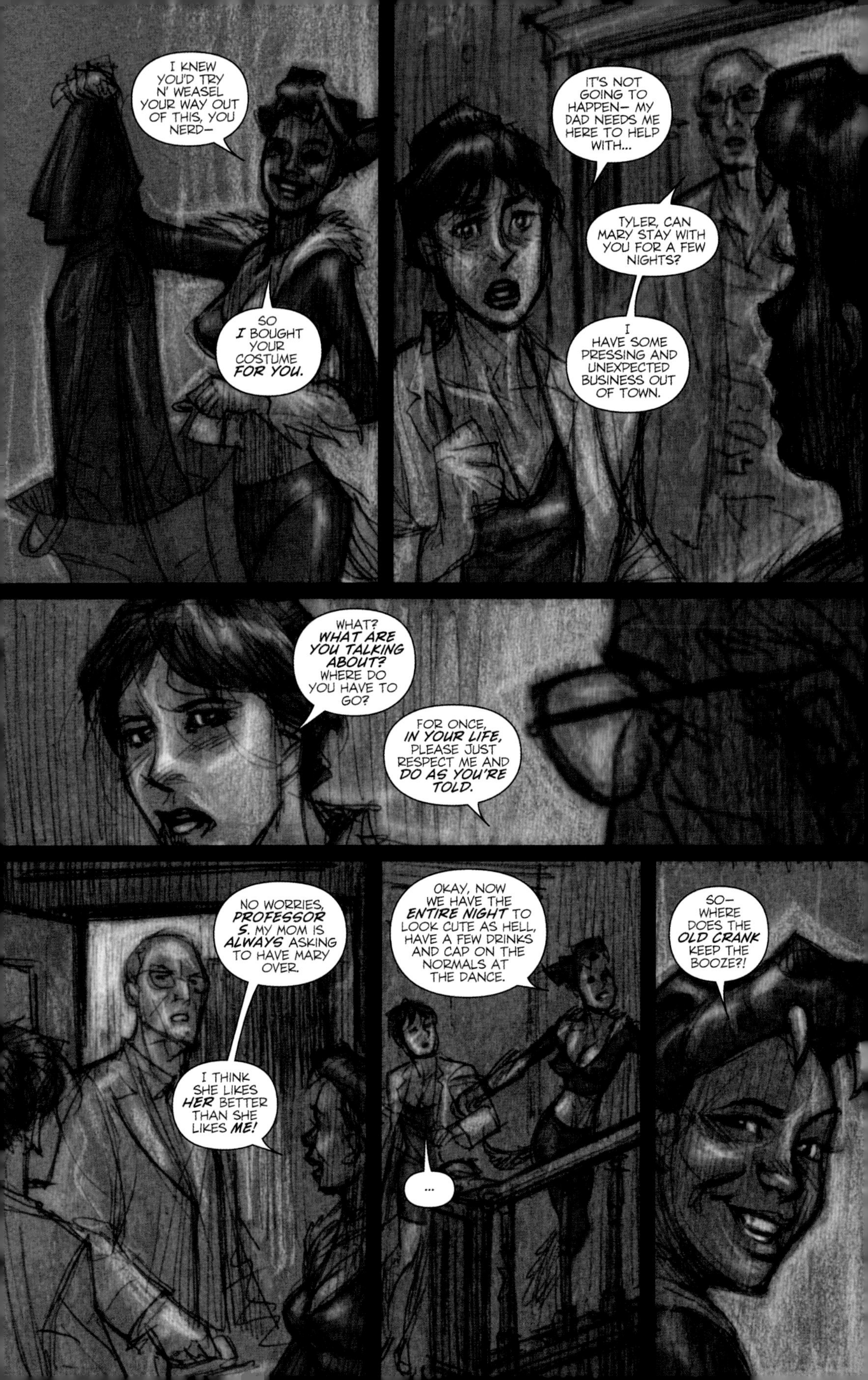
I KNEW YOU'D TRY N' WEASEL YOUR WAY OUT OF THIS, YOU NERD–
SO *I* BOUGHT YOUR COSTUME *FOR YOU.*
IT'S NOT GOING TO HAPPEN– MY DAD NEEDS ME HERE TO HELP WITH...
TYLER, CAN MARY STAY WITH YOU FOR A FEW NIGHTS?
I HAVE SOME PRESSING AND UNEXPECTED BUSINESS OUT OF TOWN.
WHAT? *WHAT ARE YOU TALKING ABOUT?* WHERE DO YOU HAVE TO GO?
FOR ONCE, *IN YOUR LIFE,* PLEASE JUST RESPECT ME AND *DO AS YOU'RE TOLD.*
NO WORRIES, *PROFESSOR S.* MY MOM IS *ALWAYS* ASKING TO HAVE MARY OVER.
I THINK SHE LIKES *HER* BETTER THAN SHE LIKES *ME!*
OKAY, NOW WE HAVE THE *ENTIRE NIGHT* TO LOOK CUTE AS HELL, HAVE A FEW DRINKS AND CAP ON THE NORMALS AT THE DANCE.
...
SO– WHERE DOES THE *OLD CRANK* KEEP THE BOOZE?!

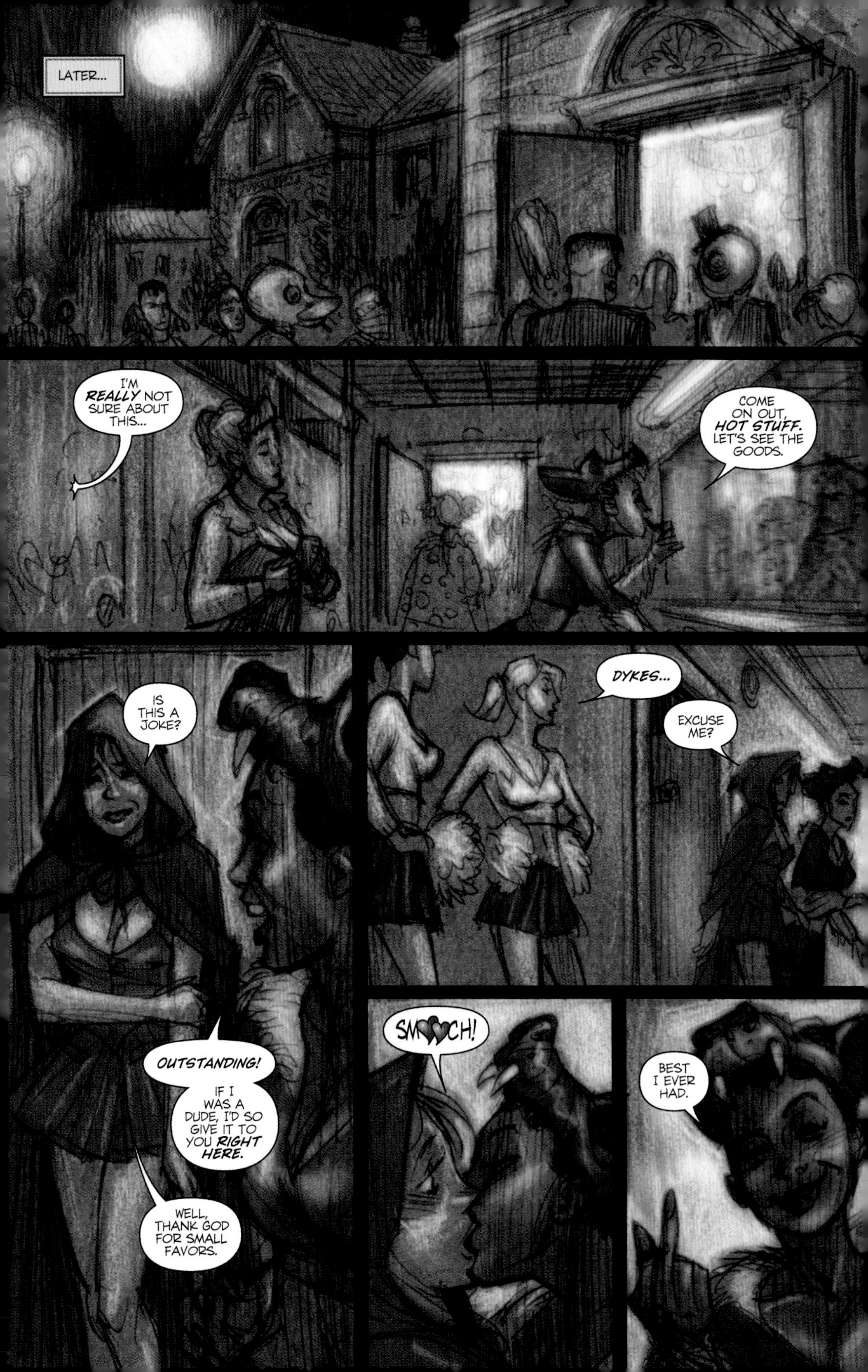
LATER...
I'M REALLY NOT SURE ABOUT THIS...
COME ON OUT, HOT STUFF. LET'S SEE THE GOODS.
IS THIS A JOKE?
OUTSTANDING!
IF I WAS A DUDE, I'D SO GIVE IT TO YOU RIGHT HERE.
WELL, THANK GOD FOR SMALL FAVORS.
DYKES...
EXCUSE ME?
SMOOCH!
BEST I EVER HAD.

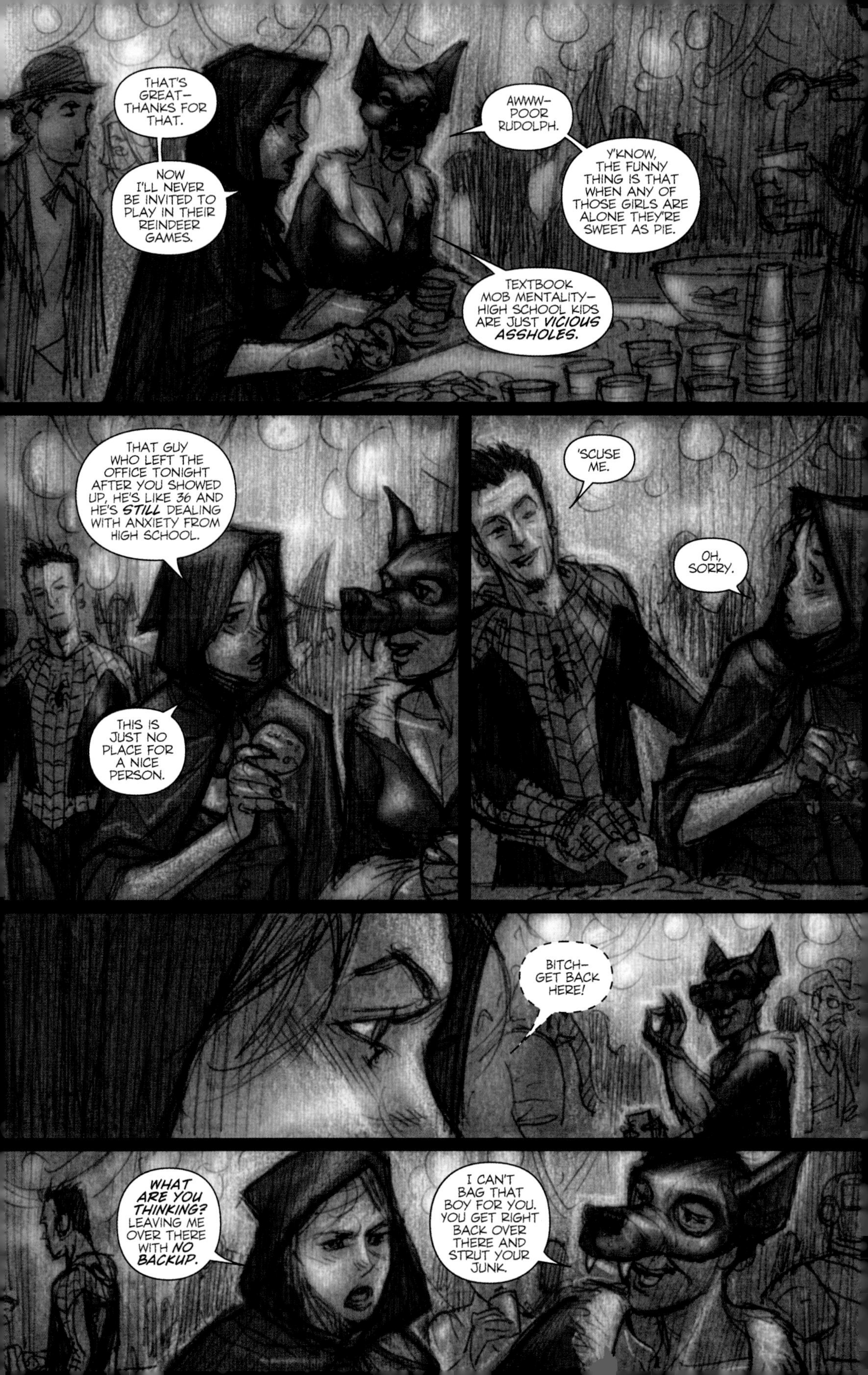
THAT'S GREAT— THANKS FOR THAT.
NOW I'LL NEVER BE INVITED TO PLAY IN THEIR REINDEER GAMES.
AWWW— POOR RUDOLPH.
Y'KNOW, THE FUNNY THING IS THAT WHEN ANY OF THOSE GIRLS ARE ALONE THEY'RE SWEET AS PIE.
TEXTBOOK MOB MENTALITY— HIGH SCHOOL KIDS ARE JUST **VICIOUS ASSHOLES.**
THAT GUY WHO LEFT THE OFFICE TONIGHT AFTER YOU SHOWED UP, HE'S LIKE 36 AND HE'S **STILL** DEALING WITH ANXIETY FROM HIGH SCHOOL.
THIS IS JUST NO PLACE FOR A NICE PERSON.
'SCUSE ME.
OH, SORRY.
BITCH— GET BACK HERE!
WHAT ARE YOU THINKING? LEAVING ME OVER THERE WITH **NO BACKUP.**
I CAN'T BAG THAT BOY FOR YOU. YOU GET RIGHT BACK OVER THERE AND STRUT YOUR JUNK.

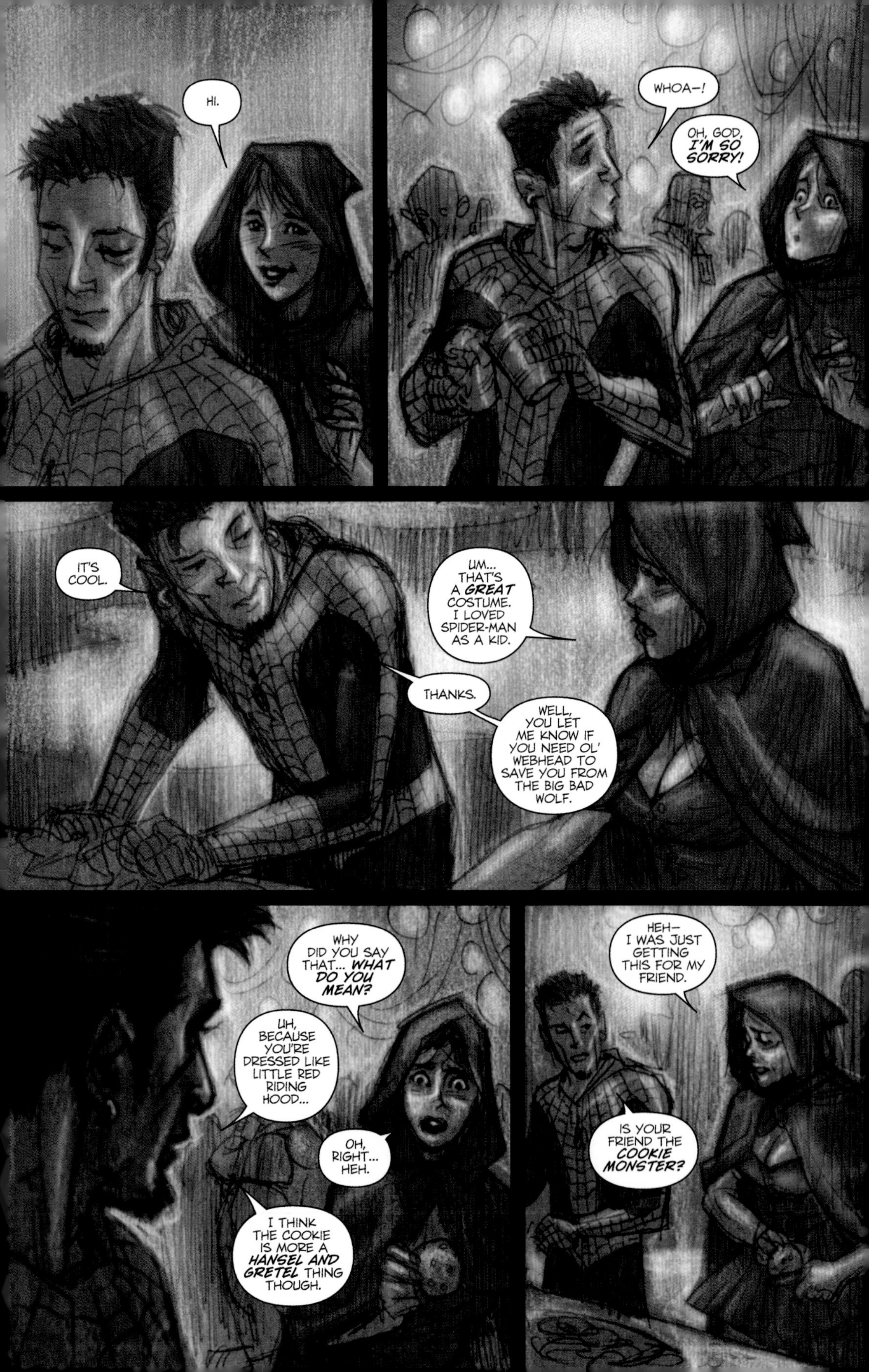
HI.
WHOA–!
OH, GOD, I'M SO SORRY!
IT'S COOL.
UM... THAT'S A GREAT COSTUME. I LOVED SPIDER-MAN AS A KID.
THANKS.
WELL, YOU LET ME KNOW IF YOU NEED OL' WEBHEAD TO SAVE YOU FROM THE BIG BAD WOLF.
WHY DID YOU SAY THAT... WHAT DO YOU MEAN?
UH, BECAUSE YOU'RE DRESSED LIKE LITTLE RED RIDING HOOD...
OH, RIGHT... HEH.
I THINK THE COOKIE IS MORE A HANSEL AND GRETEL THING THOUGH.
HEH– I WAS JUST GETTING THIS FOR MY FRIEND.
IS YOUR FRIEND THE COOKIE MONSTER?

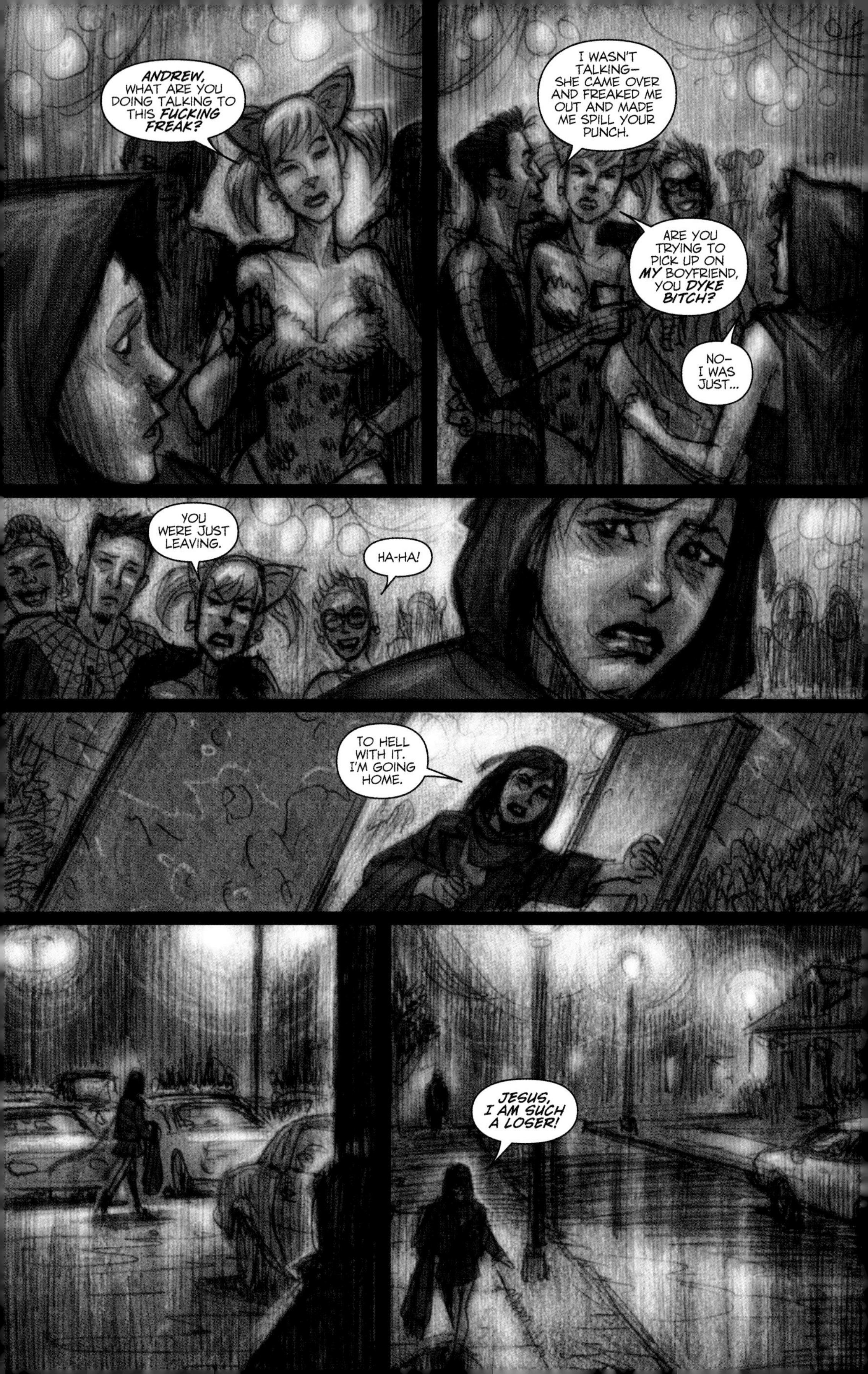
ANDREW, WHAT ARE YOU DOING TALKING TO THIS FUCKING FREAK?
I WASN'T TALKING— SHE CAME OVER AND FREAKED ME OUT AND MADE ME SPILL YOUR PUNCH.
ARE YOU TRYING TO PICK UP ON MY BOYFRIEND, YOU DYKE BITCH?
NO— I WAS JUST...
YOU WERE JUST LEAVING.
HA-HA!
TO HELL WITH IT. I'M GOING HOME.
JESUS, I AM SUCH A LOSER!

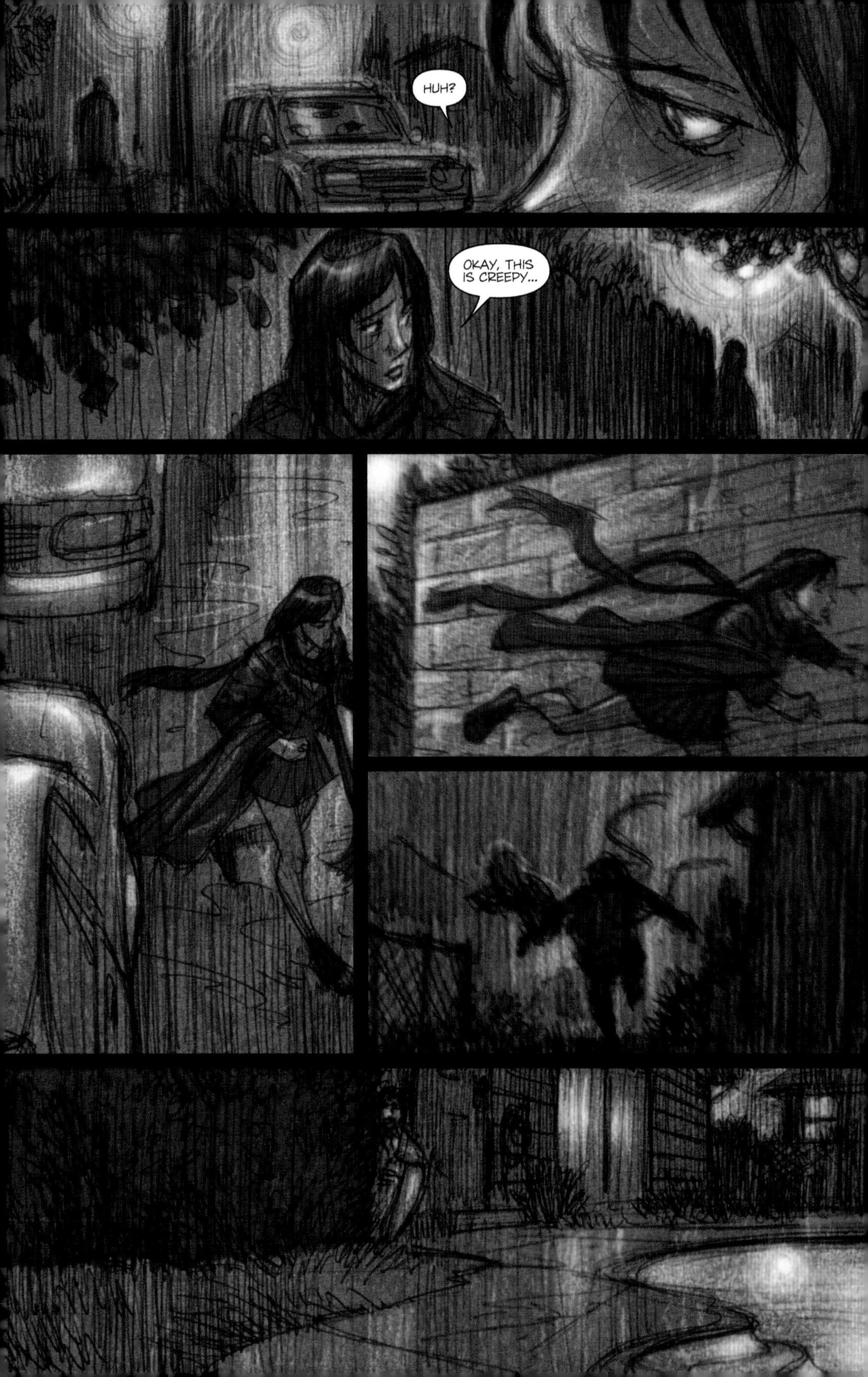
HUH?
OKAY, THIS IS CREEPY...

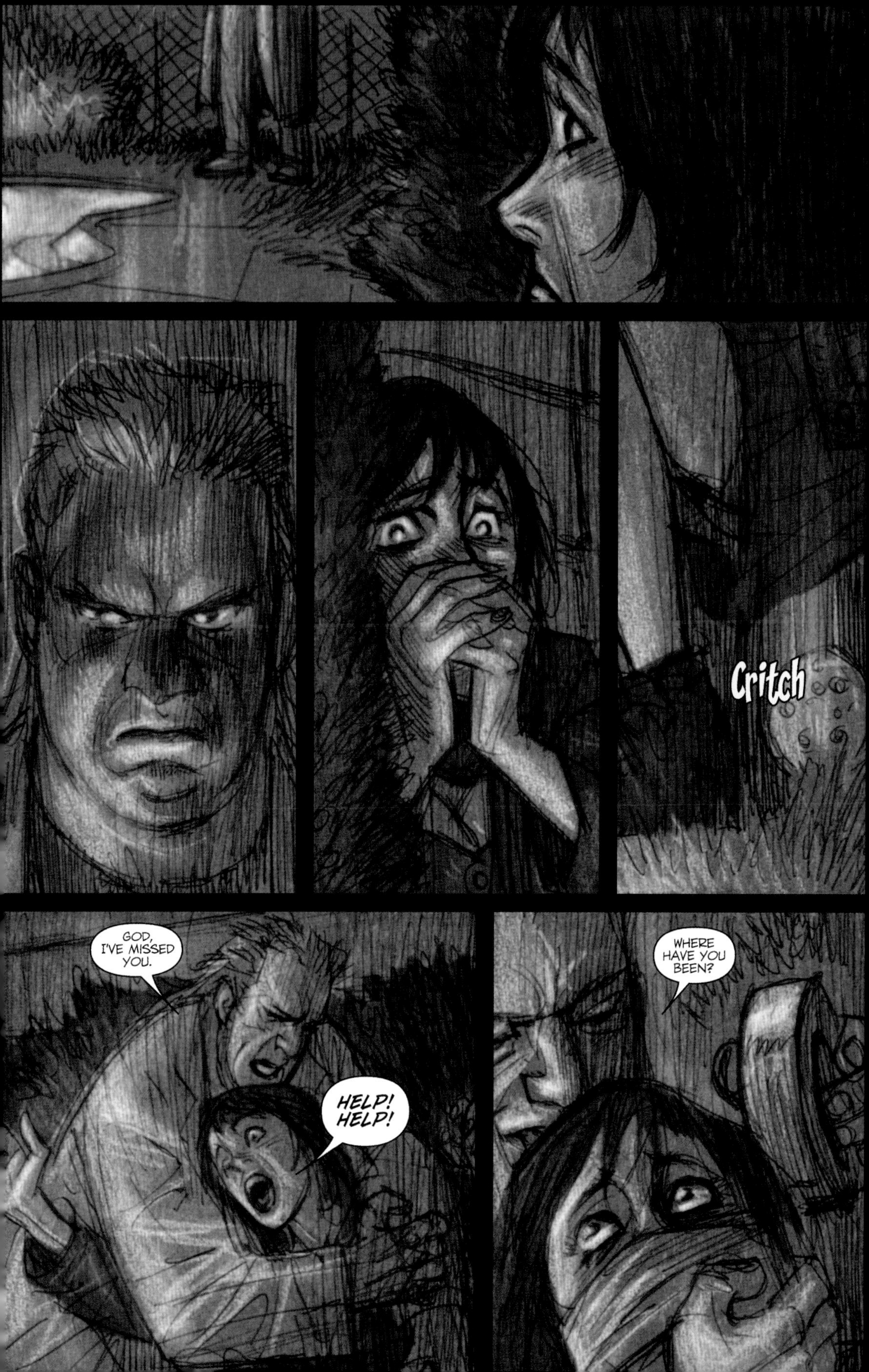
Critch
GOD, I'VE MISSED YOU.
HELP! HELP!
WHERE HAVE YOU BEEN?

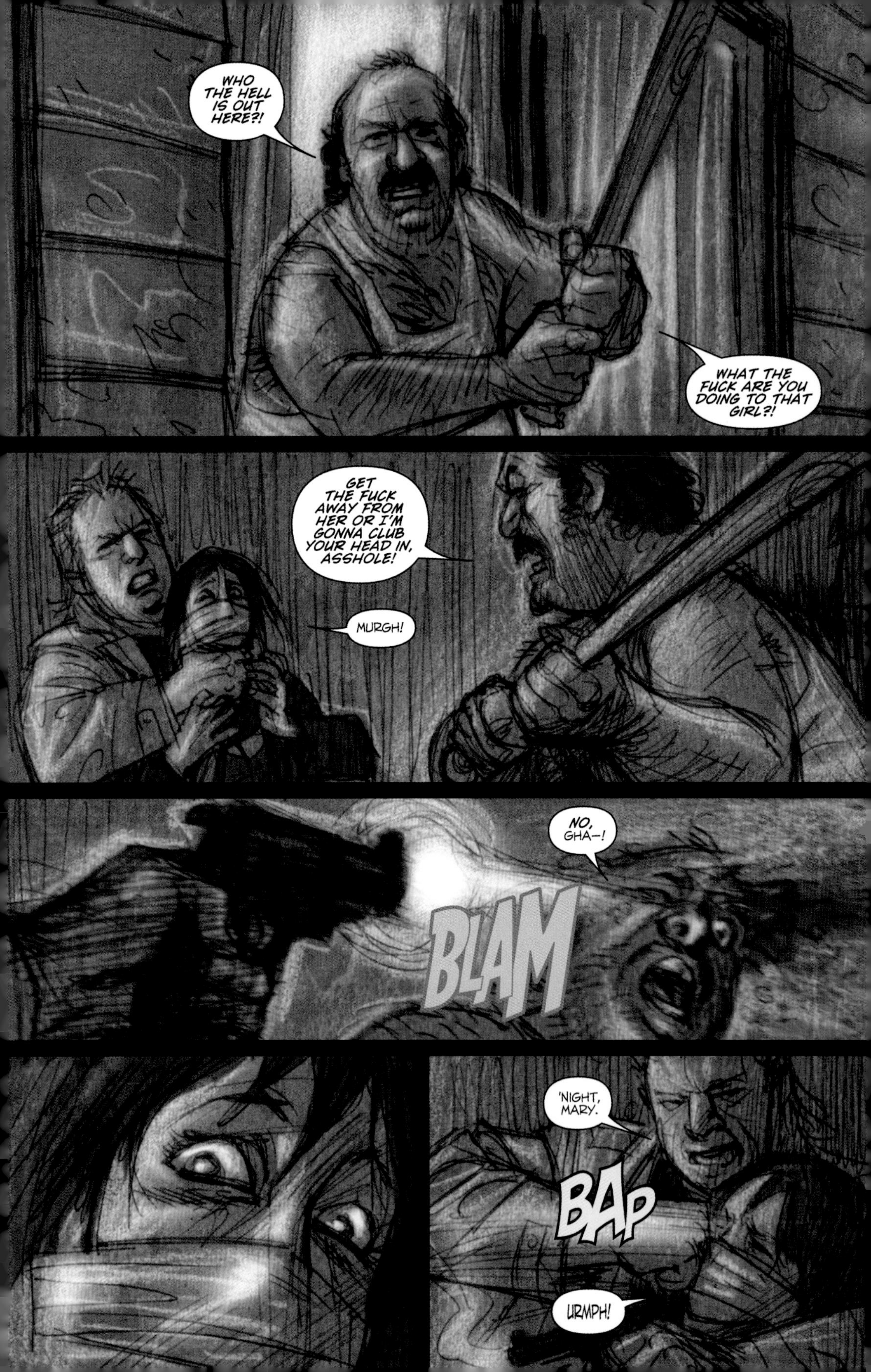
WHO THE HELL IS OUT HERE?!
WHAT THE FUCK ARE YOU DOING TO THAT GIRL?!
GET THE FUCK AWAY FROM HER OR I'M GONNA CLUB YOUR HEAD IN, ASSHOLE!
MURGH!
NO, GHA—!
BLAM
'NIGHT, MARY.
BAP
URMPH!

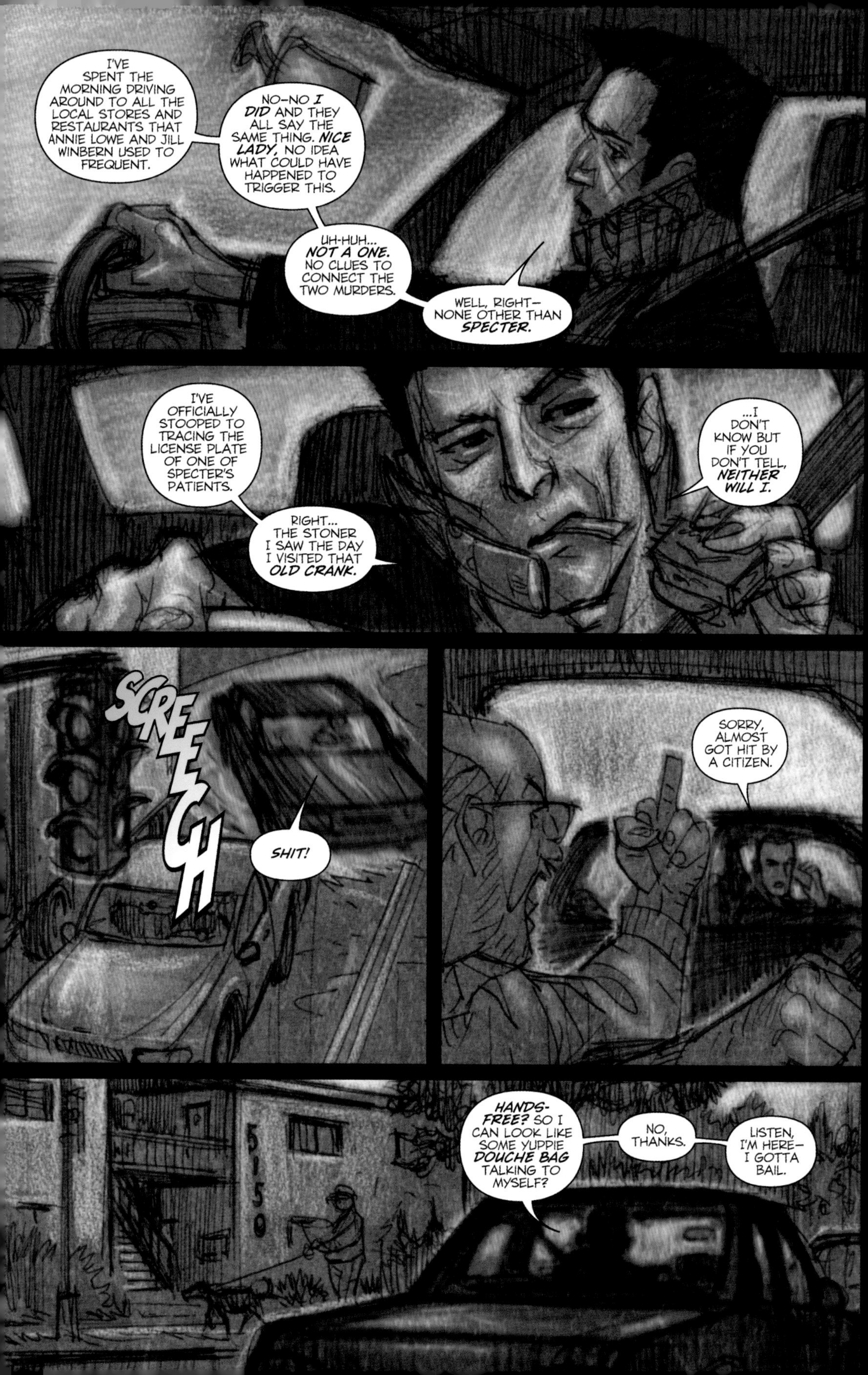
I'VE SPENT THE MORNING DRIVING AROUND TO ALL THE LOCAL STORES AND RESTAURANTS THAT ANNIE LOWE AND JILL WINBERN USED TO FREQUENT.
NO-NO *I DID* AND THEY ALL SAY THE SAME THING. *NICE LADY,* NO IDEA WHAT COULD HAVE HAPPENED TO TRIGGER THIS.
UH-HUH... *NOT A ONE.* NO CLUES TO CONNECT THE TWO MURDERS.
WELL, RIGHT-NONE OTHER THAN *SPECTER.*
I'VE OFFICIALLY STOOPED TO TRACING THE LICENSE PLATE OF ONE OF SPECTER'S PATIENTS.
RIGHT... THE STONER I SAW THE DAY I VISITED THAT *OLD CRANK.*
...I DON'T KNOW BUT IF YOU DON'T TELL, *NEITHER WILL I.*
SCREEECH
SHIT!
SORRY, ALMOST GOT HIT BY A CITIZEN.
HANDS-FREE? SO I CAN LOOK LIKE SOME YUPPIE *DOUCHE BAG* TALKING TO MYSELF?
NO, THANKS.
LISTEN, I'M HERE-I GOTTA BAIL.
5150

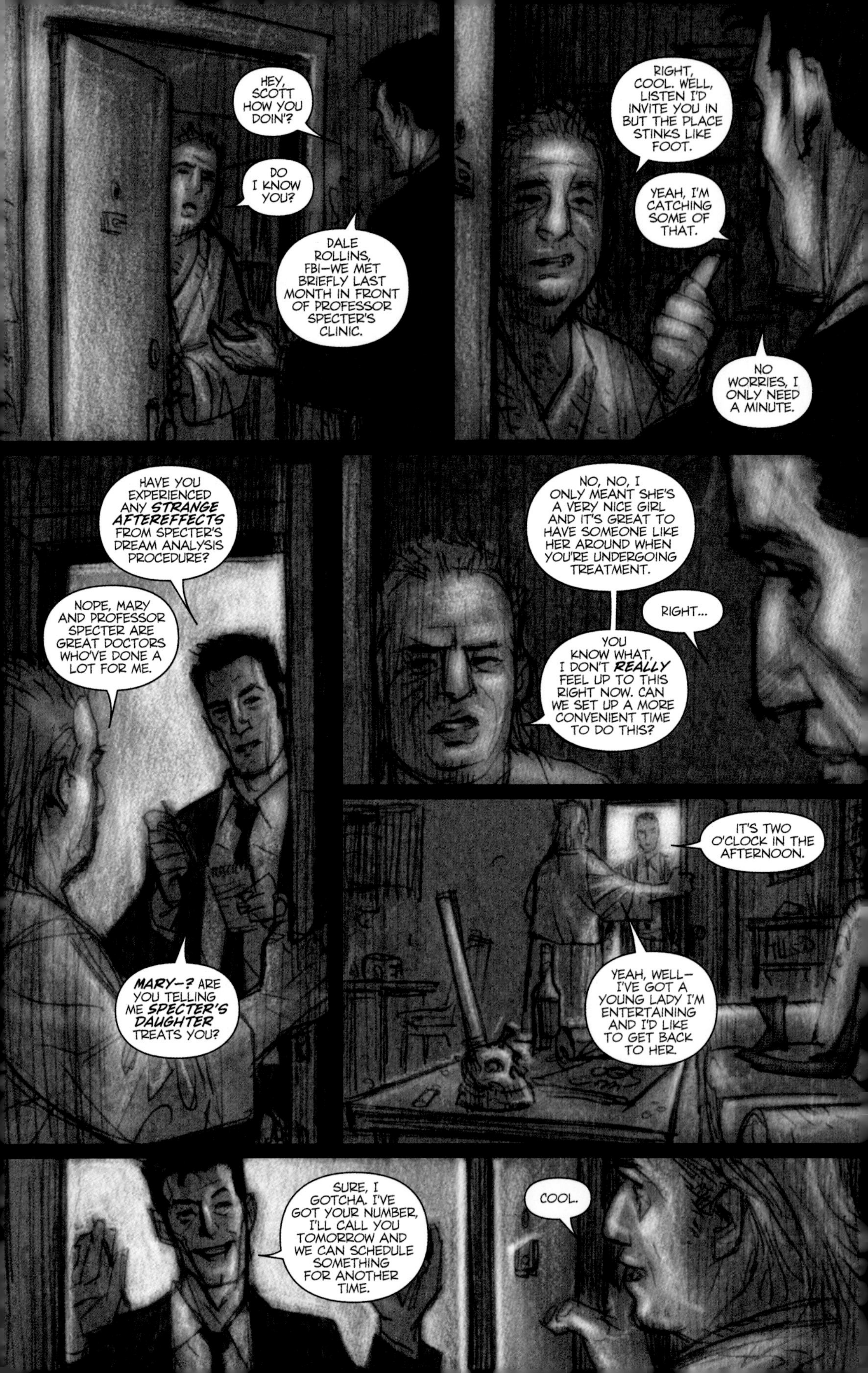
HEY, SCOTT HOW YOU DOIN'?
DO I KNOW YOU?
DALE ROLLINS, FBI—WE MET BRIEFLY LAST MONTH IN FRONT OF PROFESSOR SPECTER'S CLINIC.
RIGHT, COOL. WELL, LISTEN I'D INVITE YOU IN BUT THE PLACE STINKS LIKE FOOT.
YEAH, I'M CATCHING SOME OF THAT.
NO WORRIES, I ONLY NEED A MINUTE.
HAVE YOU EXPERIENCED ANY ***STRANGE AFTEREFFECTS*** FROM SPECTER'S DREAM ANALYSIS PROCEDURE?
NOPE, MARY AND PROFESSOR SPECTER ARE GREAT DOCTORS WHO'VE DONE A LOT FOR ME.
MARY—? ARE YOU TELLING ME ***SPECTER'S DAUGHTER*** TREATS YOU?
NO, NO, I ONLY MEANT SHE'S A VERY NICE GIRL AND IT'S GREAT TO HAVE SOMEONE LIKE HER AROUND WHEN YOU'RE UNDERGOING TREATMENT.
RIGHT...
YOU KNOW WHAT, I DON'T ***REALLY*** FEEL UP TO THIS RIGHT NOW. CAN WE SET UP A MORE CONVENIENT TIME TO DO THIS?
IT'S TWO O'CLOCK IN THE AFTERNOON.
YEAH, WELL— I'VE GOT A YOUNG LADY I'M ENTERTAINING AND I'D LIKE TO GET BACK TO HER.
SURE, I GOTCHA. I'VE GOT YOUR NUMBER, I'LL CALL YOU TOMORROW AND WE CAN SCHEDULE SOMETHING FOR ANOTHER TIME.
COOL.

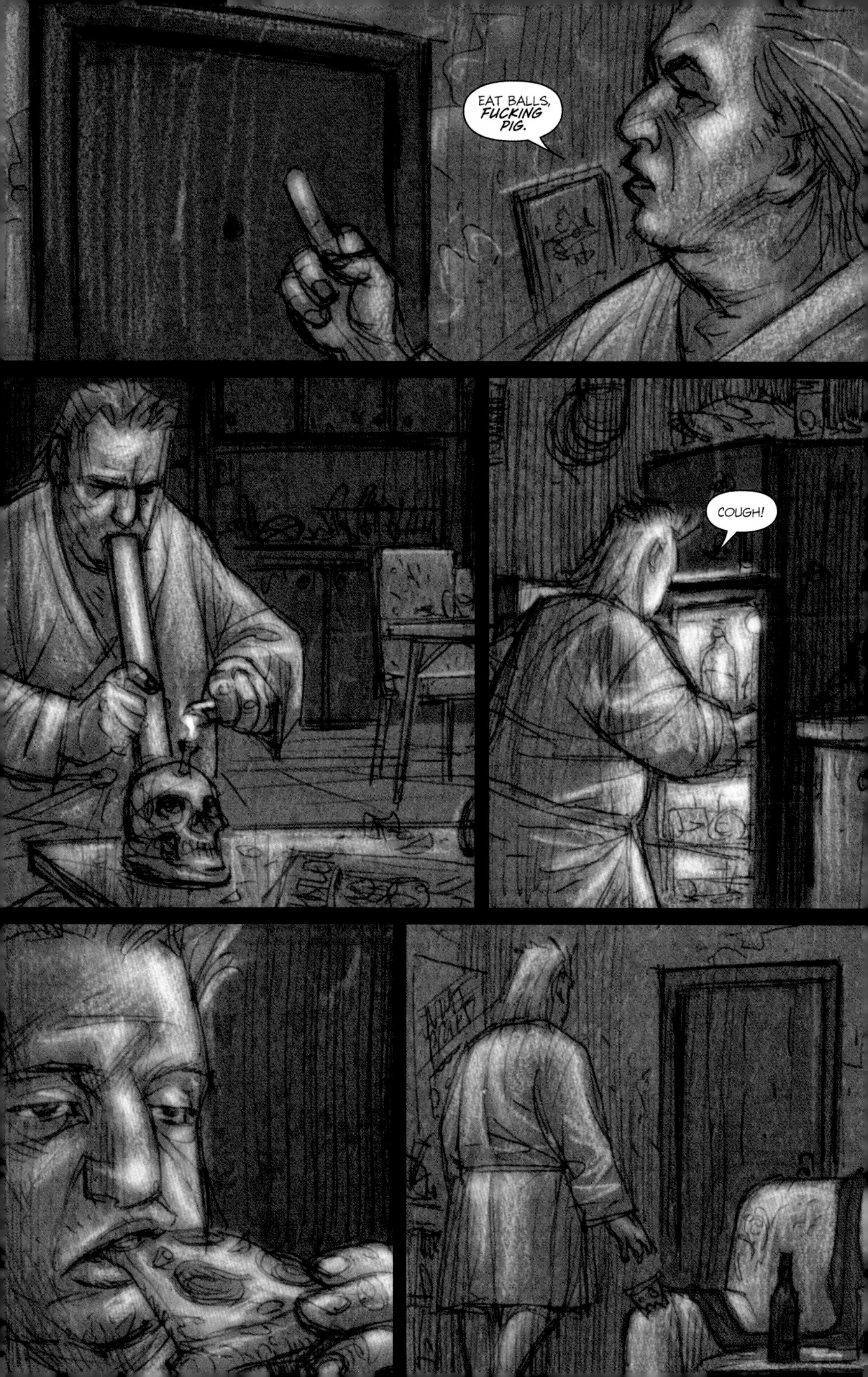
EAT BALLS, FUCKING PIG.
COUGH!

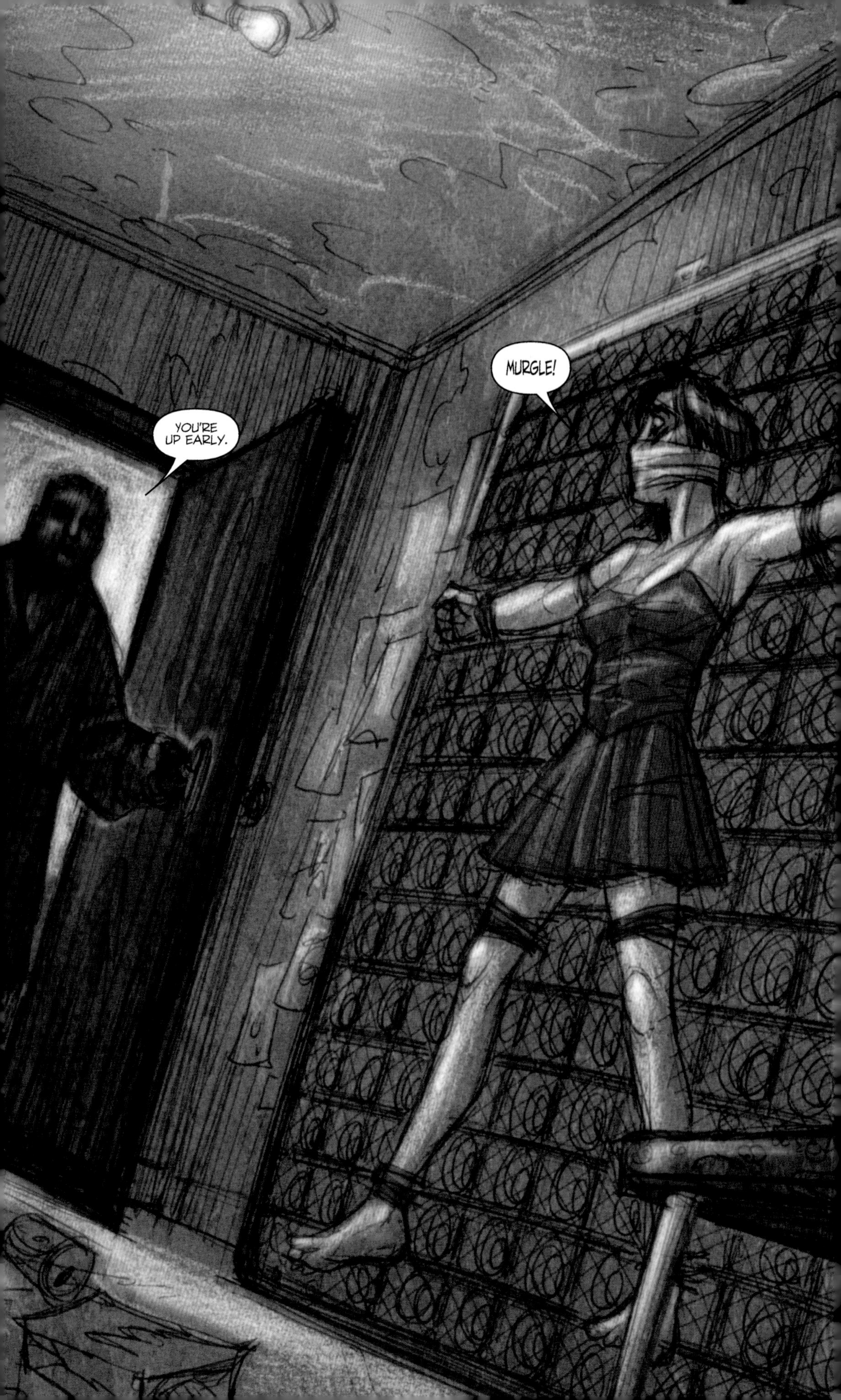
YOU'RE UP EARLY.
MURGLE!

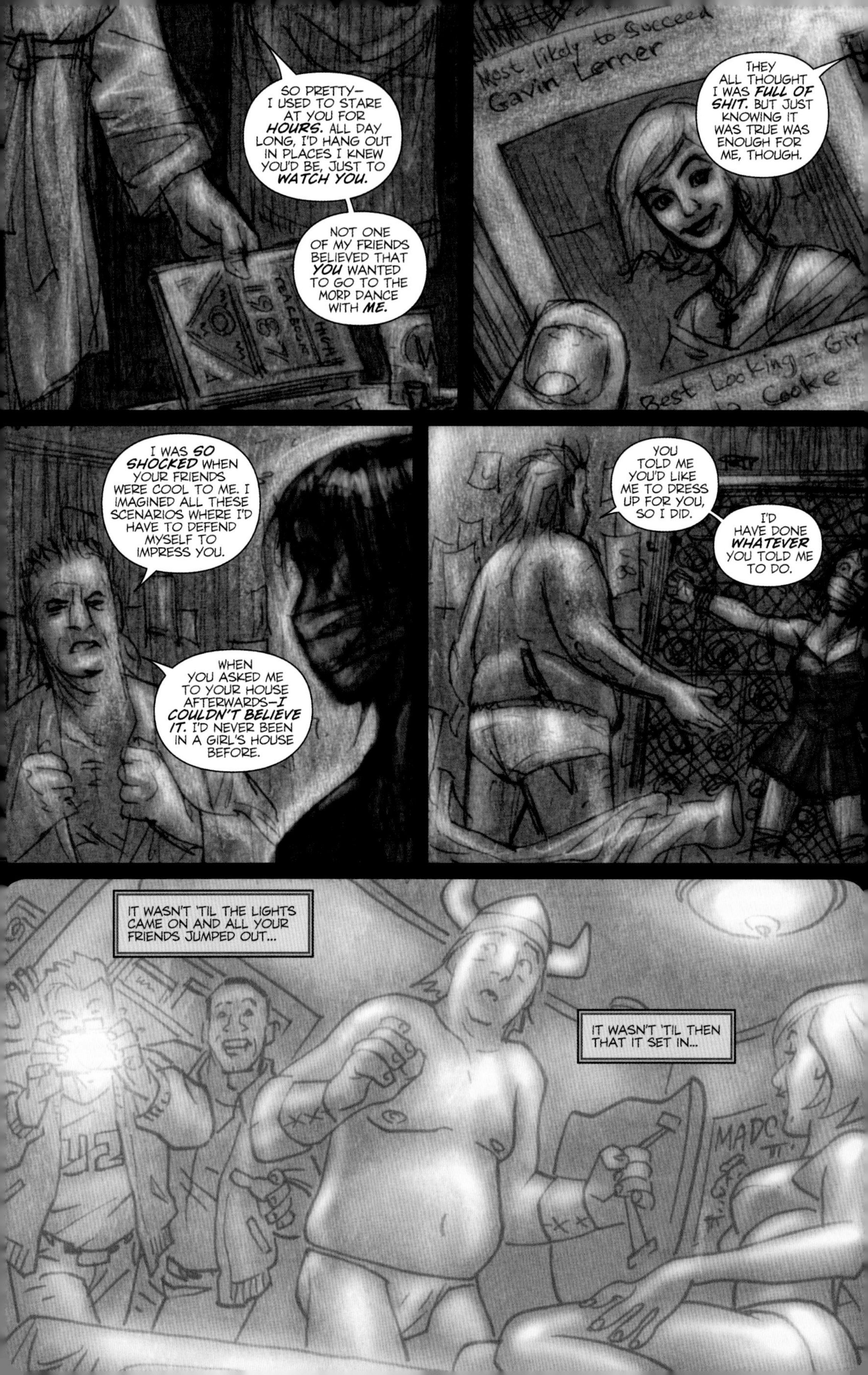

SO PRETTY— I USED TO STARE AT YOU FOR HOURS. ALL DAY LONG, I'D HANG OUT IN PLACES I KNEW YOU'D BE, JUST TO WATCH YOU.
NOT ONE OF MY FRIENDS BELIEVED THAT YOU WANTED TO GO TO THE MORP DANCE WITH ME.
Most likely to Succeed
Gavin Lerner
THEY ALL THOUGHT I WAS FULL OF SHIT. BUT JUST KNOWING IT WAS TRUE WAS ENOUGH FOR ME, THOUGH.
Best Looking - Girl
I WAS SO SHOCKED WHEN YOUR FRIENDS WERE COOL TO ME. I IMAGINED ALL THESE SCENARIOS WHERE I'D HAVE TO DEFEND MYSELF TO IMPRESS YOU.
WHEN YOU ASKED ME TO YOUR HOUSE AFTERWARDS—I COULDN'T BELIEVE IT. I'D NEVER BEEN IN A GIRL'S HOUSE BEFORE.
YOU TOLD ME YOU'D LIKE ME TO DRESS UP FOR YOU, SO I DID.
I'D HAVE DONE WHATEVER YOU TOLD ME TO DO.
IT WASN'T 'TIL THE LIGHTS CAME ON AND ALL YOUR FRIENDS JUMPED OUT...
IT WASN'T 'TIL THEN THAT IT SET IN...

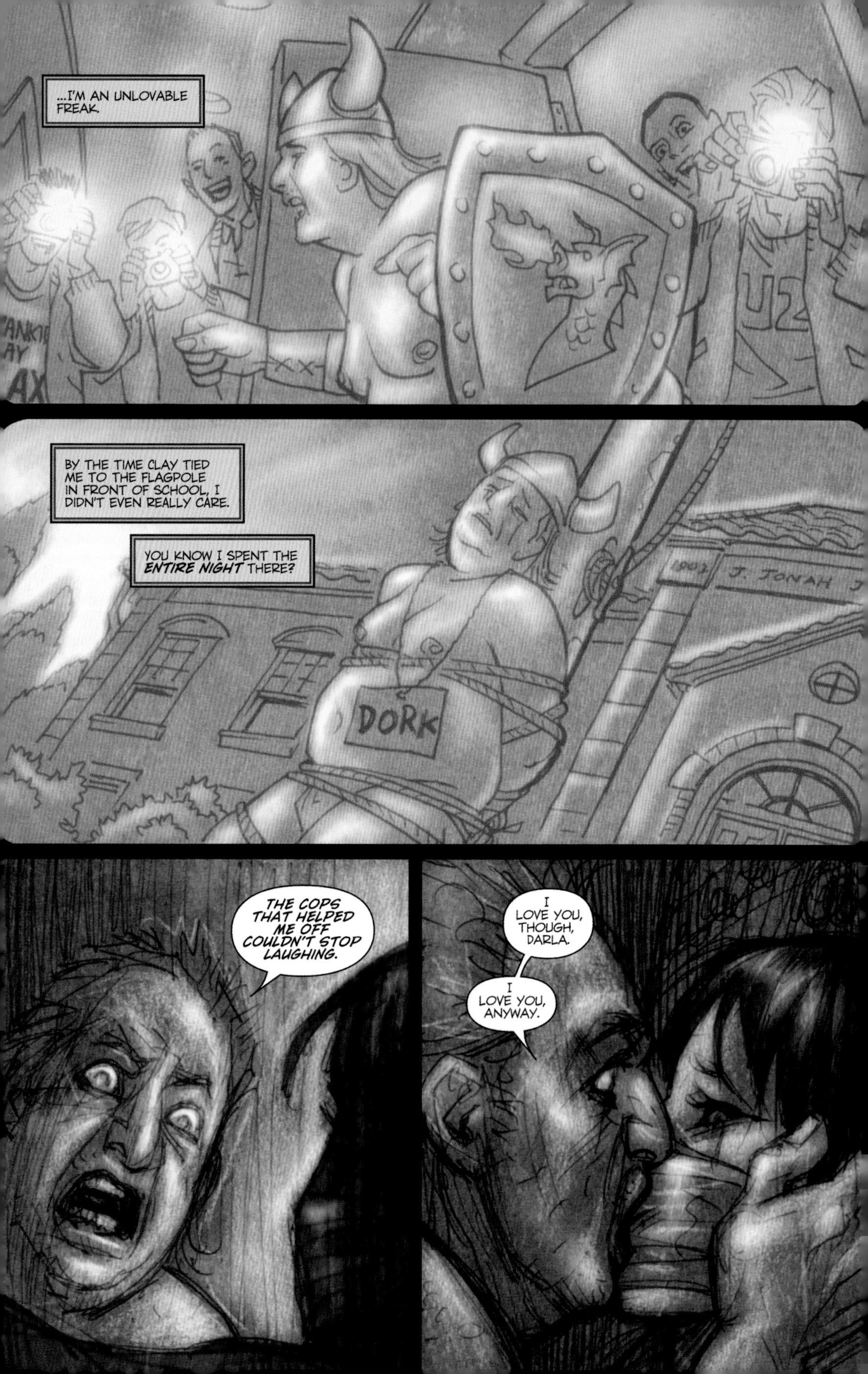
...I'M AN UNLOVABLE FREAK.
BY THE TIME CLAY TIED ME TO THE FLAGPOLE IN FRONT OF SCHOOL, I DIDN'T EVEN REALLY CARE.
YOU KNOW I SPENT THE ENTIRE NIGHT THERE?
DORK
THE COPS THAT HELPED ME OFF COULDN'T STOP LAUGHING.
I LOVE YOU, THOUGH, DARLA.
I LOVE YOU, ANYWAY.

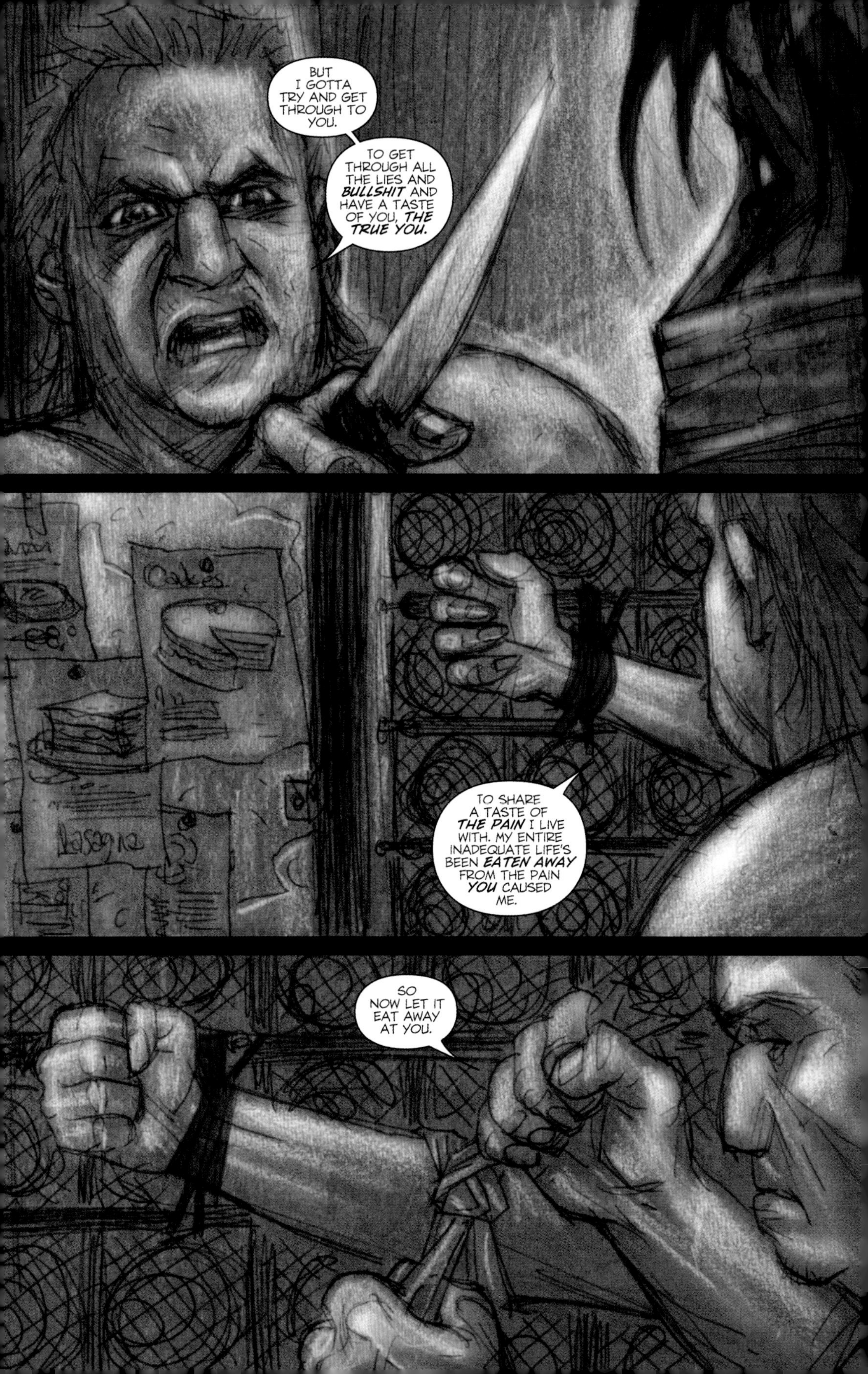
BUT I GOTTA TRY AND GET THROUGH TO YOU.
TO GET THROUGH ALL THE LIES AND ***BULLSHIT*** AND HAVE A TASTE OF YOU, ***THE TRUE YOU.***
Cakes
TO SHARE A TASTE OF ***THE PAIN*** I LIVE WITH. MY ENTIRE INADEQUATE LIFE'S BEEN ***EATEN AWAY*** FROM THE PAIN ***YOU*** CAUSED ME.
SO NOW LET IT EAT AWAY AT YOU.

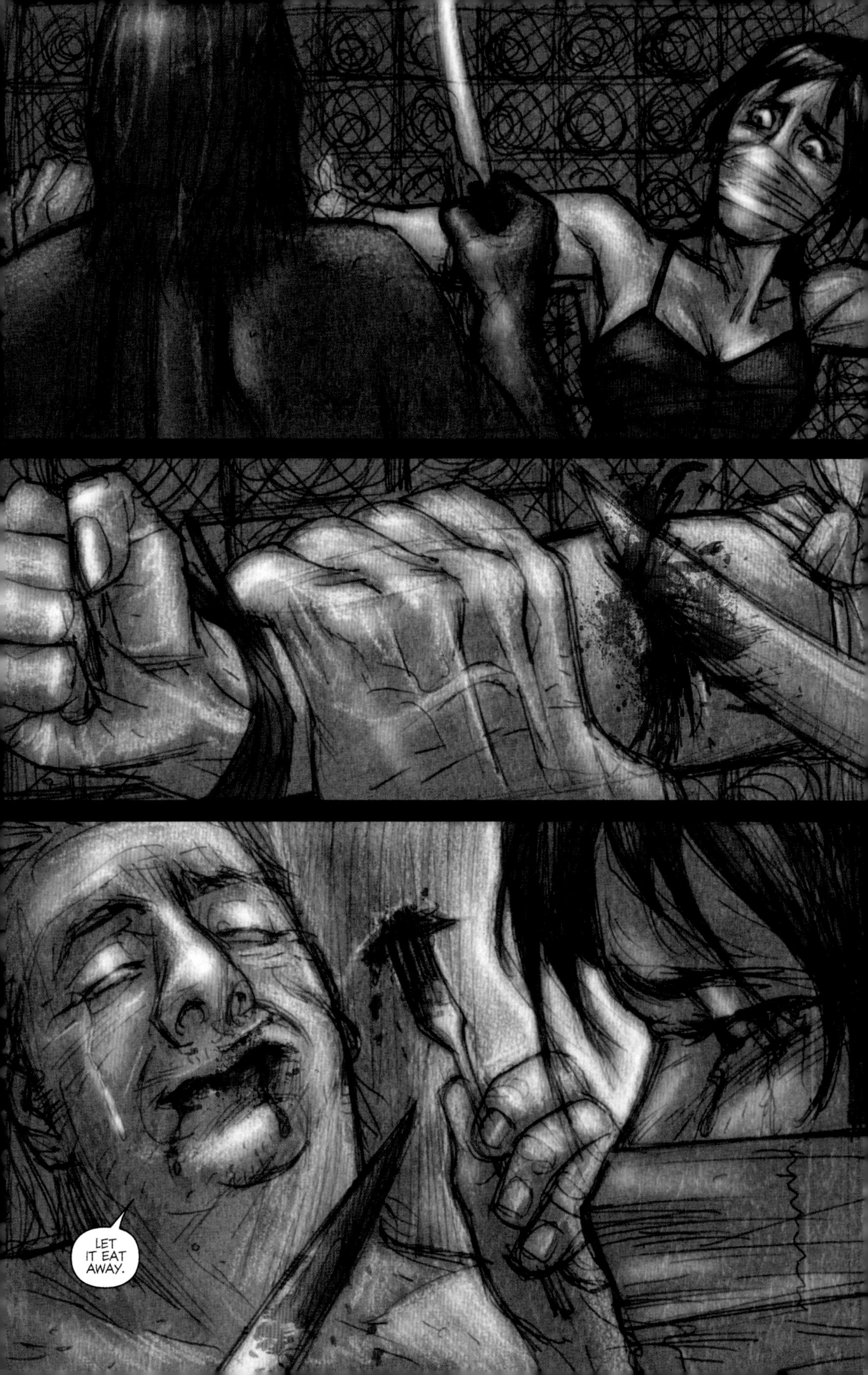
LET IT EAT AWAY.

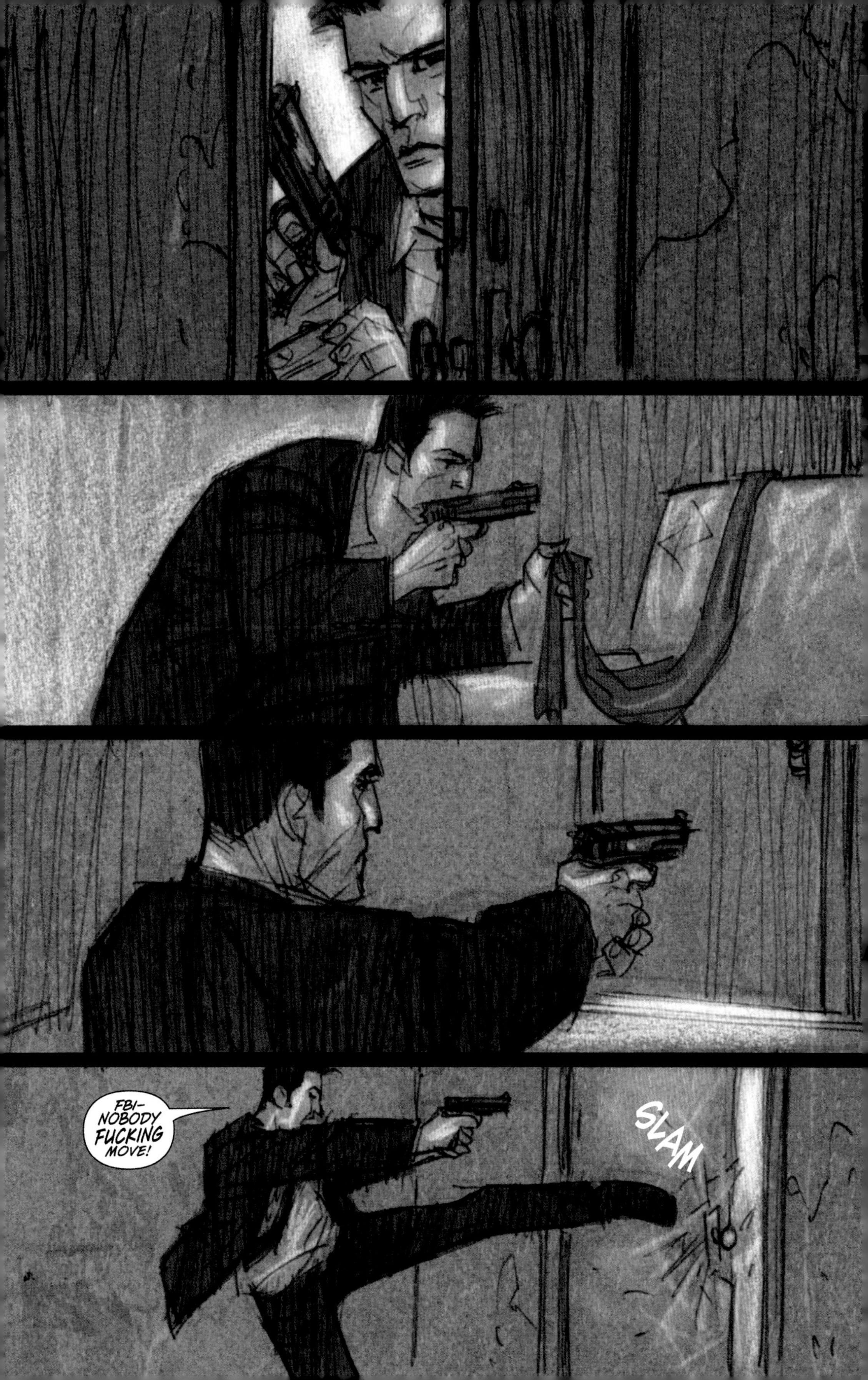
FBI-
NOBODY
FUCKING
MOVE!
SLAM

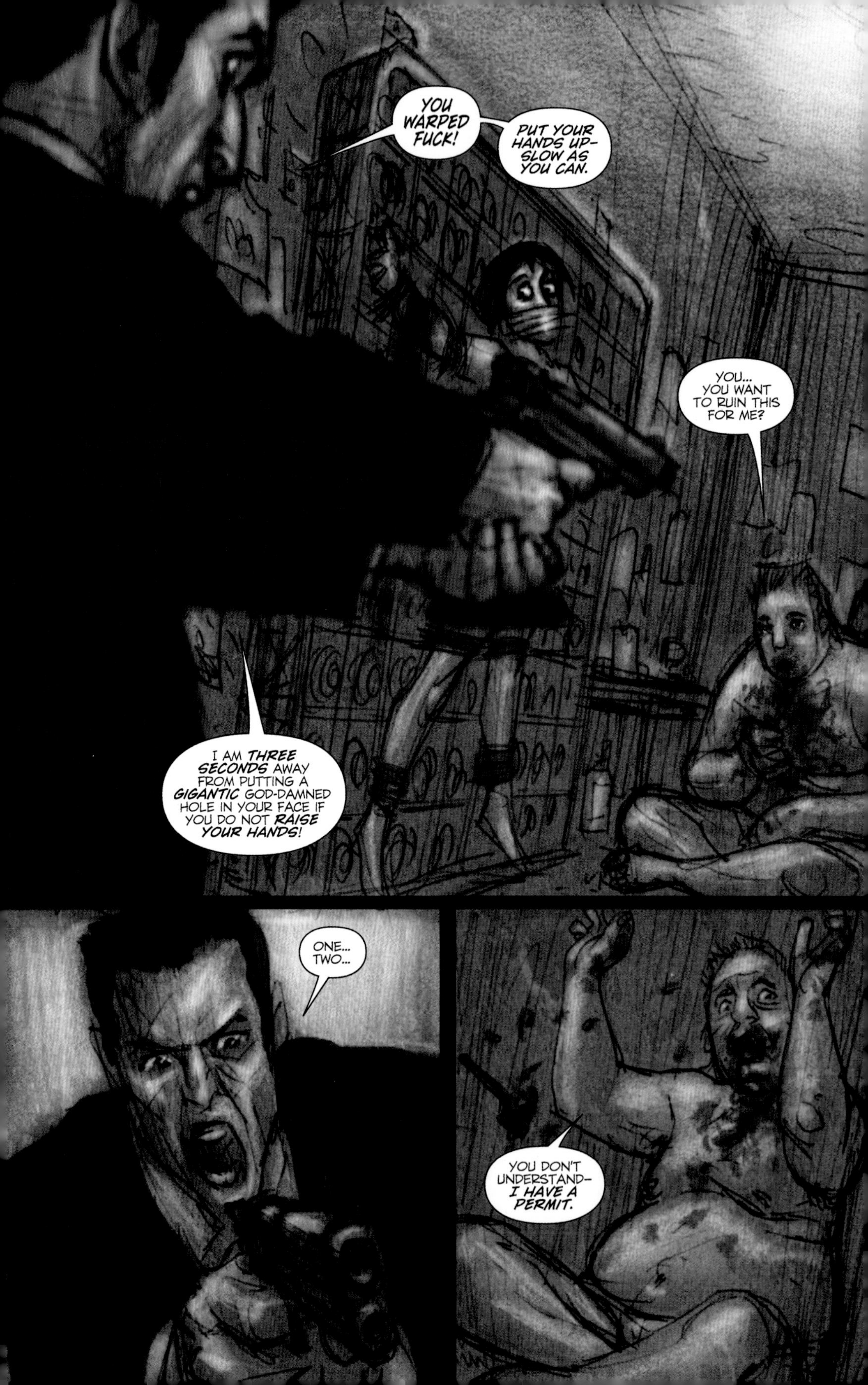
YOU WARPED FUCK!
PUT YOUR HANDS UP- SLOW AS YOU CAN.
YOU... YOU WANT TO RUIN THIS FOR ME?
I AM ***THREE SECONDS*** AWAY FROM PUTTING A ***GIGANTIC*** GOD-DAMNED HOLE IN YOUR FACE IF YOU DO NOT ***RAISE YOUR HANDS***!
ONE... TWO...
YOU DON'T UNDERSTAND– ***I HAVE A PERMIT.***

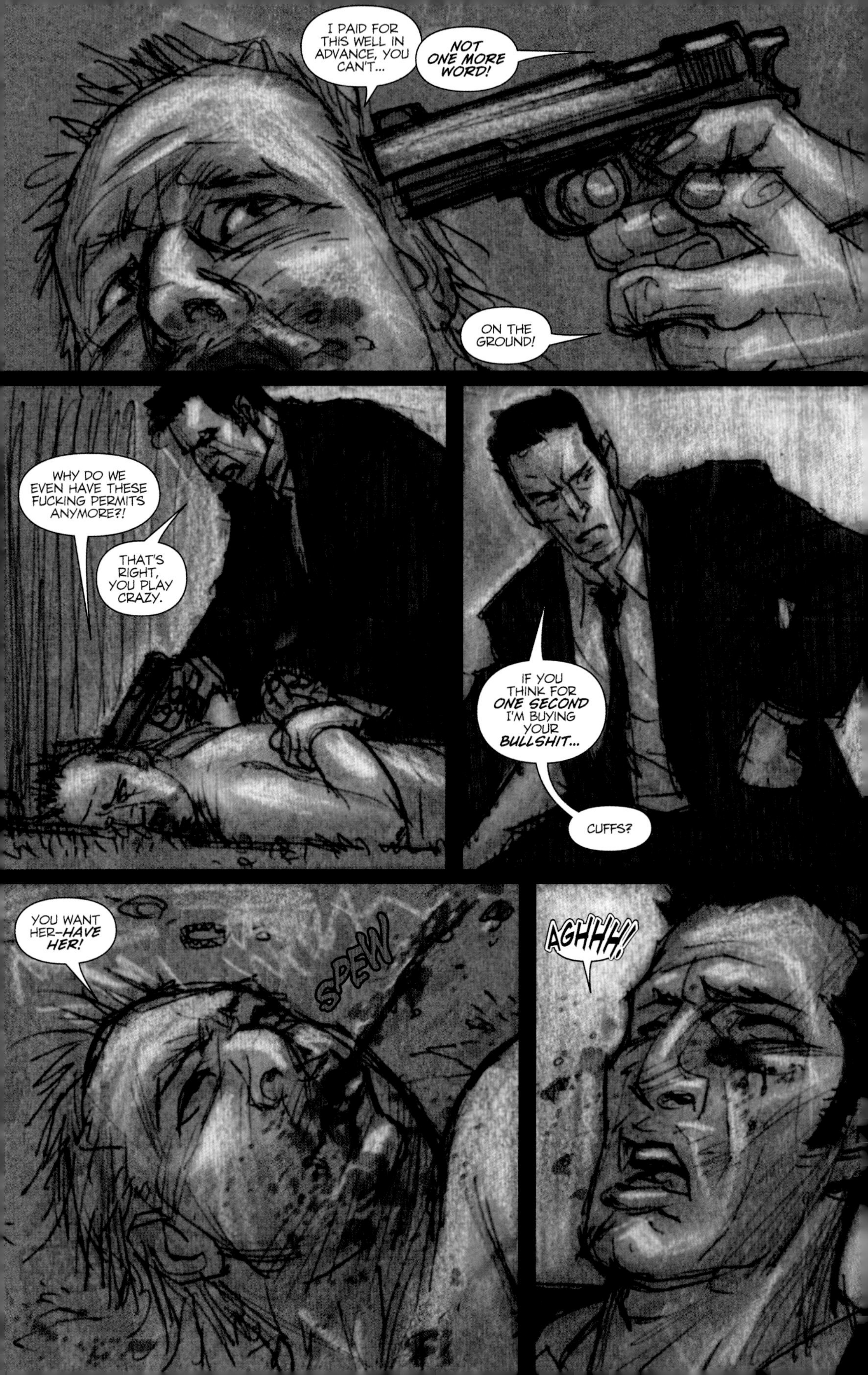

I PAID FOR THIS WELL IN ADVANCE, YOU CAN'T...
NOT ONE MORE WORD!
ON THE GROUND!
WHY DO WE EVEN HAVE THESE FUCKING PERMITS ANYMORE?!
THAT'S RIGHT, YOU PLAY CRAZY.
IF YOU THINK FOR ONE SECOND I'M BUYING YOUR BULLSHIT...
CUFFS?
YOU WANT HER–HAVE HER!
SPEW
AGHHH!!

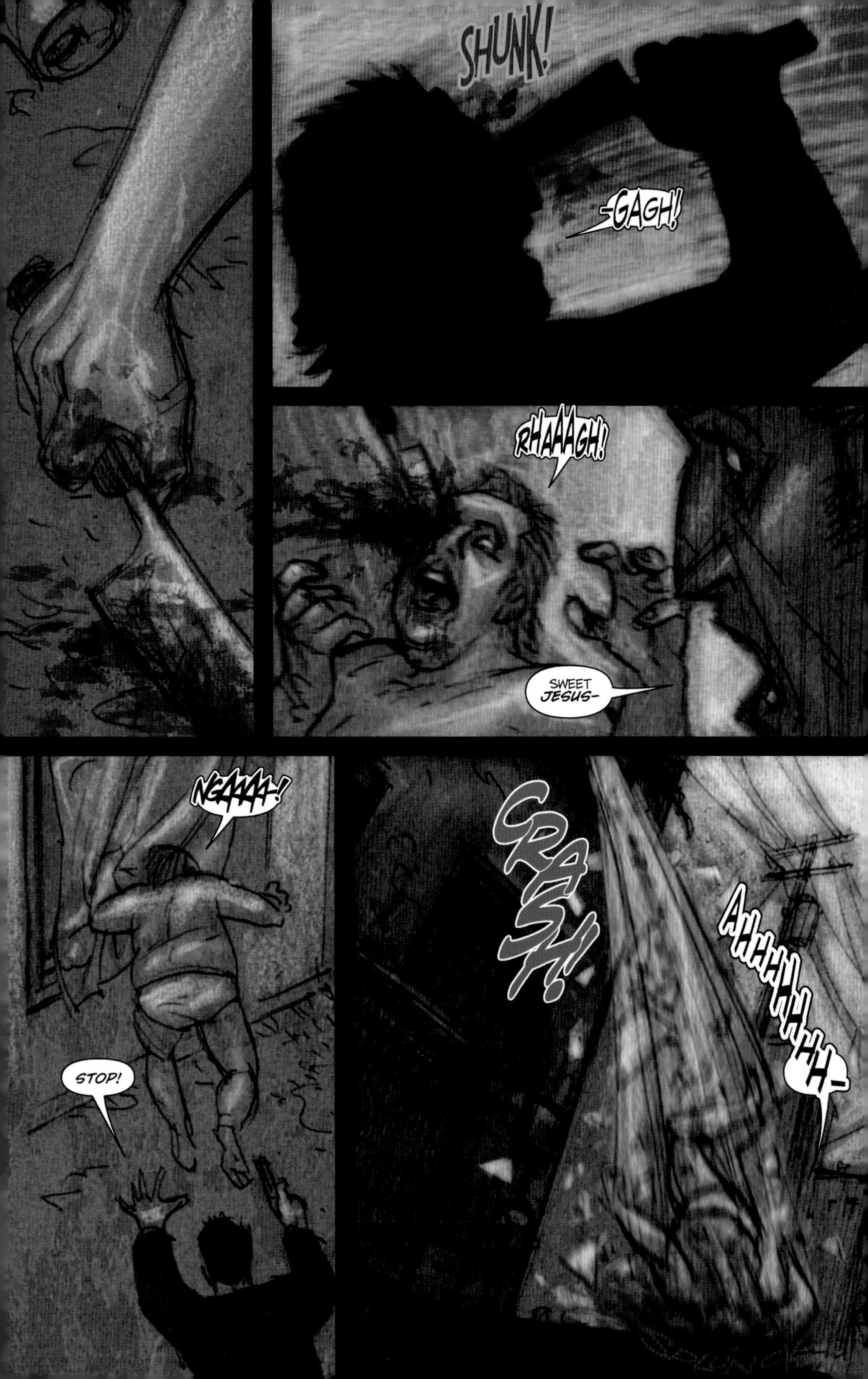
SHUNK!
-GAGH!
RHAAAGH!
SWEET JESUS-
NGAAAA!
STOP!
CRASH!
AHHHHHHHH-

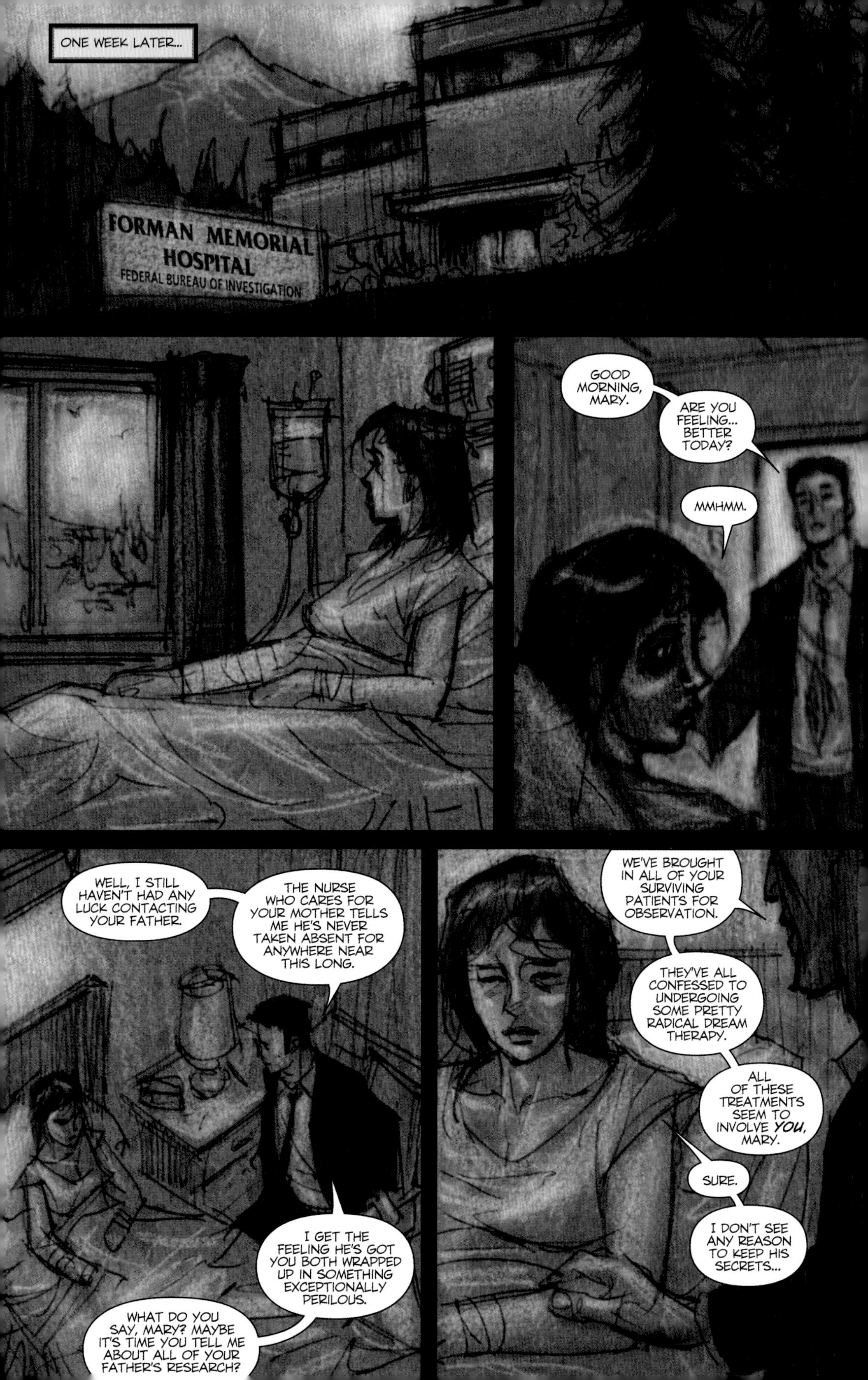
ONE WEEK LATER...
FORMAN MEMORIAL HOSPITAL
FEDERAL BUREAU OF INVESTIGATION
GOOD MORNING, MARY.
ARE YOU FEELING... BETTER TODAY?
MMHMM.
WELL, I STILL HAVEN'T HAD ANY LUCK CONTACTING YOUR FATHER.
THE NURSE WHO CARES FOR YOUR MOTHER TELLS ME HE'S NEVER TAKEN ABSENT FOR ANYWHERE NEAR THIS LONG.
I GET THE FEELING HE'S GOT YOU BOTH WRAPPED UP IN SOMETHING EXCEPTIONALLY PERILOUS.
WHAT DO YOU SAY, MARY? MAYBE IT'S TIME YOU TELL ME ABOUT ALL OF YOUR FATHER'S RESEARCH?
WE'VE BROUGHT IN ALL OF YOUR SURVIVING PATIENTS FOR OBSERVATION.
THEY'VE ALL CONFESSED TO UNDERGOING SOME PRETTY RADICAL DREAM THERAPY.
ALL OF THESE TREATMENTS SEEM TO INVOLVE *YOU,* MARY.
SURE.
I DON'T SEE ANY REASON TO KEEP HIS SECRETS...

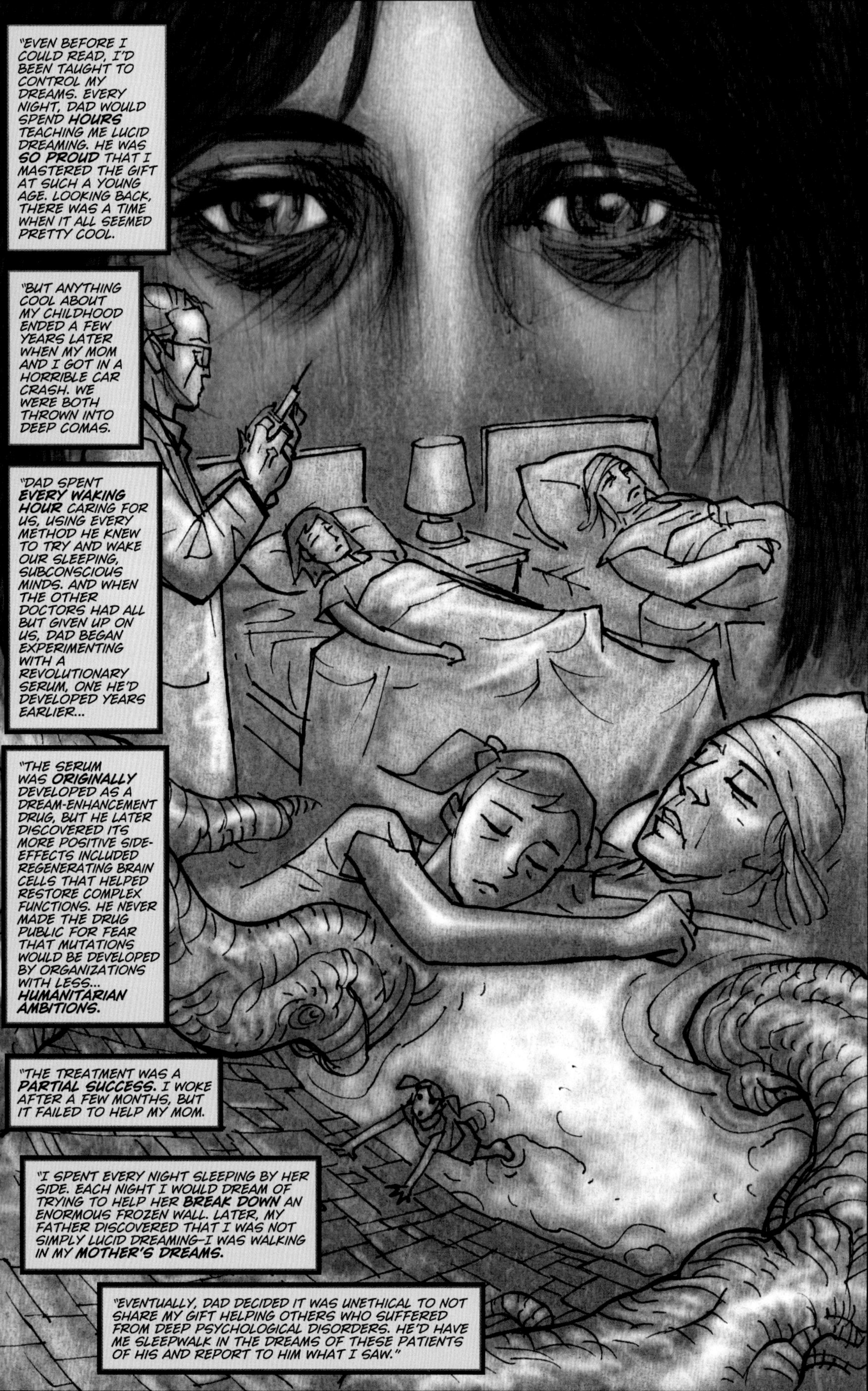
"EVEN BEFORE I COULD READ, I'D BEEN TAUGHT TO CONTROL MY DREAMS. EVERY NIGHT, DAD WOULD SPEND HOURS TEACHING ME LUCID DREAMING. HE WAS SO PROUD THAT I MASTERED THE GIFT AT SUCH A YOUNG AGE. LOOKING BACK, THERE WAS A TIME WHEN IT ALL SEEMED PRETTY COOL.
"BUT ANYTHING COOL ABOUT MY CHILDHOOD ENDED A FEW YEARS LATER WHEN MY MOM AND I GOT IN A HORRIBLE CAR CRASH. WE WERE BOTH THROWN INTO DEEP COMAS.
"DAD SPENT EVERY WAKING HOUR CARING FOR US, USING EVERY METHOD HE KNEW TO TRY AND WAKE OUR SLEEPING, SUBCONSCIOUS MINDS. AND WHEN THE OTHER DOCTORS HAD ALL BUT GIVEN UP ON US, DAD BEGAN EXPERIMENTING WITH A REVOLUTIONARY SERUM, ONE HE'D DEVELOPED YEARS EARLIER...
"THE SERUM WAS ORIGINALLY DEVELOPED AS A DREAM-ENHANCEMENT DRUG, BUT HE LATER DISCOVERED ITS MORE POSITIVE SIDE-EFFECTS INCLUDED REGENERATING BRAIN CELLS THAT HELPED RESTORE COMPLEX FUNCTIONS. HE NEVER MADE THE DRUG PUBLIC FOR FEAR THAT MUTATIONS WOULD BE DEVELOPED BY ORGANIZATIONS WITH LESS... HUMANITARIAN AMBITIONS.
"THE TREATMENT WAS A PARTIAL SUCCESS. I WOKE AFTER A FEW MONTHS, BUT IT FAILED TO HELP MY MOM.
"I SPENT EVERY NIGHT SLEEPING BY HER SIDE. EACH NIGHT I WOULD DREAM OF TRYING TO HELP HER BREAK DOWN AN ENORMOUS FROZEN WALL. LATER, MY FATHER DISCOVERED THAT I WAS NOT SIMPLY LUCID DREAMING—I WAS WALKING IN MY MOTHER'S DREAMS.
"EVENTUALLY, DAD DECIDED IT WAS UNETHICAL TO NOT SHARE MY GIFT HELPING OTHERS WHO SUFFERED FROM DEEP PSYCHOLOGICAL DISORDERS. HE'D HAVE ME SLEEPWALK IN THE DREAMS OF THESE PATIENTS OF HIS AND REPORT TO HIM WHAT I SAW."

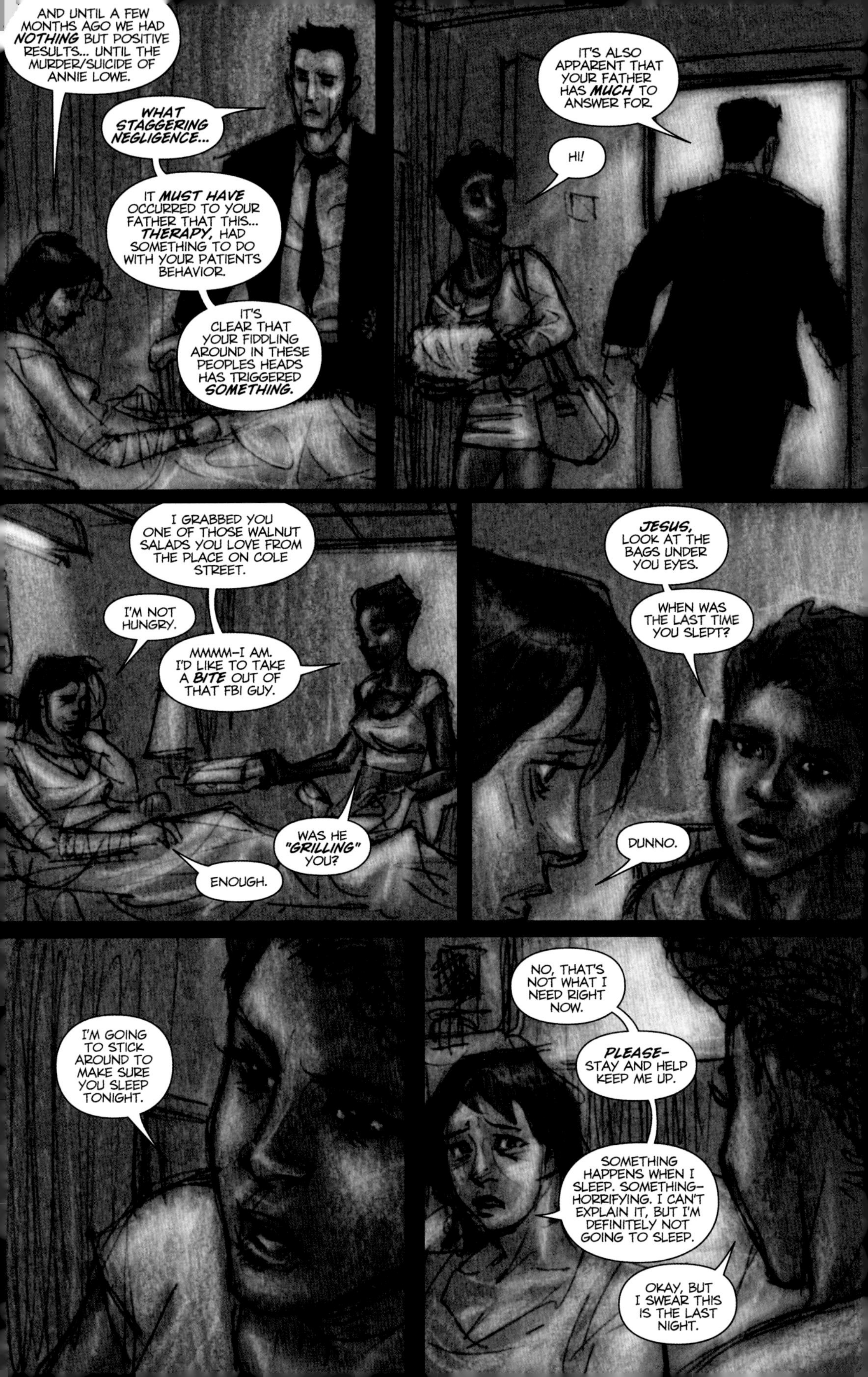
AND UNTIL A FEW MONTHS AGO WE HAD NOTHING BUT POSITIVE RESULTS... UNTIL THE MURDER/SUICIDE OF ANNIE LOWE.
WHAT STAGGERING NEGLIGENCE...
IT MUST HAVE OCCURRED TO YOUR FATHER THAT THIS... THERAPY, HAD SOMETHING TO DO WITH YOUR PATIENTS BEHAVIOR.
IT'S CLEAR THAT YOUR FIDDLING AROUND IN THESE PEOPLES HEADS HAS TRIGGERED SOMETHING.
IT'S ALSO APPARENT THAT YOUR FATHER HAS MUCH TO ANSWER FOR.
HI!
I GRABBED YOU ONE OF THOSE WALNUT SALADS YOU LOVE FROM THE PLACE ON COLE STREET.
I'M NOT HUNGRY.
MMMM–I AM. I'D LIKE TO TAKE A BITE OUT OF THAT FBI GUY.
WAS HE "GRILLING" YOU?
ENOUGH.
JESUS, LOOK AT THE BAGS UNDER YOU EYES.
WHEN WAS THE LAST TIME YOU SLEPT?
DUNNO.
I'M GOING TO STICK AROUND TO MAKE SURE YOU SLEEP TONIGHT.
NO, THAT'S NOT WHAT I NEED RIGHT NOW.
PLEASE- STAY AND HELP KEEP ME UP.
SOMETHING HAPPENS WHEN I SLEEP. SOMETHING- HORRIFYING. I CAN'T EXPLAIN IT, BUT I'M DEFINITELY NOT GOING TO SLEEP.
OKAY, BUT I SWEAR THIS IS THE LAST NIGHT.

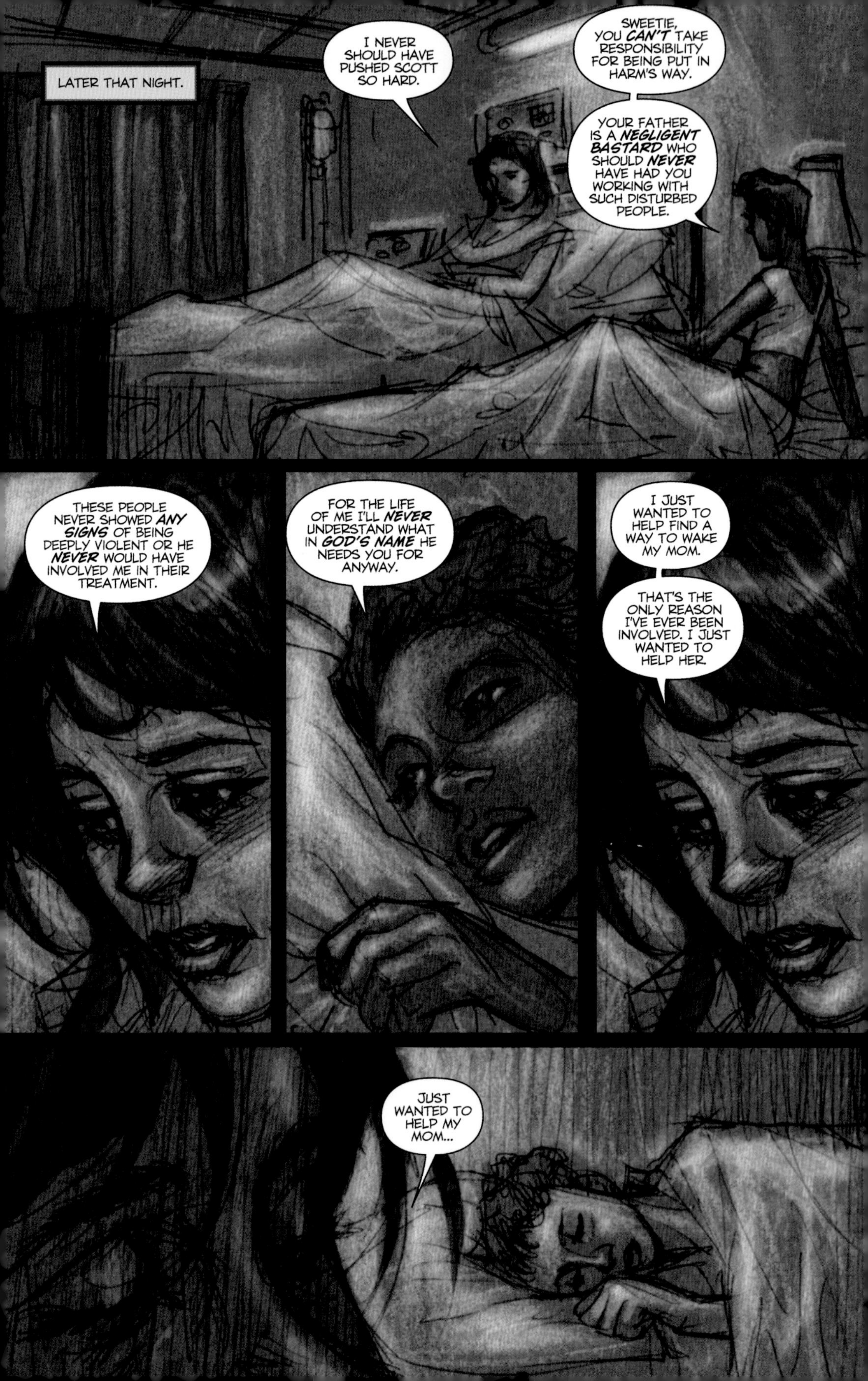
LATER THAT NIGHT.
I NEVER SHOULD HAVE PUSHED SCOTT SO HARD.
SWEETIE, YOU CAN'T TAKE RESPONSIBILITY FOR BEING PUT IN HARM'S WAY.
YOUR FATHER IS A NEGLIGENT BASTARD WHO SHOULD NEVER HAVE HAD YOU WORKING WITH SUCH DISTURBED PEOPLE.
THESE PEOPLE NEVER SHOWED ANY SIGNS OF BEING DEEPLY VIOLENT OR HE NEVER WOULD HAVE INVOLVED ME IN THEIR TREATMENT.
FOR THE LIFE OF ME I'LL NEVER UNDERSTAND WHAT IN GOD'S NAME HE NEEDS YOU FOR ANYWAY.
I JUST WANTED TO HELP FIND A WAY TO WAKE MY MOM.
THAT'S THE ONLY REASON I'VE EVER BEEN INVOLVED. I JUST WANTED TO HELP HER.
JUST WANTED TO HELP MY MOM...

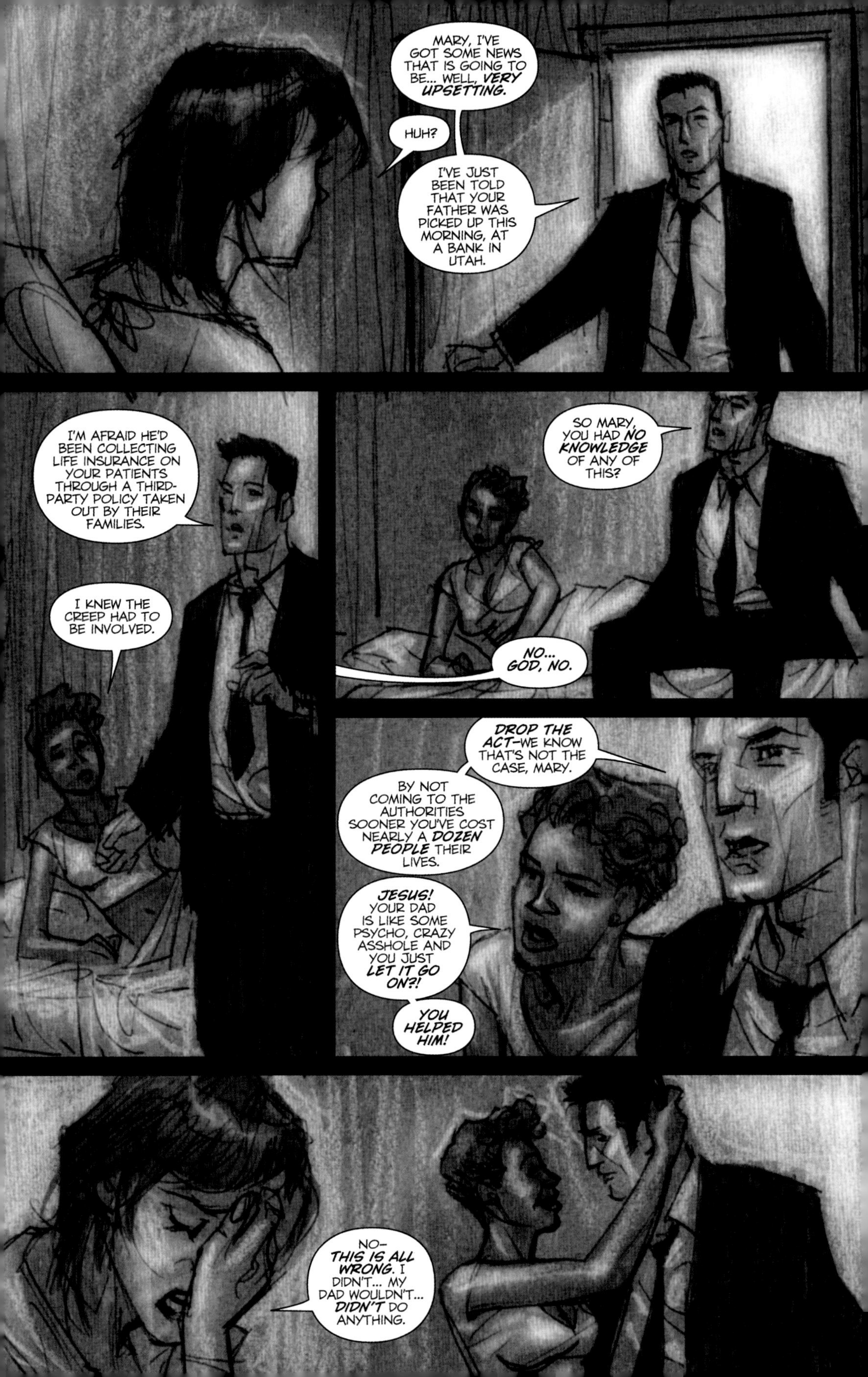

MARY, I'VE GOT SOME NEWS THAT IS GOING TO BE... WELL, *VERY UPSETTING.*
HUH?
I'VE JUST BEEN TOLD THAT YOUR FATHER WAS PICKED UP THIS MORNING, AT A BANK IN UTAH.
I'M AFRAID HE'D BEEN COLLECTING LIFE INSURANCE ON YOUR PATIENTS THROUGH A THIRD-PARTY POLICY TAKEN OUT BY THEIR FAMILIES.
I KNEW THE CREEP HAD TO BE INVOLVED.
SO MARY, YOU HAD *NO KNOWLEDGE* OF ANY OF THIS?
NO... GOD, NO.
DROP THE ACT—WE KNOW THAT'S NOT THE CASE, MARY.
BY NOT COMING TO THE AUTHORITIES SOONER YOU'VE COST NEARLY A *DOZEN PEOPLE* THEIR LIVES.
JESUS! YOUR DAD IS LIKE SOME PSYCHO, CRAZY ASSHOLE AND YOU JUST *LET IT GO ON?!*
YOU HELPED HIM!
NO— *THIS IS ALL WRONG.* I DIDN'T... MY DAD WOULDN'T... *DIDN'T* DO ANYTHING.

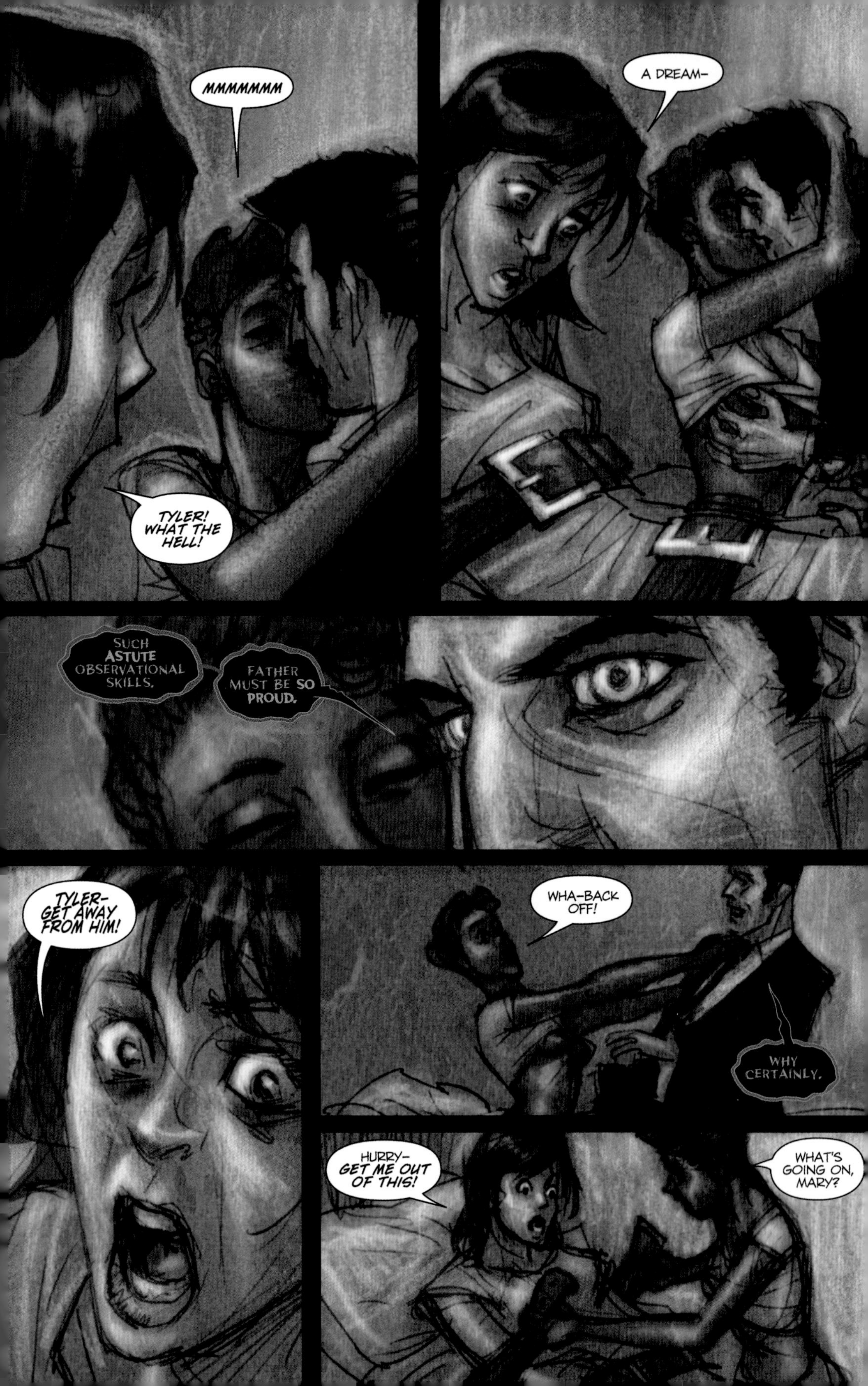
MMMMMMM
TYLER! WHAT THE HELL!
A DREAM-
SUCH ASTUTE OBSERVATIONAL SKILLS.
FATHER MUST BE SO PROUD.
TYLER- GET AWAY FROM HIM!
WHA-BACK OFF!
WHY CERTAINLY.
HURRY- GET ME OUT OF THIS!
WHAT'S GOING ON, MARY?

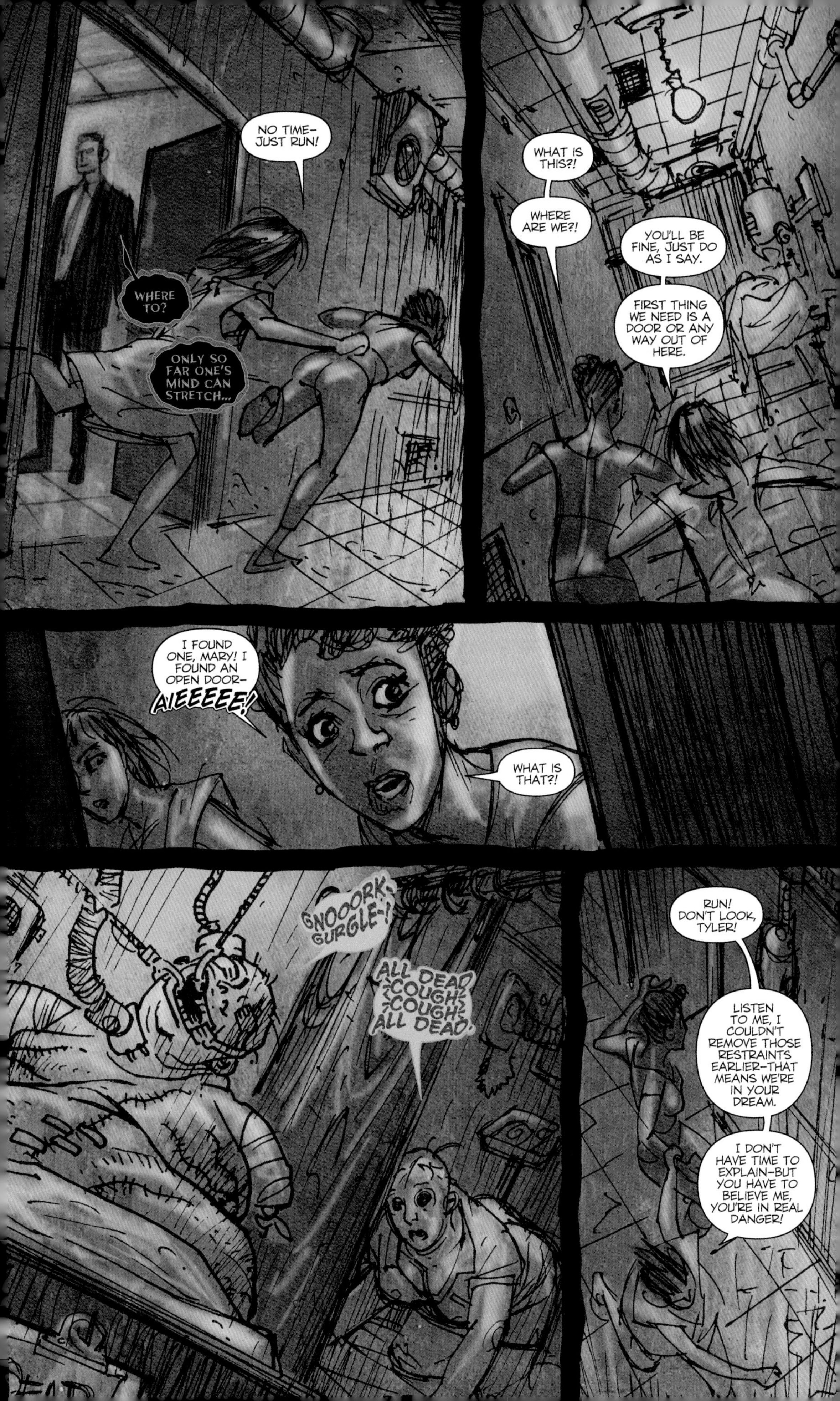

NO TIME– JUST RUN!
WHERE TO?
ONLY SO FAR ONE'S MIND CAN STRETCH...
WHAT IS THIS?!
WHERE ARE WE?!
YOU'LL BE FINE, JUST DO AS I SAY.
FIRST THING WE NEED IS A DOOR OR ANY WAY OUT OF HERE.
I FOUND ONE, MARY! I FOUND AN OPEN DOOR–
AIEEEEE!
WHAT IS THAT?!
GNOOORK-GURGLE-!
ALL DEAD -COUGH- -COUGH- ALL DEAD.
RUN! DON'T LOOK, TYLER!
LISTEN TO ME, I COULDN'T REMOVE THOSE RESTRAINTS EARLIER–THAT MEANS WE'RE IN YOUR DREAM.
I DON'T HAVE TIME TO EXPLAIN–BUT YOU HAVE TO BELIEVE ME, YOU'RE IN REAL DANGER!

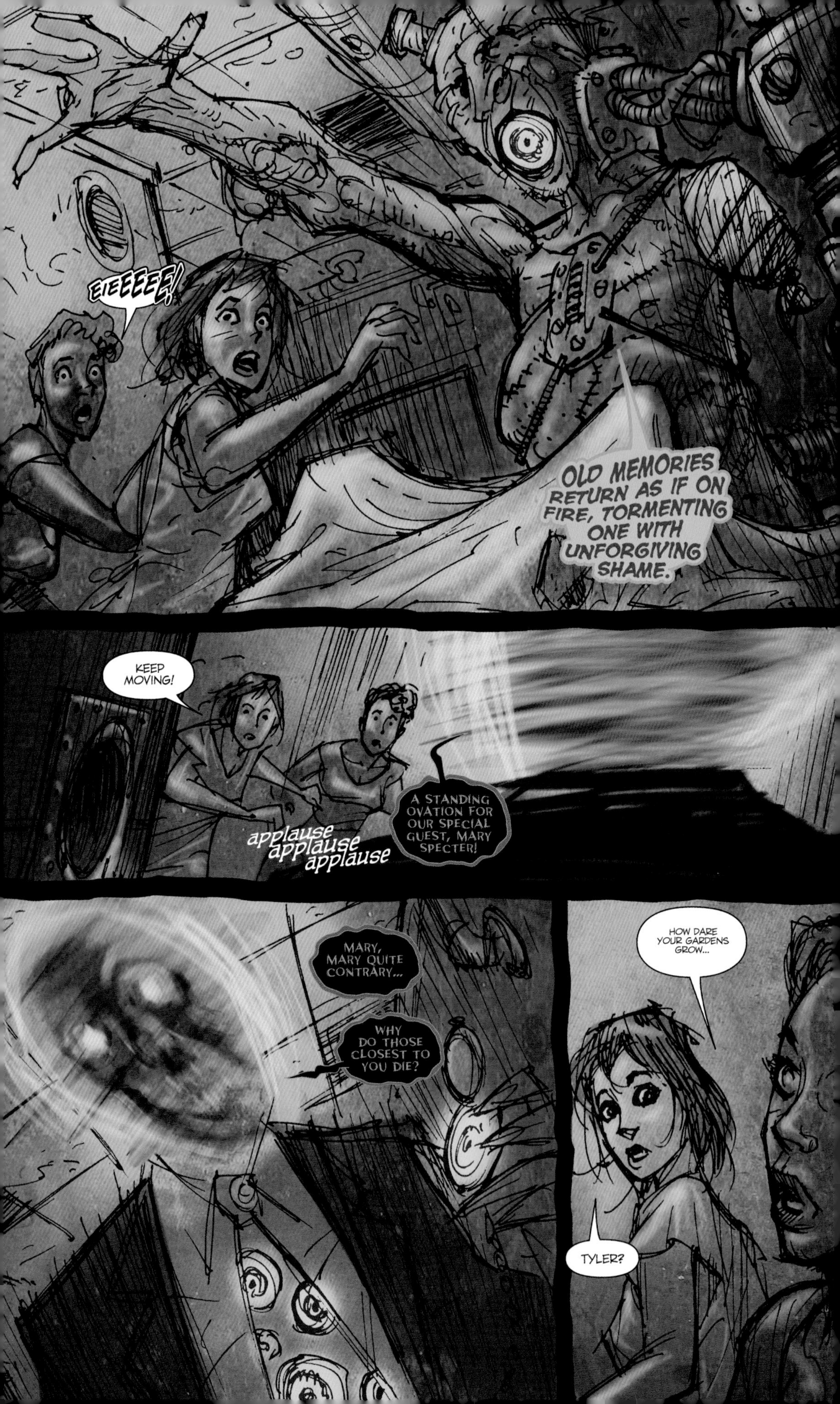
EIEEEEE!
OLD MEMORIES RETURN AS IF ON FIRE, TORMENTING ONE WITH UNFORGIVING SHAME.
KEEP MOVING!
applause applause applause
A STANDING OVATION FOR OUR SPECIAL GUEST, MARY SPECTER!
MARY, MARY QUITE CONTRARY...
WHY DO THOSE CLOSEST TO YOU DIE?
HOW DARE YOUR GARDENS GROW...
TYLER?

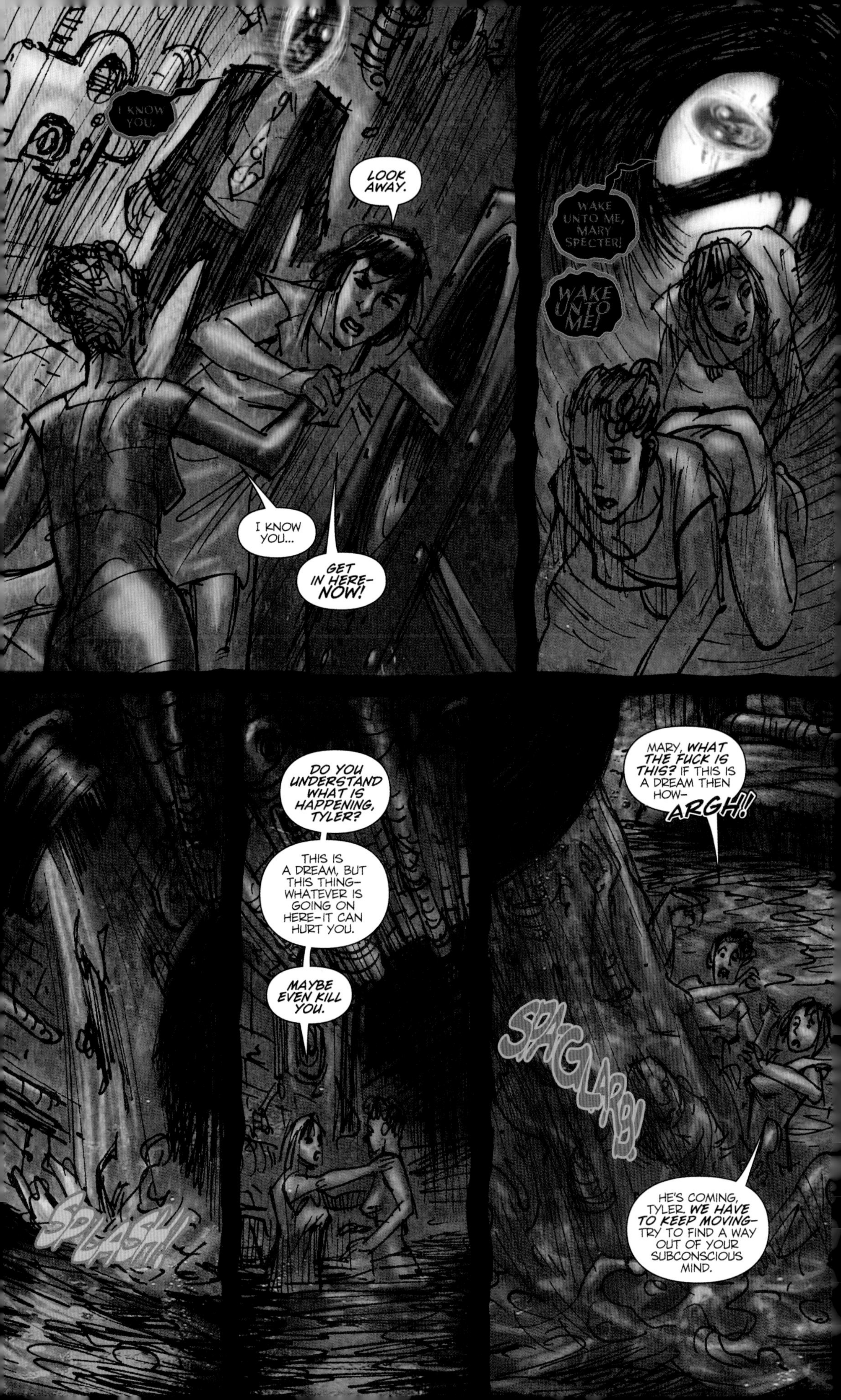
I KNOW YOU.
LOOK AWAY.
I KNOW YOU...
GET IN HERE- NOW!
WAKE UNTO ME, MARY SPECTER!
WAKE UNTO ME!
SPLASH
DO YOU UNDERSTAND WHAT IS HAPPENING, TYLER?
THIS IS A DREAM, BUT THIS THING- WHATEVER IS GOING ON HERE-IT CAN HURT YOU.
MAYBE EVEN KILL YOU.
MARY, WHAT THE FUCK IS THIS? IF THIS IS A DREAM THEN HOW- ARGH!!
SPLAGLARB!
HE'S COMING, TYLER. WE HAVE TO KEEP MOVING- TRY TO FIND A WAY OUT OF YOUR SUBCONSCIOUS MIND.

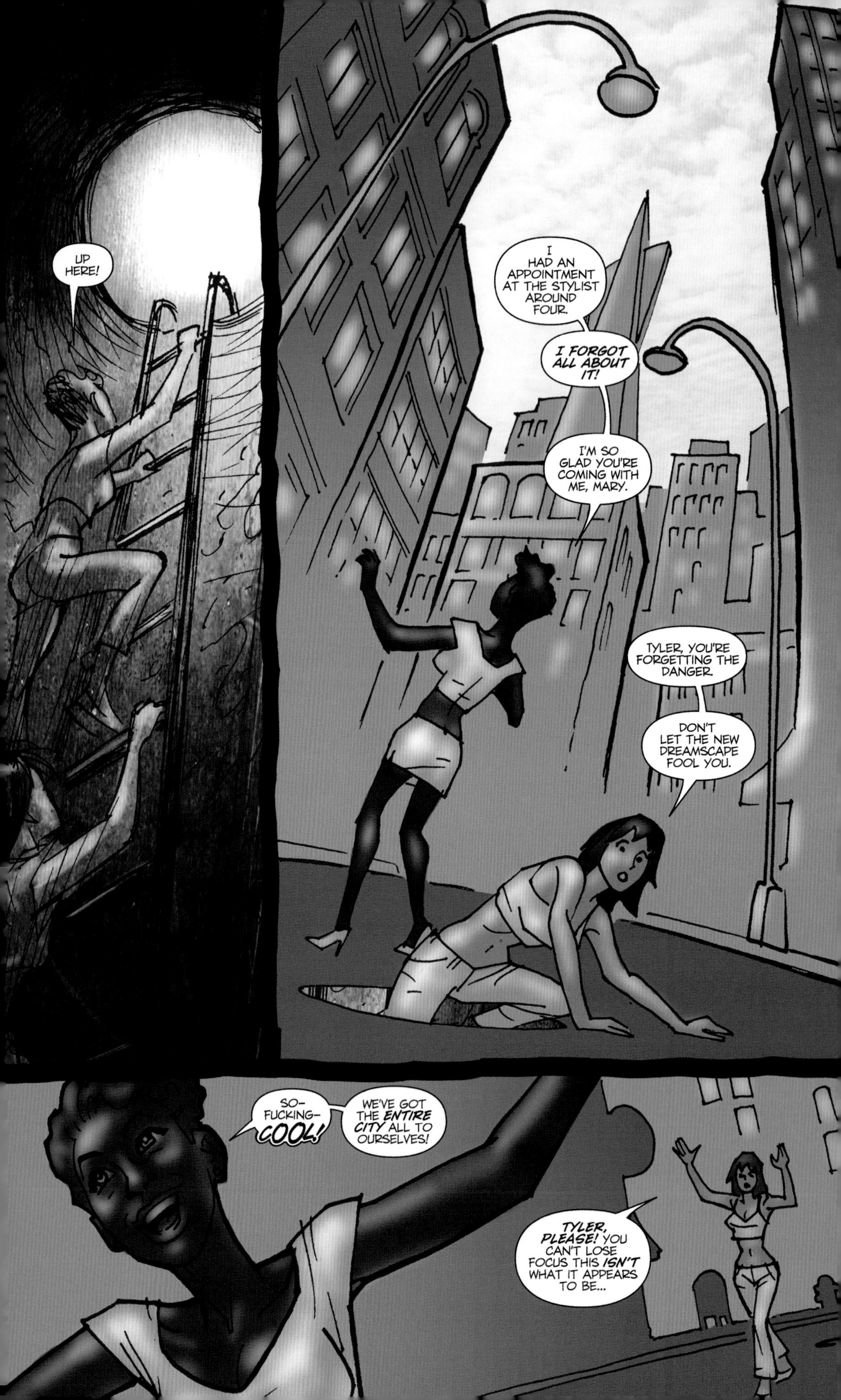

UP HERE!
I HAD AN APPOINTMENT AT THE STYLIST AROUND FOUR.
I FORGOT ALL ABOUT IT!
I'M SO GLAD YOU'RE COMING WITH ME, MARY.
TYLER, YOU'RE FORGETTING THE DANGER.
DON'T LET THE NEW DREAMSCAPE FOOL YOU.
SO-FUCKING-COOL!
WE'VE GOT THE ENTIRE CITY ALL TO OURSELVES!
TYLER, PLEASE! YOU CAN'T LOSE FOCUS THIS ISN'T WHAT IT APPEARS TO BE...

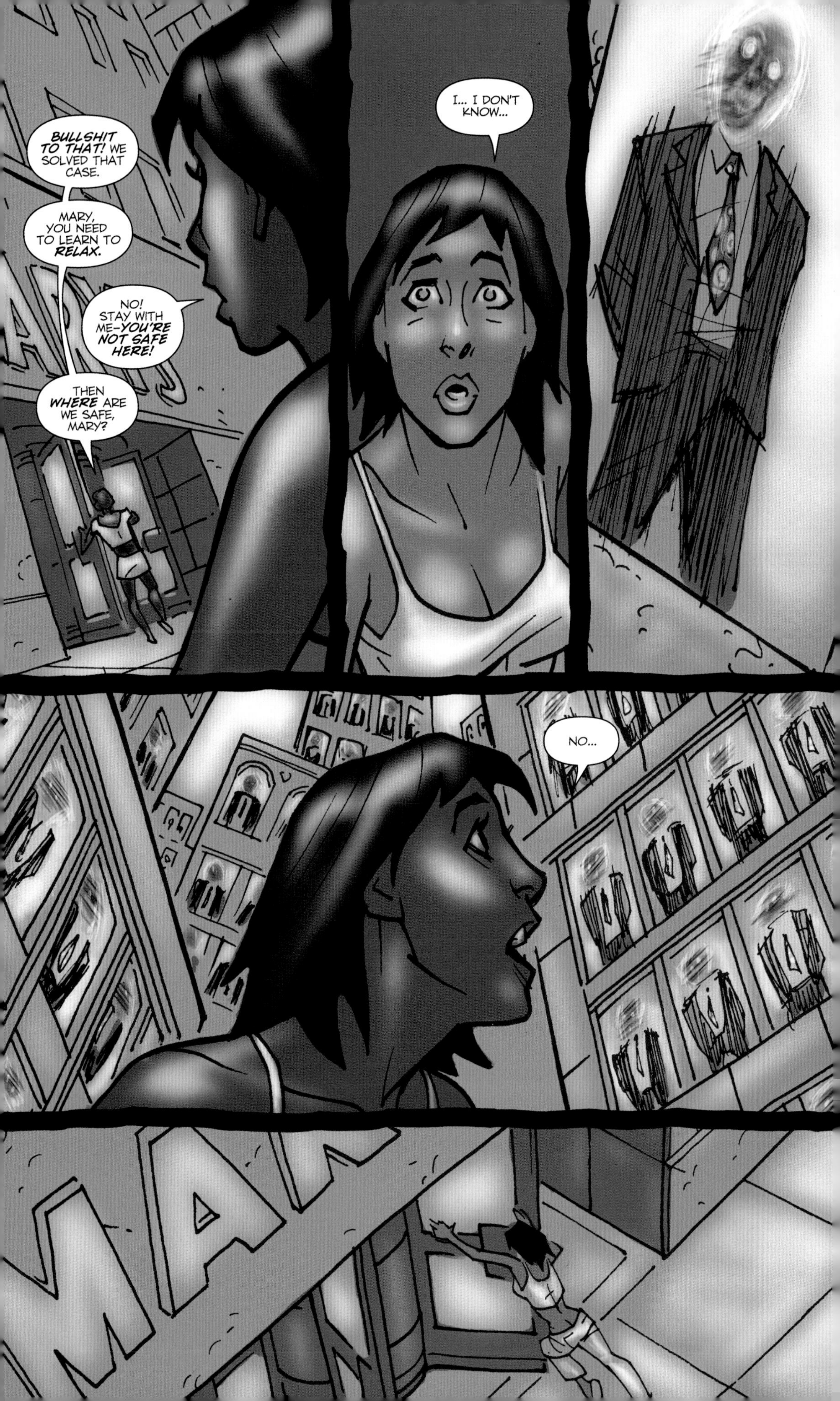
BULLSHIT TO THAT! WE SOLVED THAT CASE.
MARY, YOU NEED TO LEARN TO RELAX.
NO! STAY WITH ME--YOU'RE NOT SAFE HERE!
THEN WHERE ARE WE SAFE, MARY?
I... I DON'T KNOW...
NO...

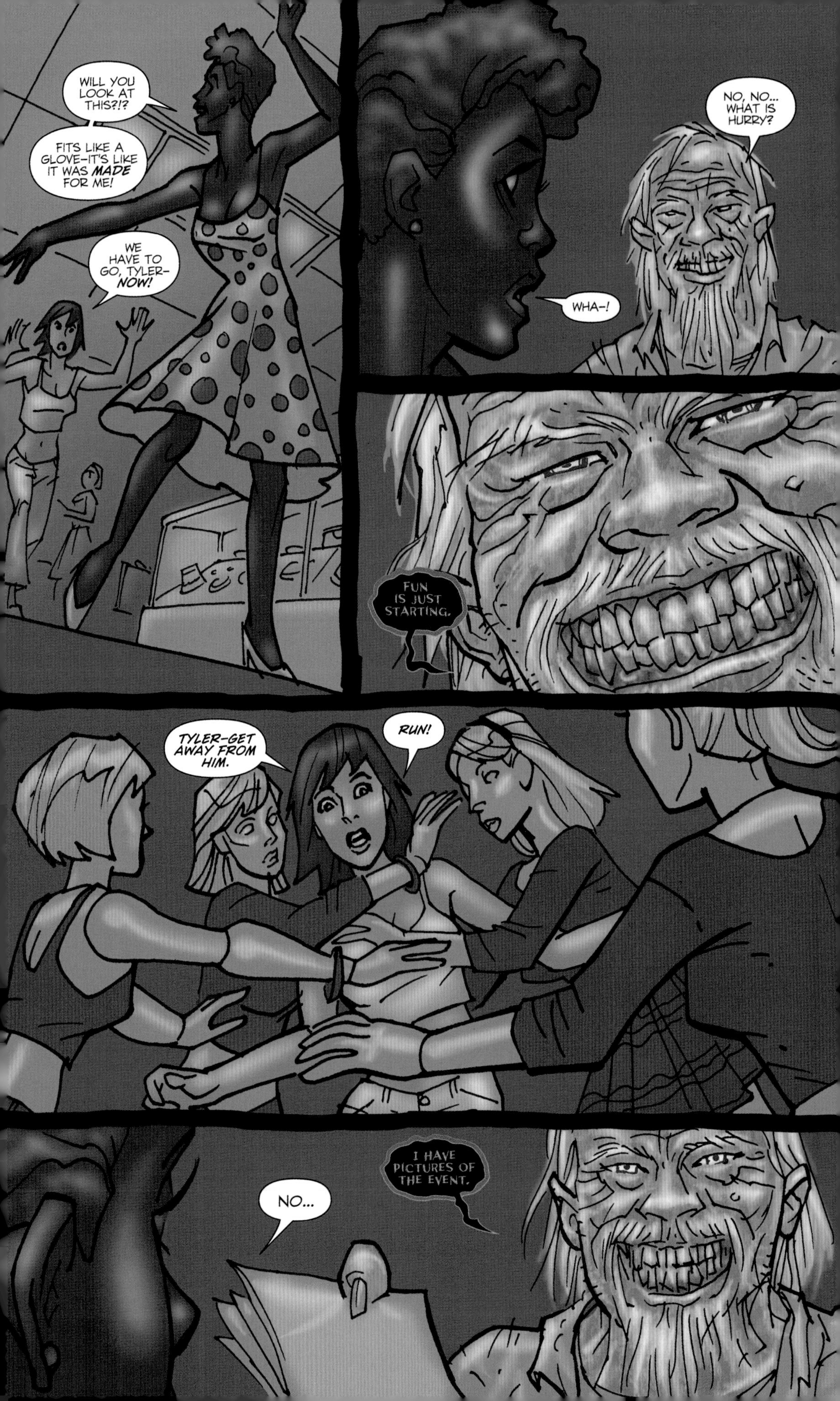
WILL YOU LOOK AT THIS?!?
FITS LIKE A GLOVE–IT'S LIKE IT WAS **MADE** FOR ME!
WE HAVE TO GO, TYLER–**NOW!**
NO, NO... WHAT IS HURRY?
WHA–!
FUN IS JUST STARTING.
TYLER–GET AWAY FROM HIM.
RUN!
I HAVE PICTURES OF THE EVENT.
NO...

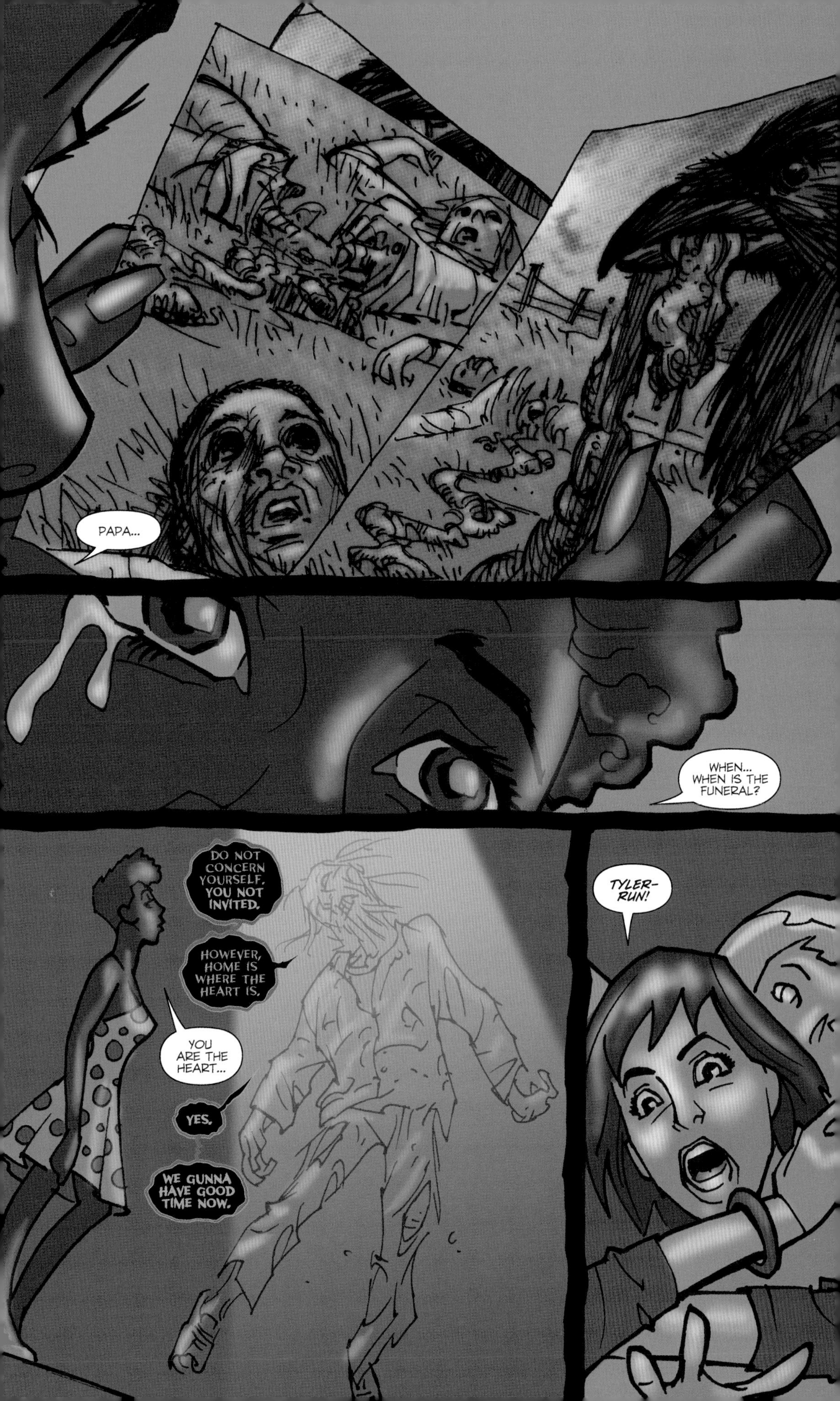
PAPA...
WHEN... WHEN IS THE FUNERAL?
DO NOT CONCERN YOURSELF. YOU NOT INVITED.
HOWEVER, HOME IS WHERE THE HEART IS.
YOU ARE THE HEART...
YES.
WE GUNNA HAVE GOOD TIME NOW.
TYLER-RUN!

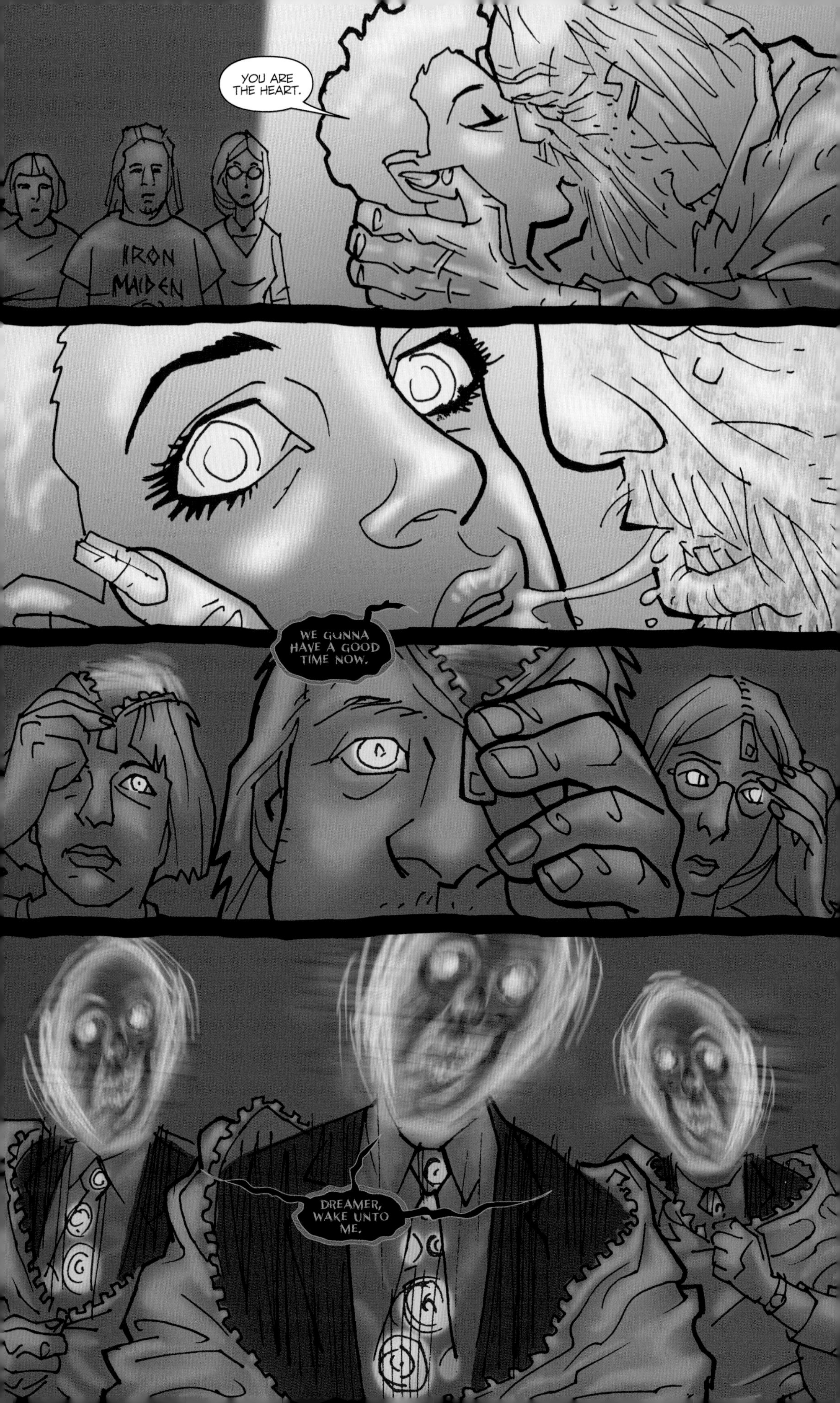
YOU ARE THE HEART.
IRON MAIDEN
WE GUNNA HAVE A GOOD TIME NOW.
DREAMER, WAKE UNTO ME.

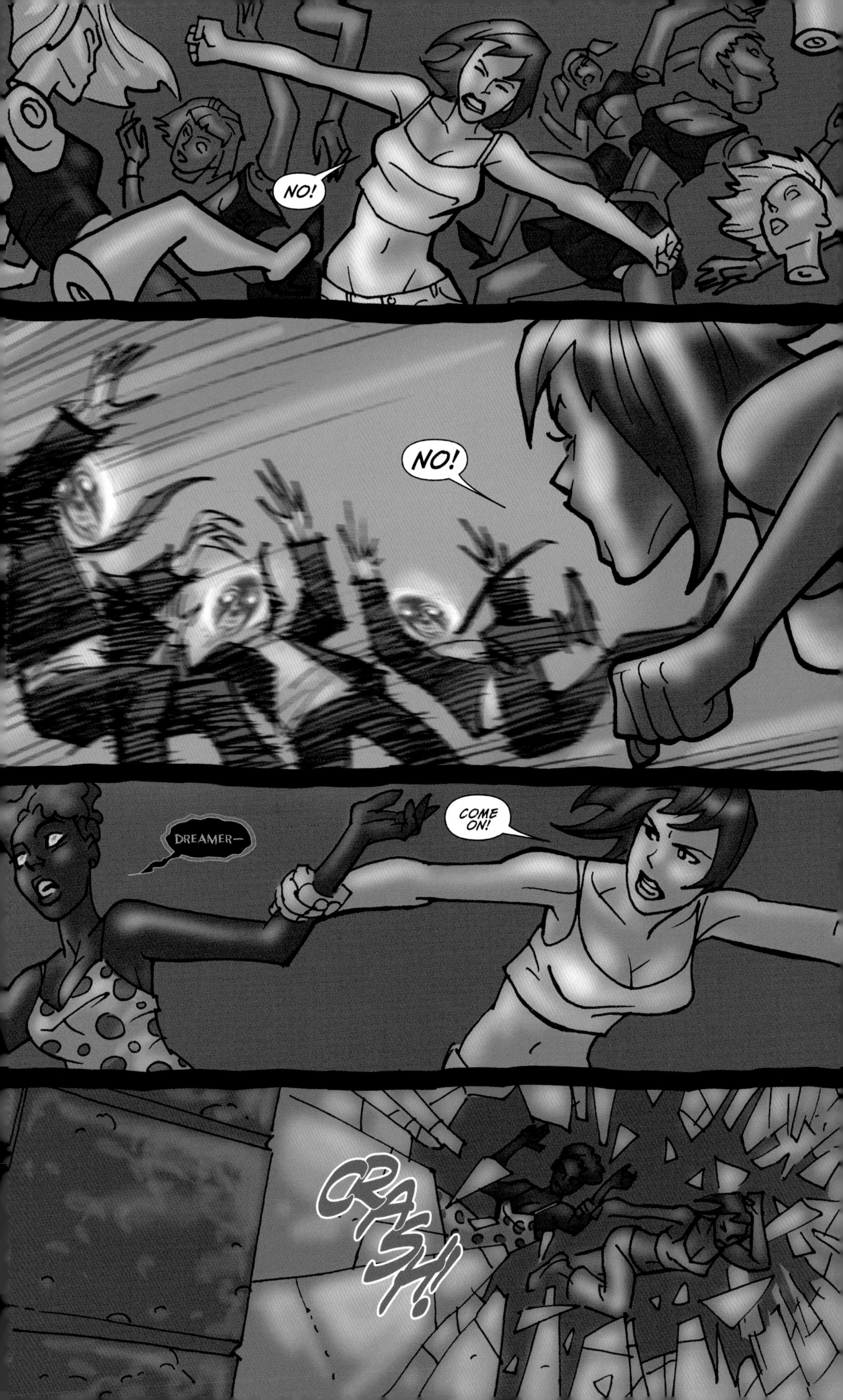
NO!
NO!
DREAMER—
COME ON!
CRASH!

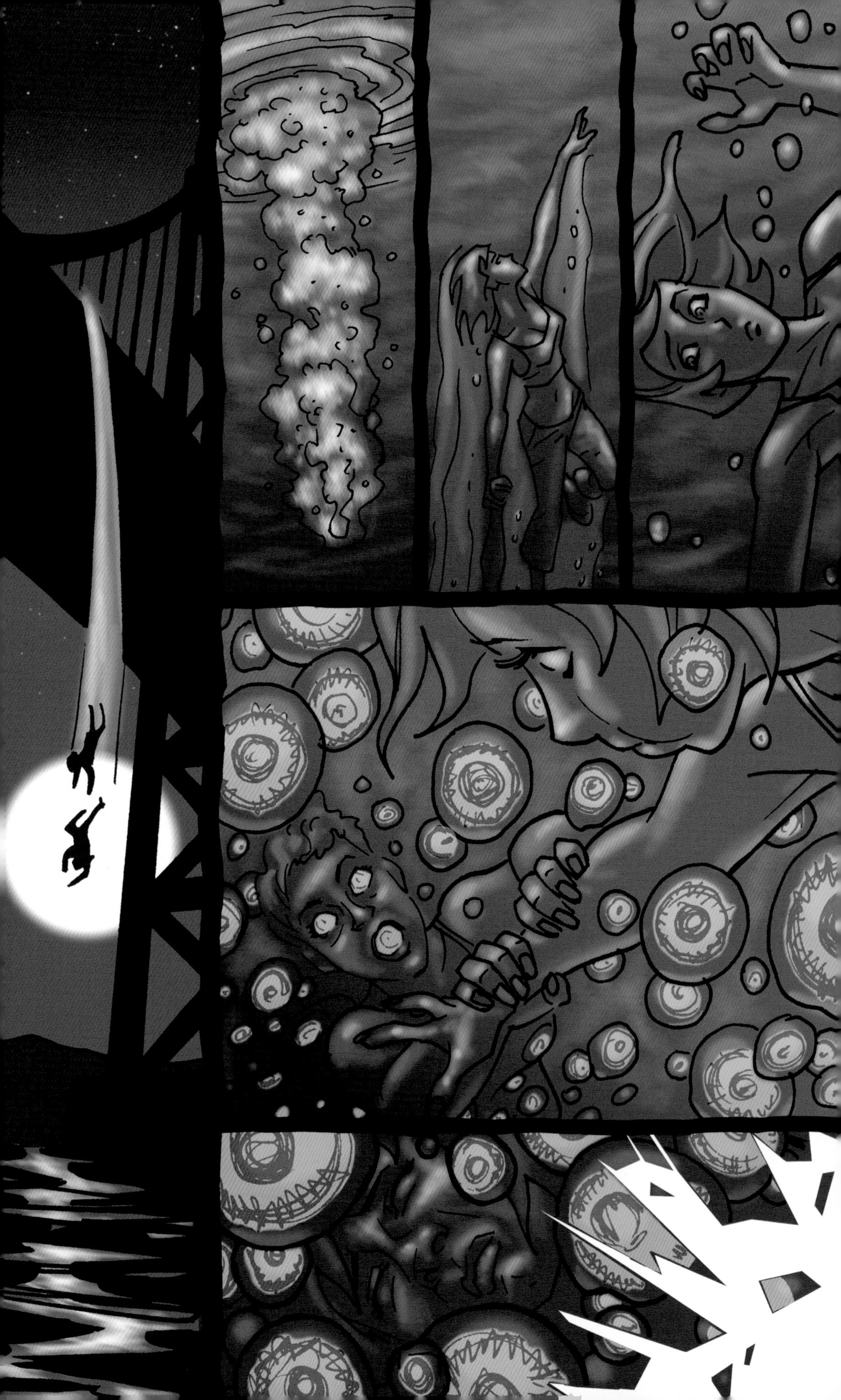

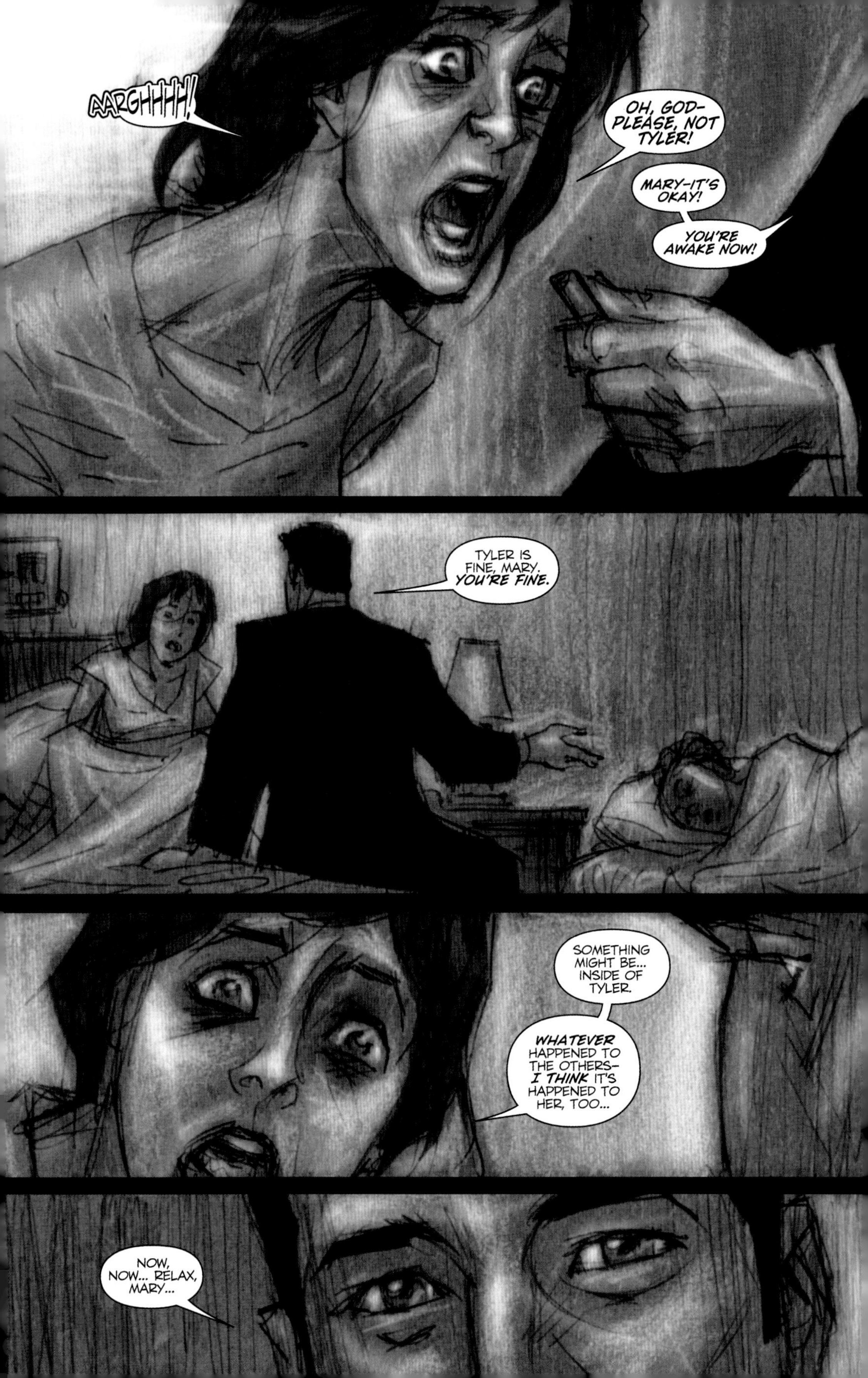
AARGHHHH!
OH, GOD- PLEASE, NOT TYLER!
MARY-IT'S OKAY!
YOU'RE AWAKE NOW!
TYLER IS FINE, MARY. YOU'RE FINE.
SOMETHING MIGHT BE... INSIDE OF TYLER.
WHATEVER HAPPENED TO THE OTHERS- I THINK IT'S HAPPENED TO HER, TOO...
NOW, NOW... RELAX, MARY...

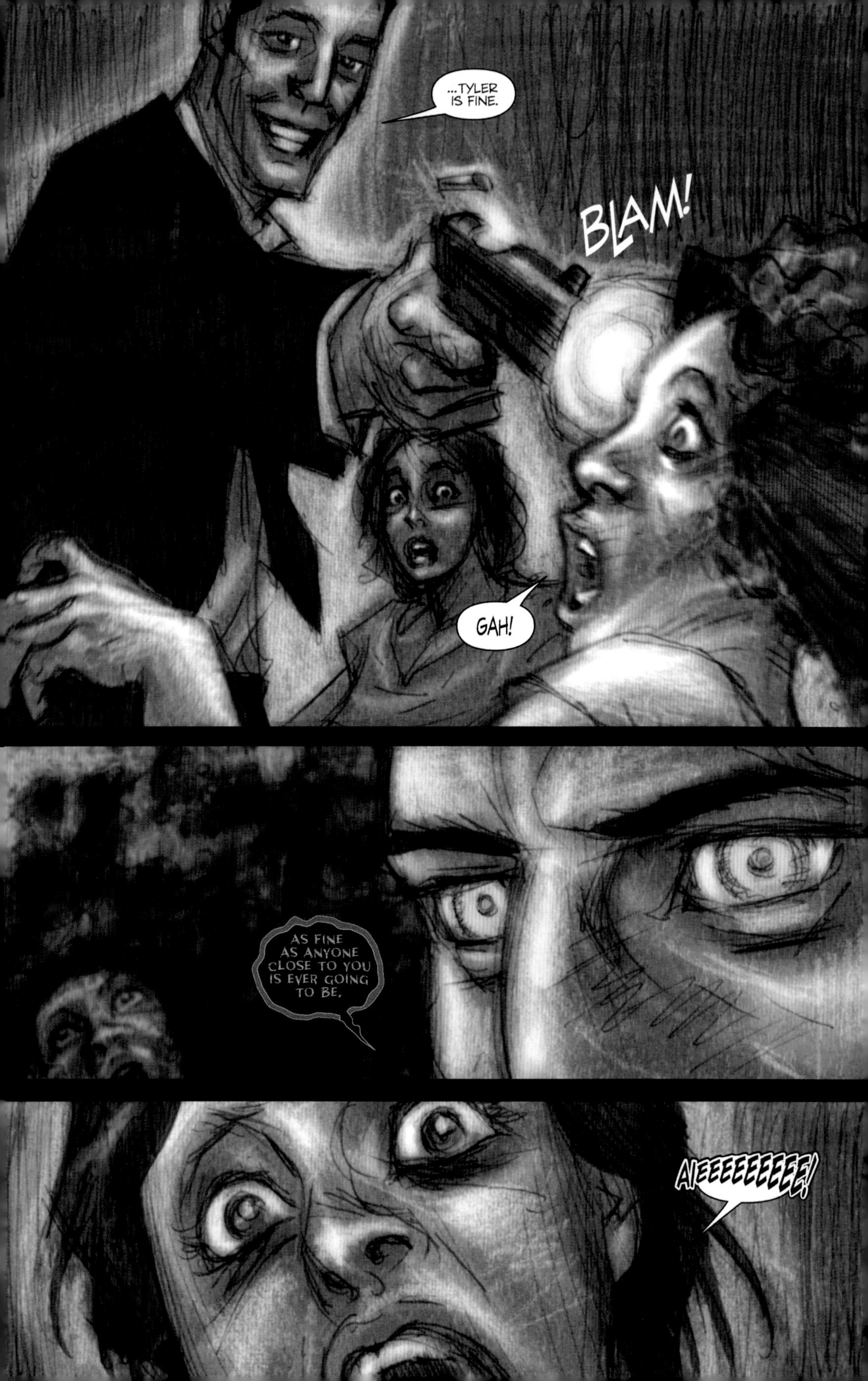
...TYLER IS FINE.
BLAM!
GAH!
AS FINE AS ANYONE CLOSE TO YOU IS EVER GOING TO BE.
AIEEEEEEEEEE!

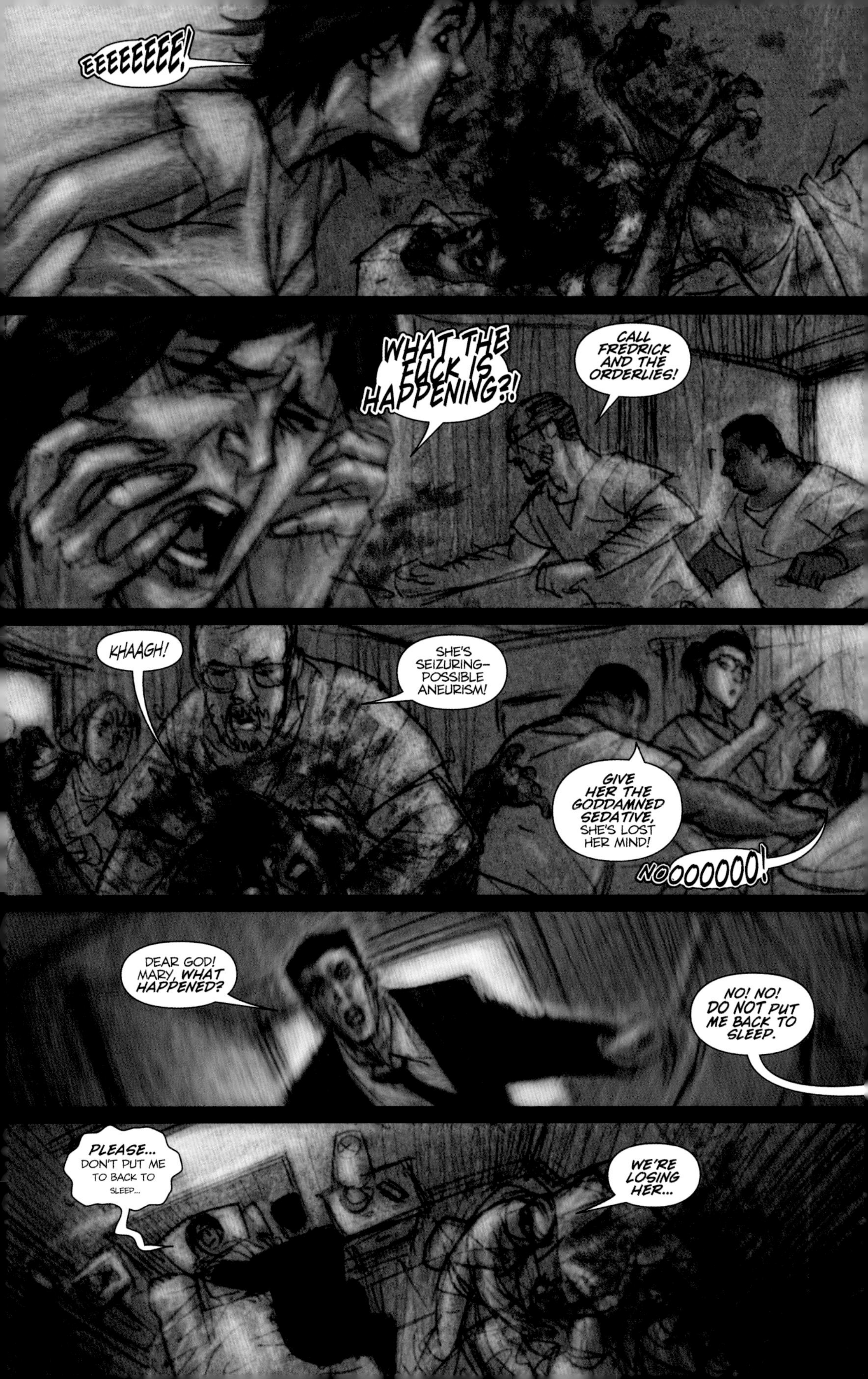
EEEEEEEE!
WHAT THE FUCK IS HAPPENING?!
CALL FREDRICK AND THE ORDERLIES!
KHAAGH!
SHE'S SEIZURING--POSSIBLE ANEURISM!
GIVE HER THE GODDAMNED SEDATIVE, SHE'S LOST HER MIND!
NOOOOOOO!
DEAR GOD! MARY, WHAT HAPPENED?
NO! NO! DO NOT PUT ME BACK TO SLEEP.
PLEASE... DON'T PUT ME TO BACK TO SLEEP...
WE'RE LOSING HER...

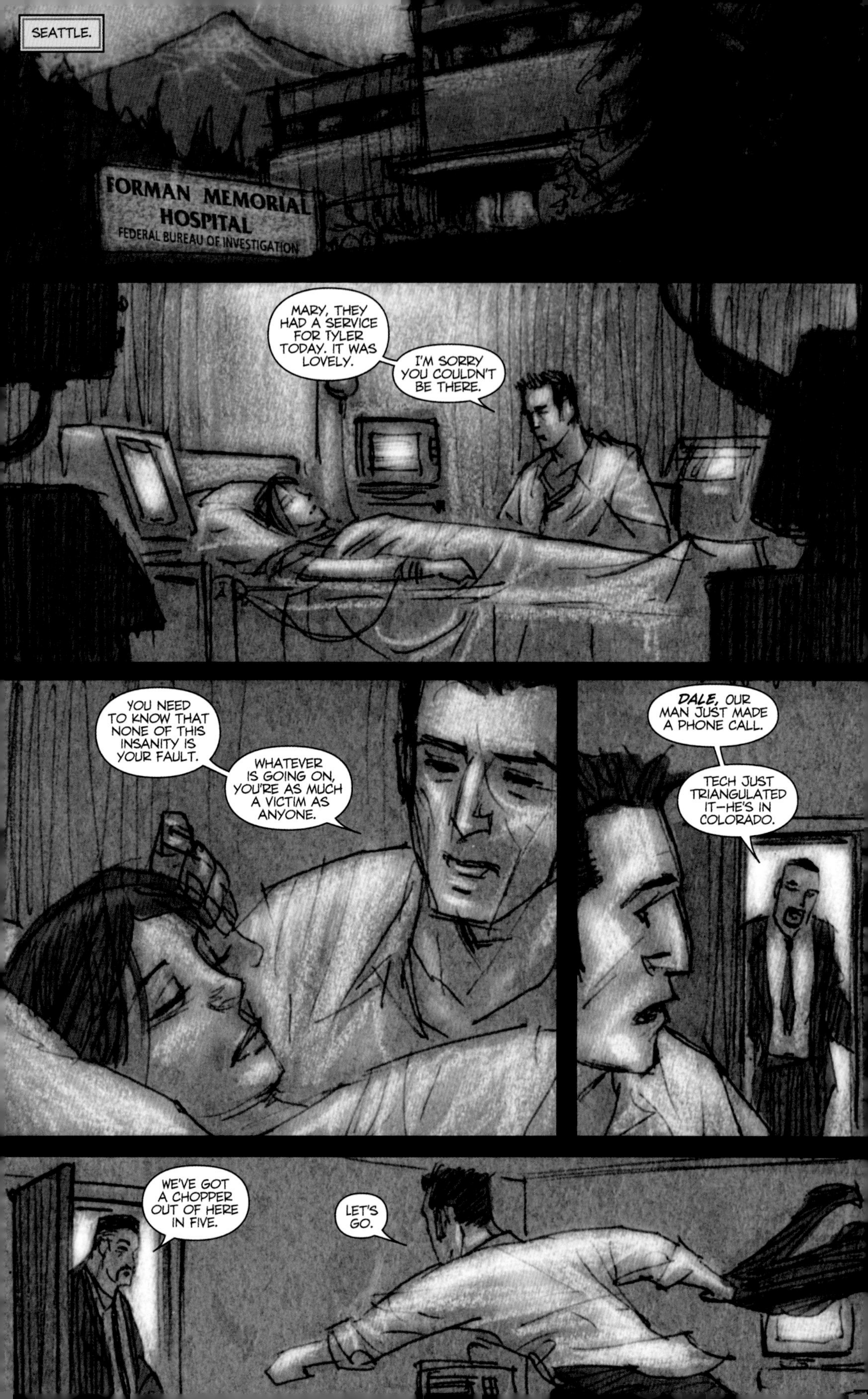
SEATTLE.
FORMAN MEMORIAL HOSPITAL
FEDERAL BUREAU OF INVESTIGATION
MARY, THEY HAD A SERVICE FOR TYLER TODAY. IT WAS LOVELY.
I'M SORRY YOU COULDN'T BE THERE.
YOU NEED TO KNOW THAT NONE OF THIS INSANITY IS YOUR FAULT.
WHATEVER IS GOING ON, YOU'RE AS MUCH A VICTIM AS ANYONE.
DALE, OUR MAN JUST MADE A PHONE CALL.
TECH JUST TRIANGULATED IT—HE'S IN COLORADO.
WE'VE GOT A CHOPPER OUT OF HERE IN FIVE.
LET'S GO.

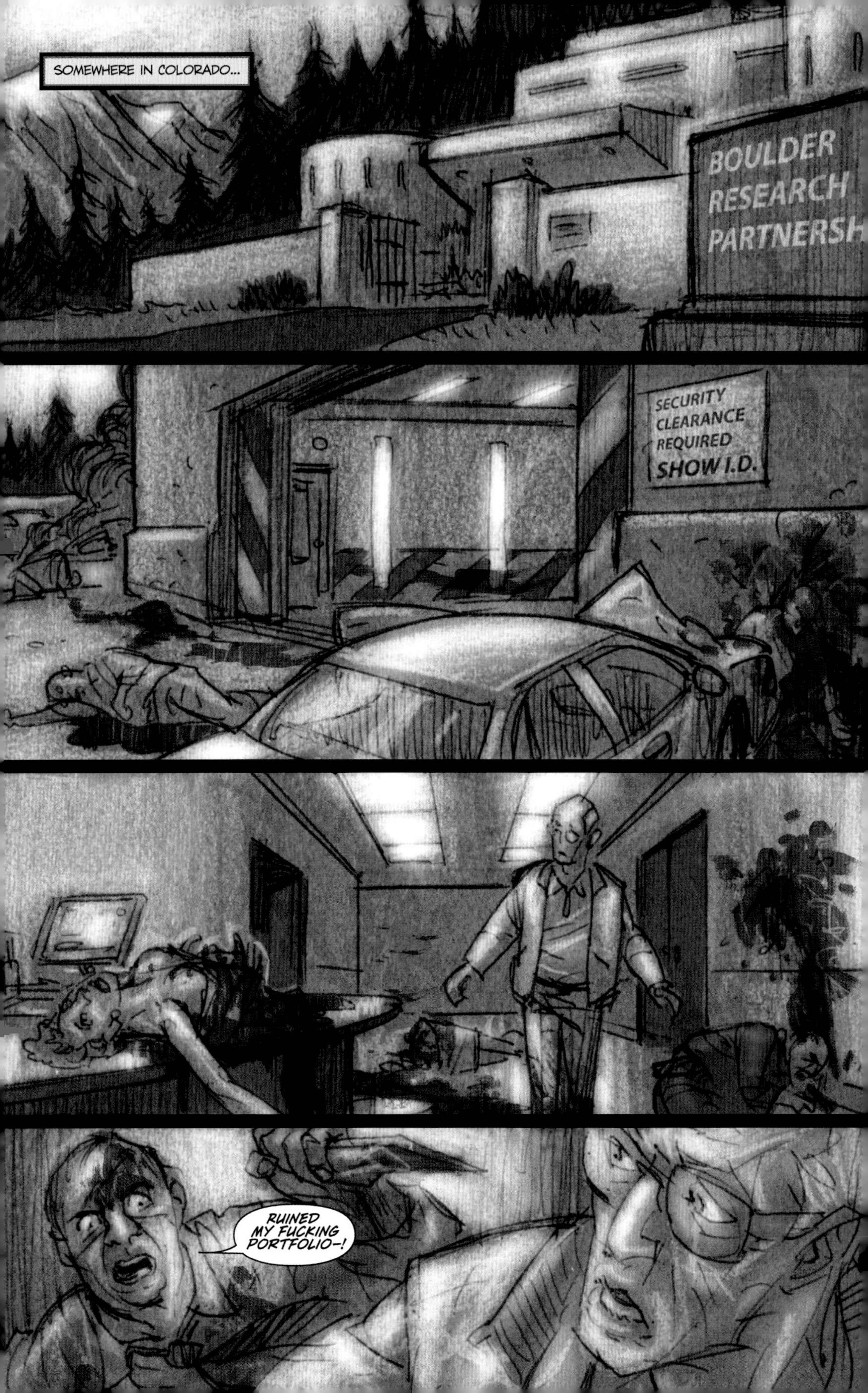
SOMEWHERE IN COLORADO...
BOULDER RESEARCH PARTNERSH
SECURITY CLEARANCE REQUIRED SHOW I.D.
RUINED MY FUCKING PORTFOLIO-!

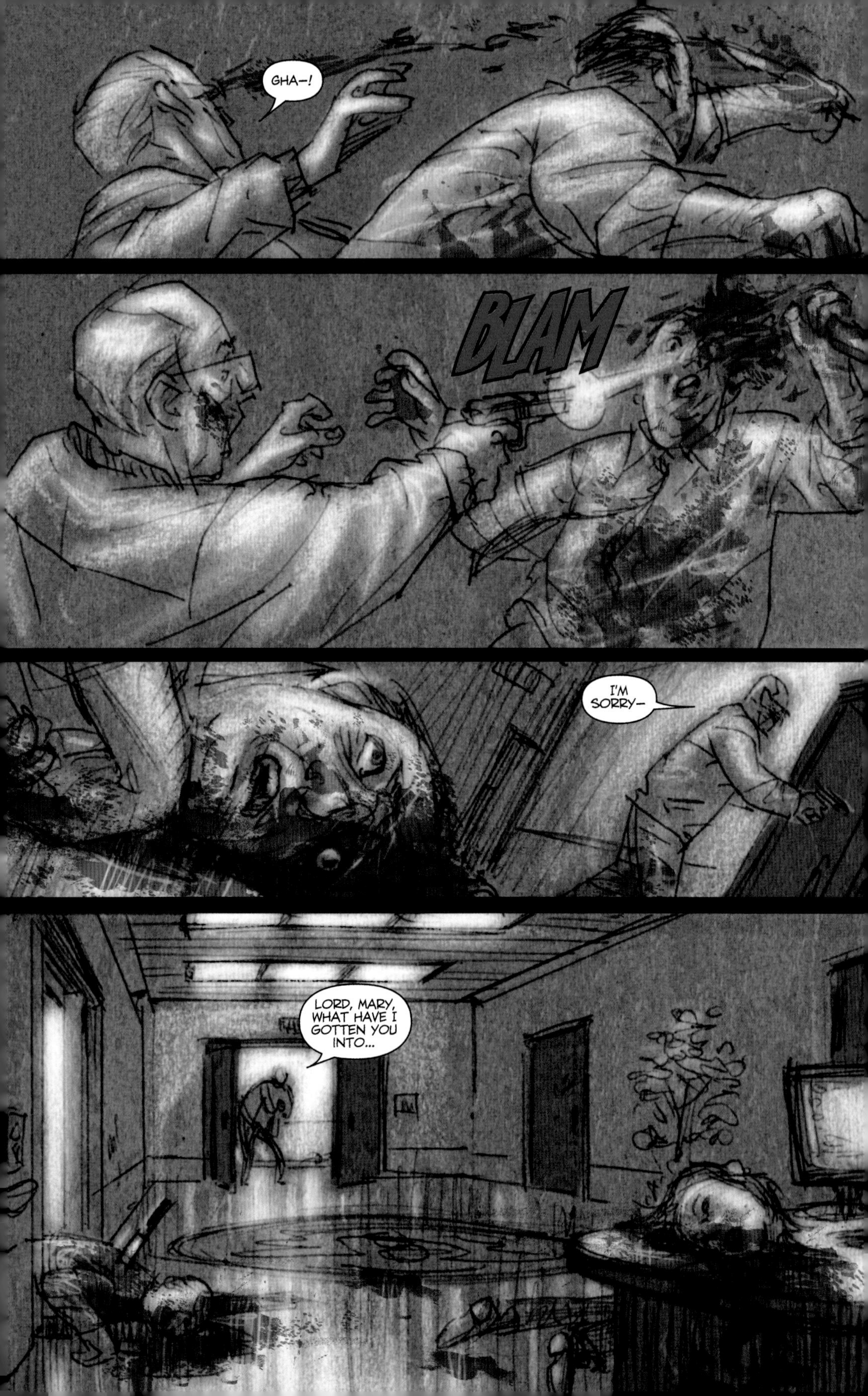
GHA–!
BLAM
I'M SORRY–
LORD, MARY, WHAT HAVE I GOTTEN YOU INTO...

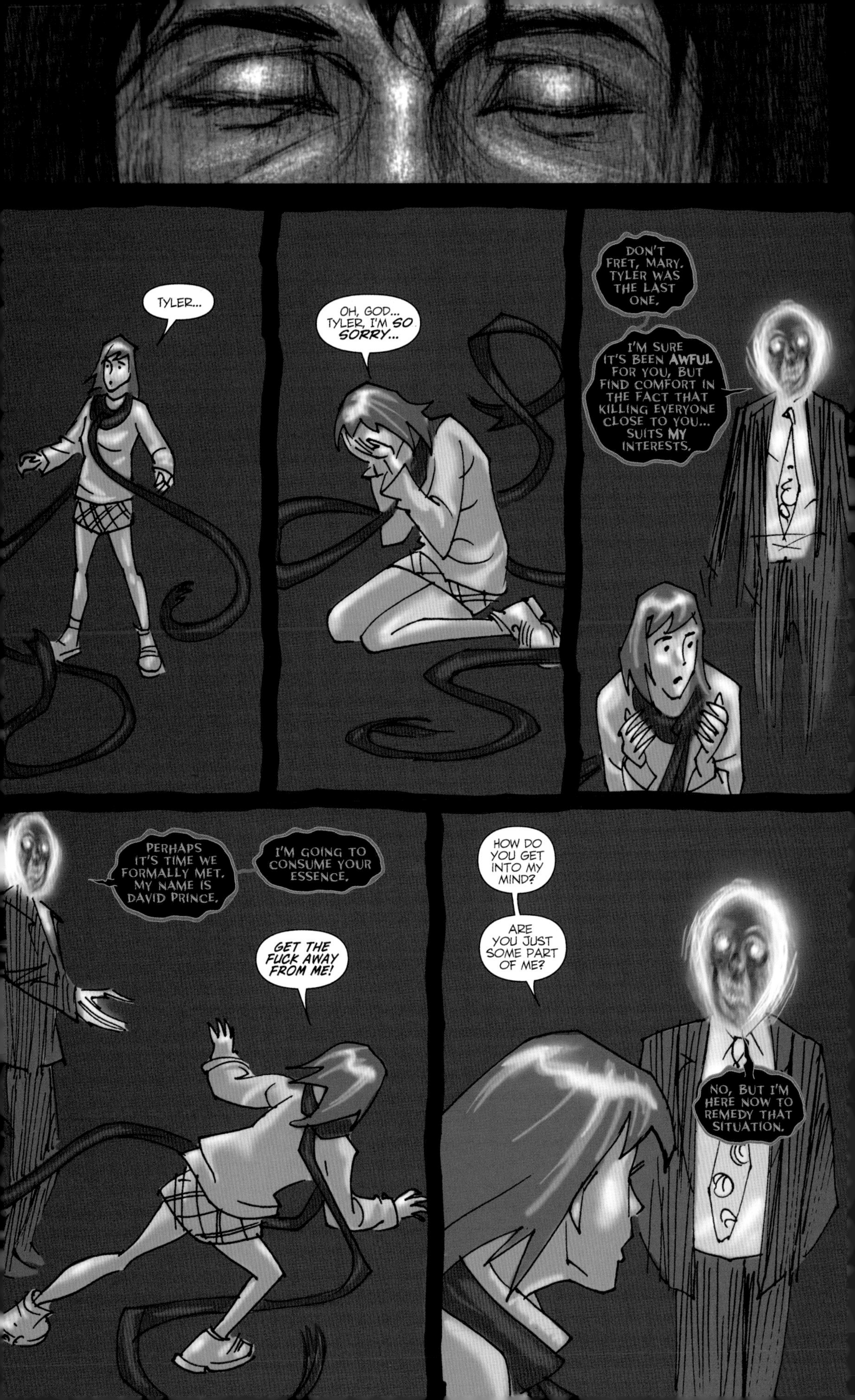
TYLER...
OH, GOD... TYLER, I'M SO SORRY...
DON'T FRET, MARY. TYLER WAS THE LAST ONE.
I'M SURE IT'S BEEN AWFUL FOR YOU, BUT FIND COMFORT IN THE FACT THAT KILLING EVERYONE CLOSE TO YOU... SUITS MY INTERESTS.
PERHAPS IT'S TIME WE FORMALLY MET. MY NAME IS DAVID PRINCE.
I'M GOING TO CONSUME YOUR ESSENCE.
GET THE FUCK AWAY FROM ME!
HOW DO YOU GET INTO MY MIND?
ARE YOU JUST SOME PART OF ME?
NO, BUT I'M HERE NOW TO REMEDY THAT SITUATION.

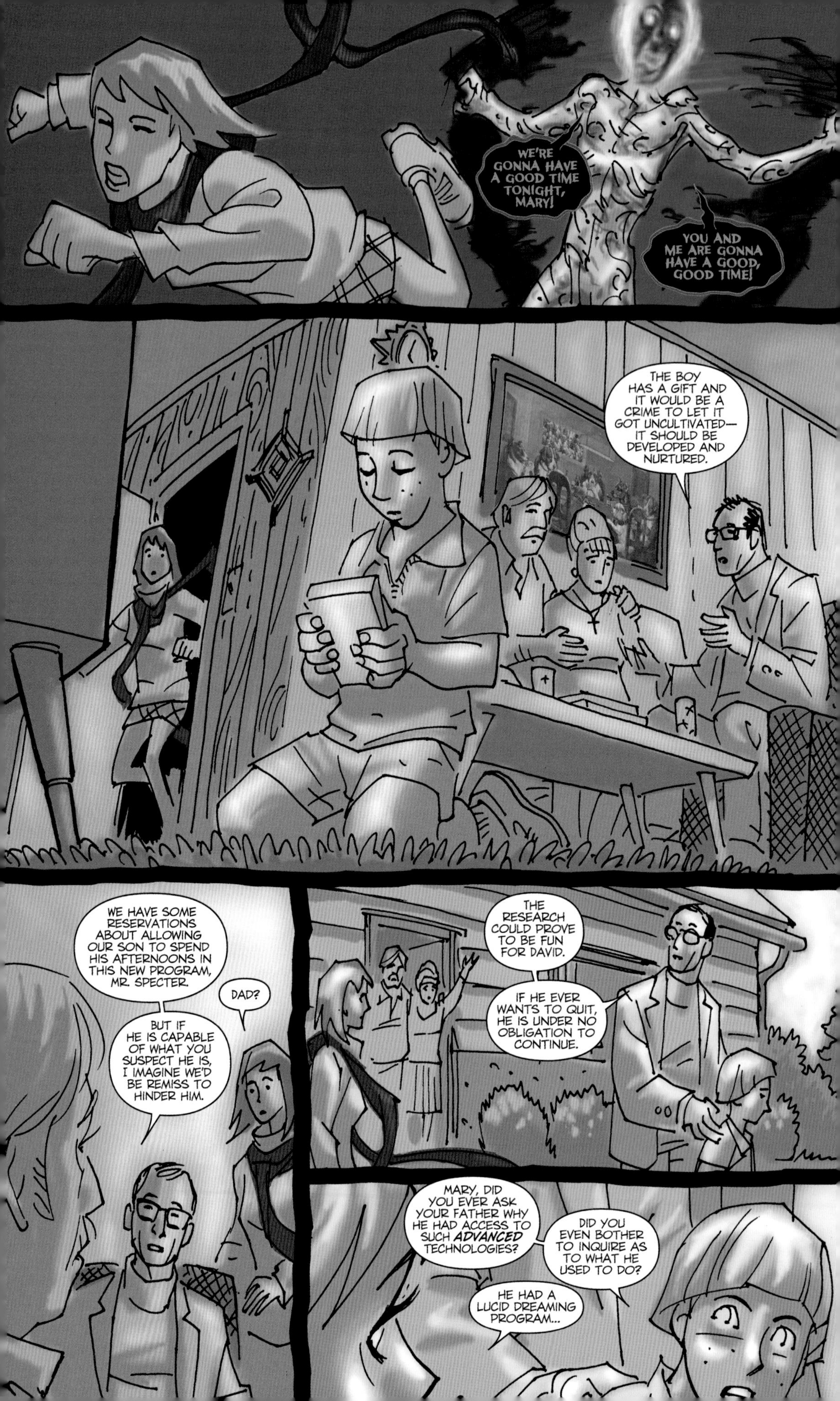
WE'RE GONNA HAVE A GOOD TIME TONIGHT, MARY!
YOU AND ME ARE GONNA HAVE A GOOD, GOOD TIME!
THE BOY HAS A GIFT AND IT WOULD BE A CRIME TO LET IT GOT UNCULTIVATED— IT SHOULD BE DEVELOPED AND NURTURED.
WE HAVE SOME RESERVATIONS ABOUT ALLOWING OUR SON TO SPEND HIS AFTERNOONS IN THIS NEW PROGRAM, MR. SPECTER.
BUT IF HE IS CAPABLE OF WHAT YOU SUSPECT HE IS, I IMAGINE WE'D BE REMISS TO HINDER HIM.
DAD?
THE RESEARCH COULD PROVE TO BE FUN FOR DAVID.
IF HE EVER WANTS TO QUIT, HE IS UNDER NO OBLIGATION TO CONTINUE.
MARY, DID YOU EVER ASK YOUR FATHER WHY HE HAD ACCESS TO SUCH ADVANCED TECHNOLOGIES?
DID YOU EVEN BOTHER TO INQUIRE AS TO WHAT HE USED TO DO?
HE HAD A LUCID DREAMING PROGRAM...

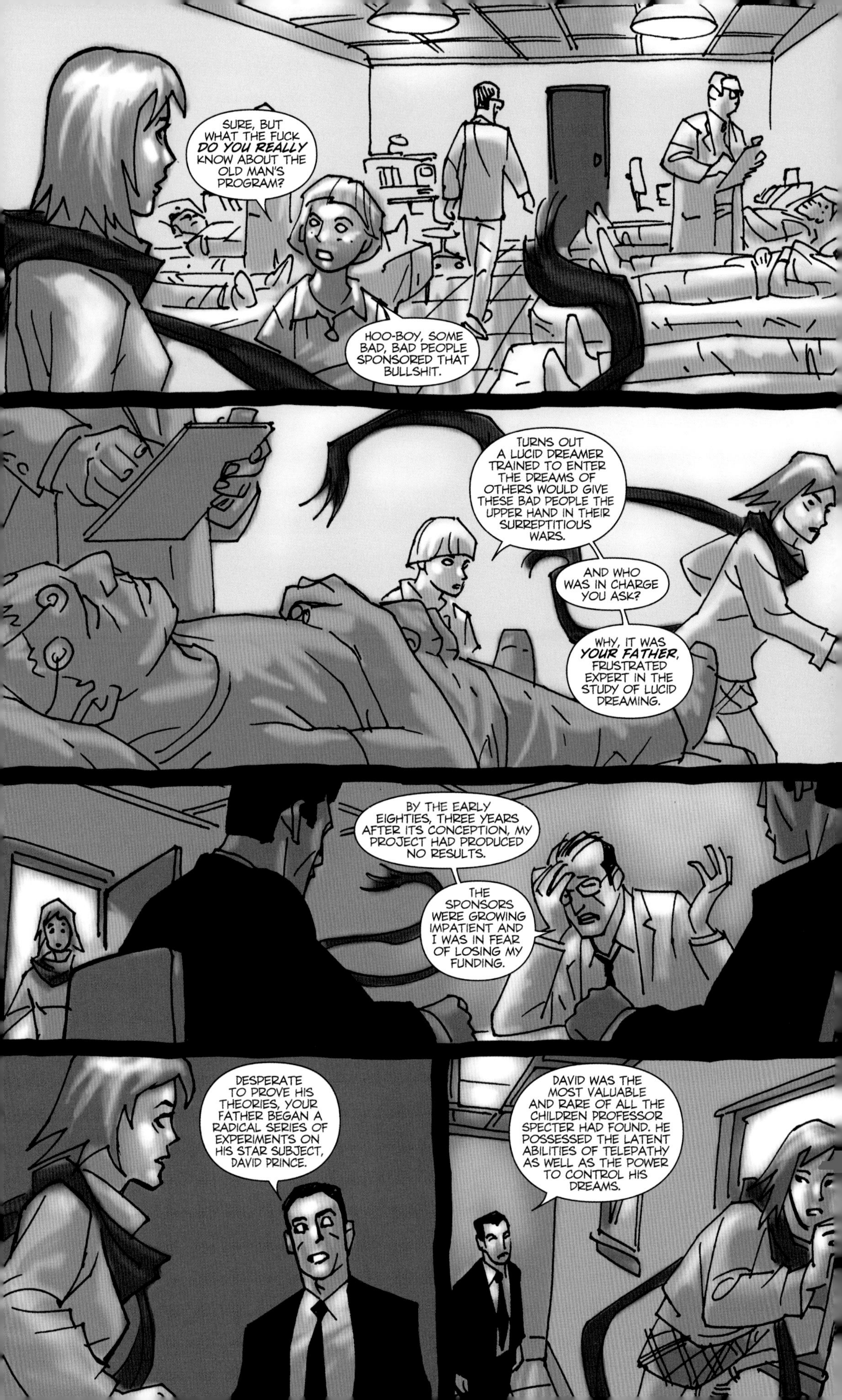
SURE, BUT WHAT THE FUCK *DO YOU REALLY* KNOW ABOUT THE OLD MAN'S PROGRAM?
HOO-BOY, SOME BAD, BAD PEOPLE SPONSORED THAT BULLSHIT.
TURNS OUT A LUCID DREAMER TRAINED TO ENTER THE DREAMS OF OTHERS WOULD GIVE THESE BAD PEOPLE THE UPPER HAND IN THEIR SURREPTITIOUS WARS.
AND WHO WAS IN CHARGE YOU ASK?
WHY, IT WAS *YOUR FATHER*, FRUSTRATED EXPERT IN THE STUDY OF LUCID DREAMING.
BY THE EARLY EIGHTIES, THREE YEARS AFTER ITS CONCEPTION, MY PROJECT HAD PRODUCED NO RESULTS.
THE SPONSORS WERE GROWING IMPATIENT AND I WAS IN FEAR OF LOSING MY FUNDING.
DESPERATE TO PROVE HIS THEORIES, YOUR FATHER BEGAN A RADICAL SERIES OF EXPERIMENTS ON HIS STAR SUBJECT, DAVID PRINCE.
DAVID WAS THE MOST VALUABLE AND RARE OF ALL THE CHILDREN PROFESSOR SPECTER HAD FOUND. HE POSSESSED THE LATENT ABILITIES OF TELEPATHY AS WELL AS THE POWER TO CONTROL HIS DREAMS.

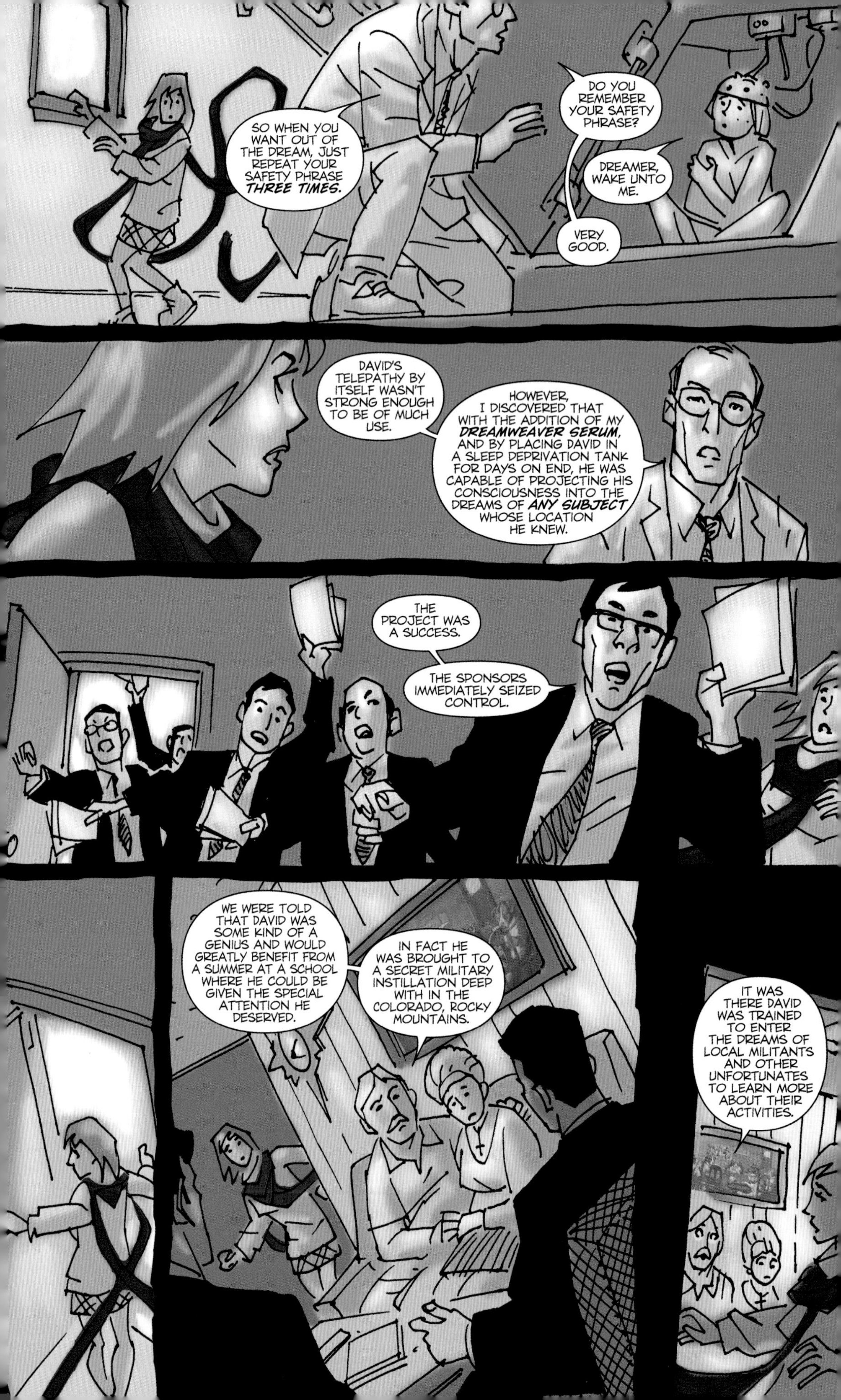
SO WHEN YOU WANT OUT OF THE DREAM, JUST REPEAT YOUR SAFETY PHRASE ***THREE TIMES.***
DO YOU REMEMBER YOUR SAFETY PHRASE?
DREAMER, WAKE UNTO ME.
VERY GOOD.
DAVID'S TELEPATHY BY ITSELF WASN'T STRONG ENOUGH TO BE OF MUCH USE.
HOWEVER, I DISCOVERED THAT WITH THE ADDITION OF MY ***DREAMWEAVER SERUM***, AND BY PLACING DAVID IN A SLEEP DEPRIVATION TANK FOR DAYS ON END, HE WAS CAPABLE OF PROJECTING HIS CONSCIOUSNESS INTO THE DREAMS OF ***ANY SUBJECT*** WHOSE LOCATION HE KNEW.
THE PROJECT WAS A SUCCESS.
THE SPONSORS IMMEDIATELY SEIZED CONTROL.
WE WERE TOLD THAT DAVID WAS SOME KIND OF A GENIUS AND WOULD GREATLY BENEFIT FROM A SUMMER AT A SCHOOL WHERE HE COULD BE GIVEN THE SPECIAL ATTENTION HE DESERVED.
IN FACT HE WAS BROUGHT TO A SECRET MILITARY INSTILLATION DEEP WITH IN THE COLORADO, ROCKY MOUNTAINS.
IT WAS THERE DAVID WAS TRAINED TO ENTER THE DREAMS OF LOCAL MILITANTS AND OTHER UNFORTUNATES TO LEARN MORE ABOUT THEIR ACTIVITIES.

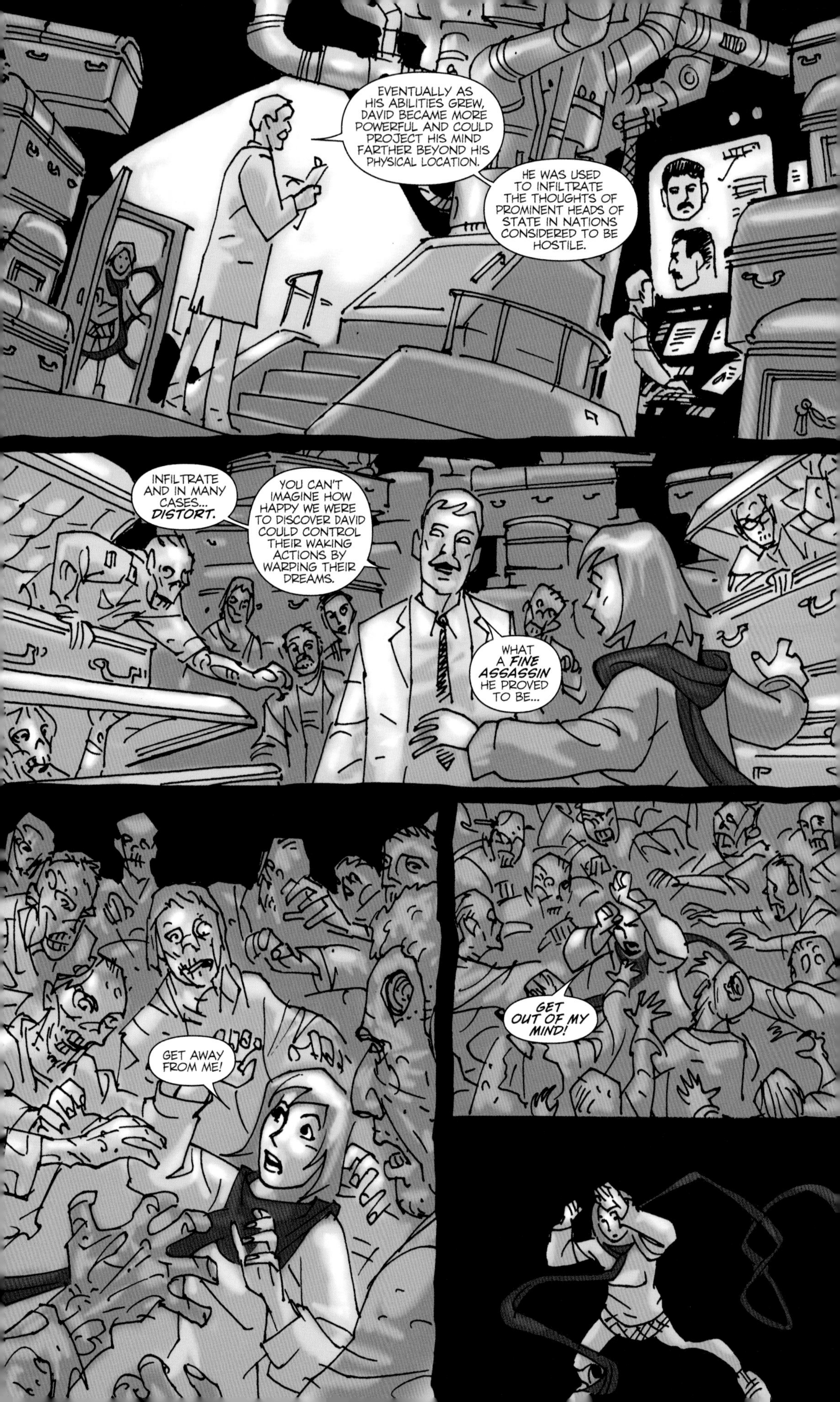
EVENTUALLY AS HIS ABILITIES GREW, DAVID BECAME MORE POWERFUL AND COULD PROJECT HIS MIND FARTHER BEYOND HIS PHYSICAL LOCATION.
HE WAS USED TO INFILTRATE THE THOUGHTS OF PROMINENT HEADS OF STATE IN NATIONS CONSIDERED TO BE HOSTILE.
INFILTRATE AND IN MANY CASES... *DISTORT*.
YOU CAN'T IMAGINE HOW HAPPY WE WERE TO DISCOVER DAVID COULD CONTROL THEIR WAKING ACTIONS BY WARPING THEIR DREAMS.
WHAT A *FINE ASSASSIN* HE PROVED TO BE...
GET AWAY FROM ME!
GET OUT OF MY MIND!

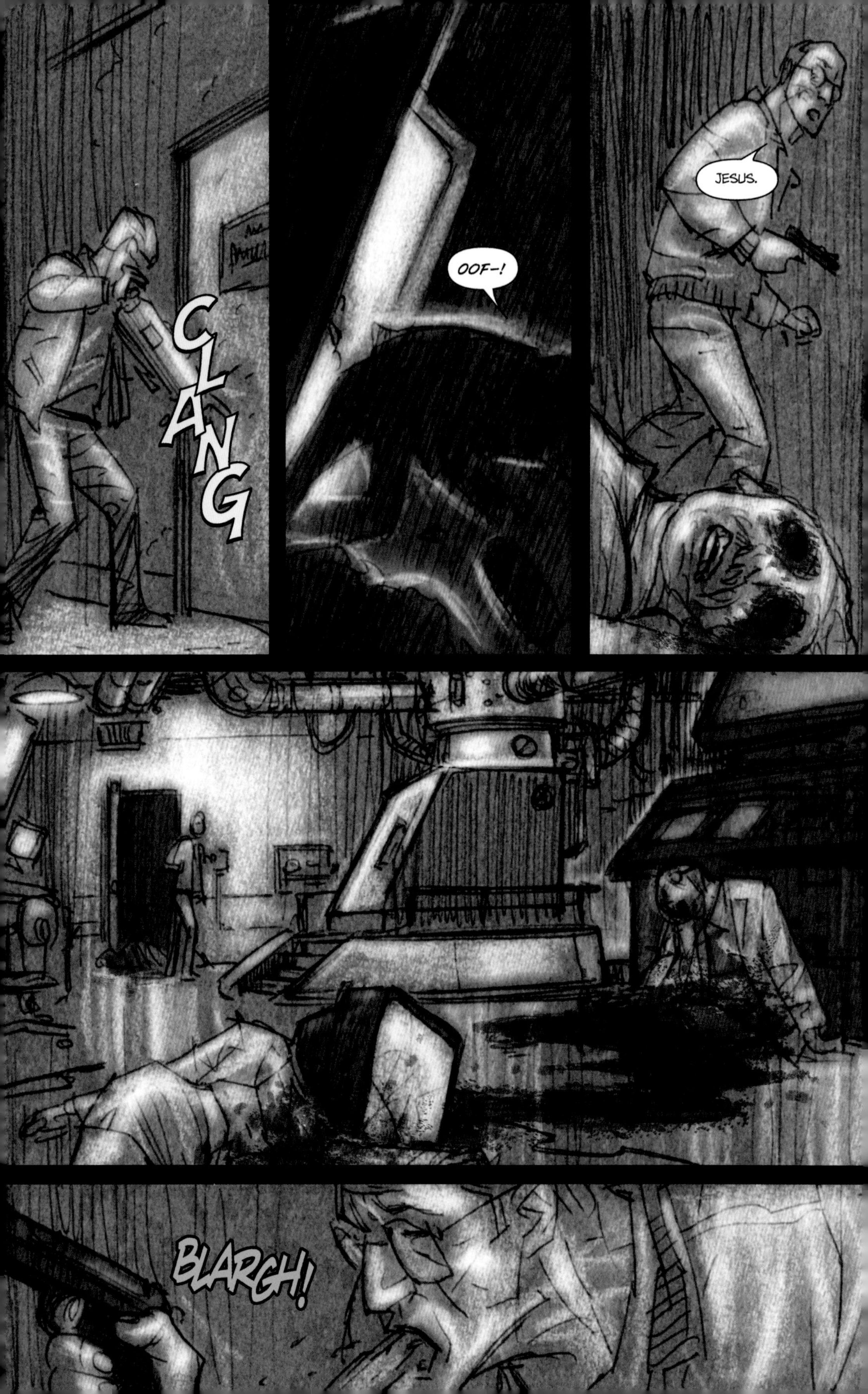
CLANG
OOF–!
JESUS.
BLARGH!

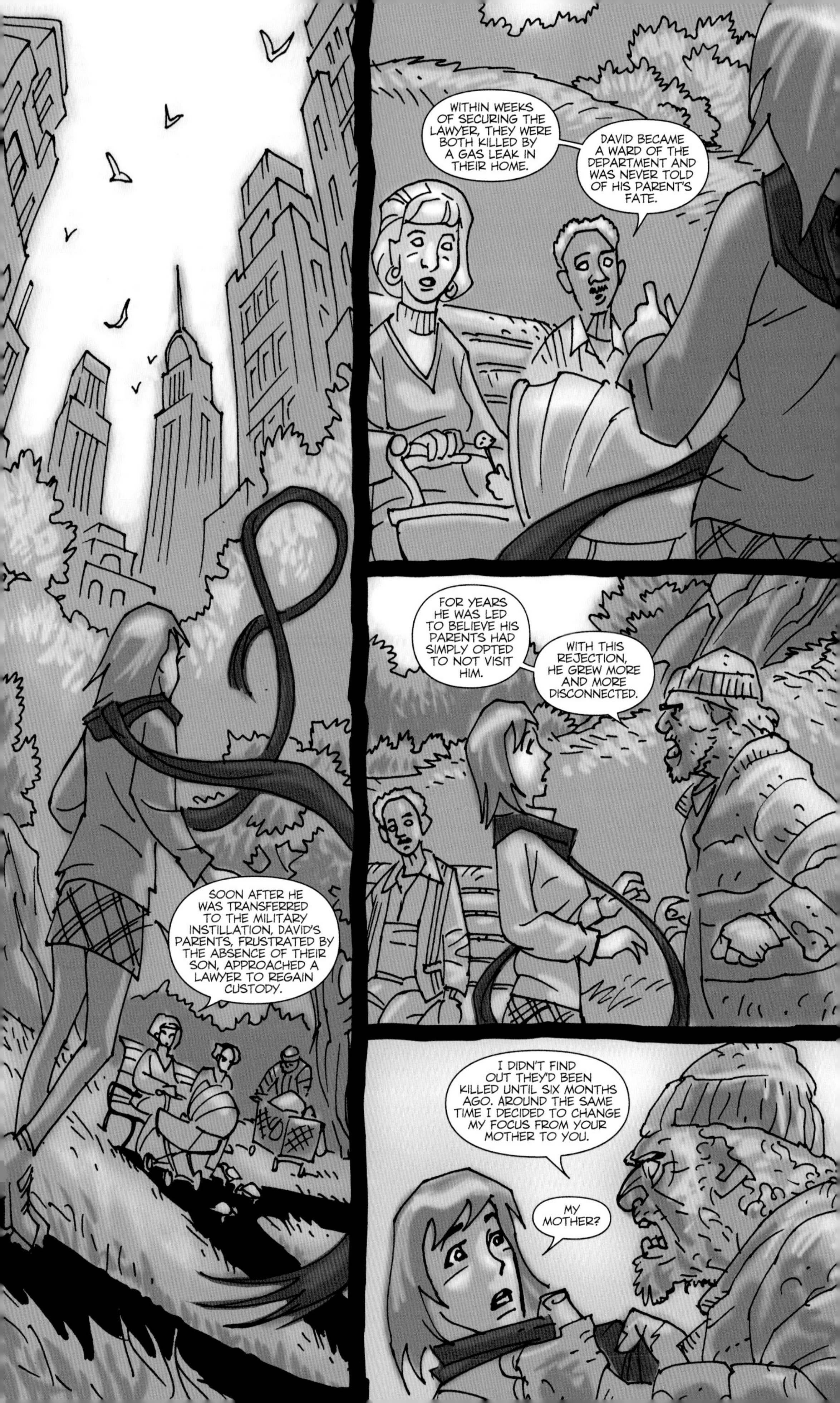
SOON AFTER HE WAS TRANSFERRED TO THE MILITARY INSTILLATION, DAVID'S PARENTS, FRUSTRATED BY THE ABSENCE OF THEIR SON, APPROACHED A LAWYER TO REGAIN CUSTODY.
WITHIN WEEKS OF SECURING THE LAWYER, THEY WERE BOTH KILLED BY A GAS LEAK IN THEIR HOME.
DAVID BECAME A WARD OF THE DEPARTMENT AND WAS NEVER TOLD OF HIS PARENT'S FATE.
FOR YEARS HE WAS LED TO BELIEVE HIS PARENTS HAD SIMPLY OPTED TO NOT VISIT HIM.
WITH THIS REJECTION, HE GREW MORE AND MORE DISCONNECTED.
I DIDN'T FIND OUT THEY'D BEEN KILLED UNTIL SIX MONTHS AGO. AROUND THE SAME TIME I DECIDED TO CHANGE MY FOCUS FROM YOUR MOTHER TO YOU.
MY MOTHER?

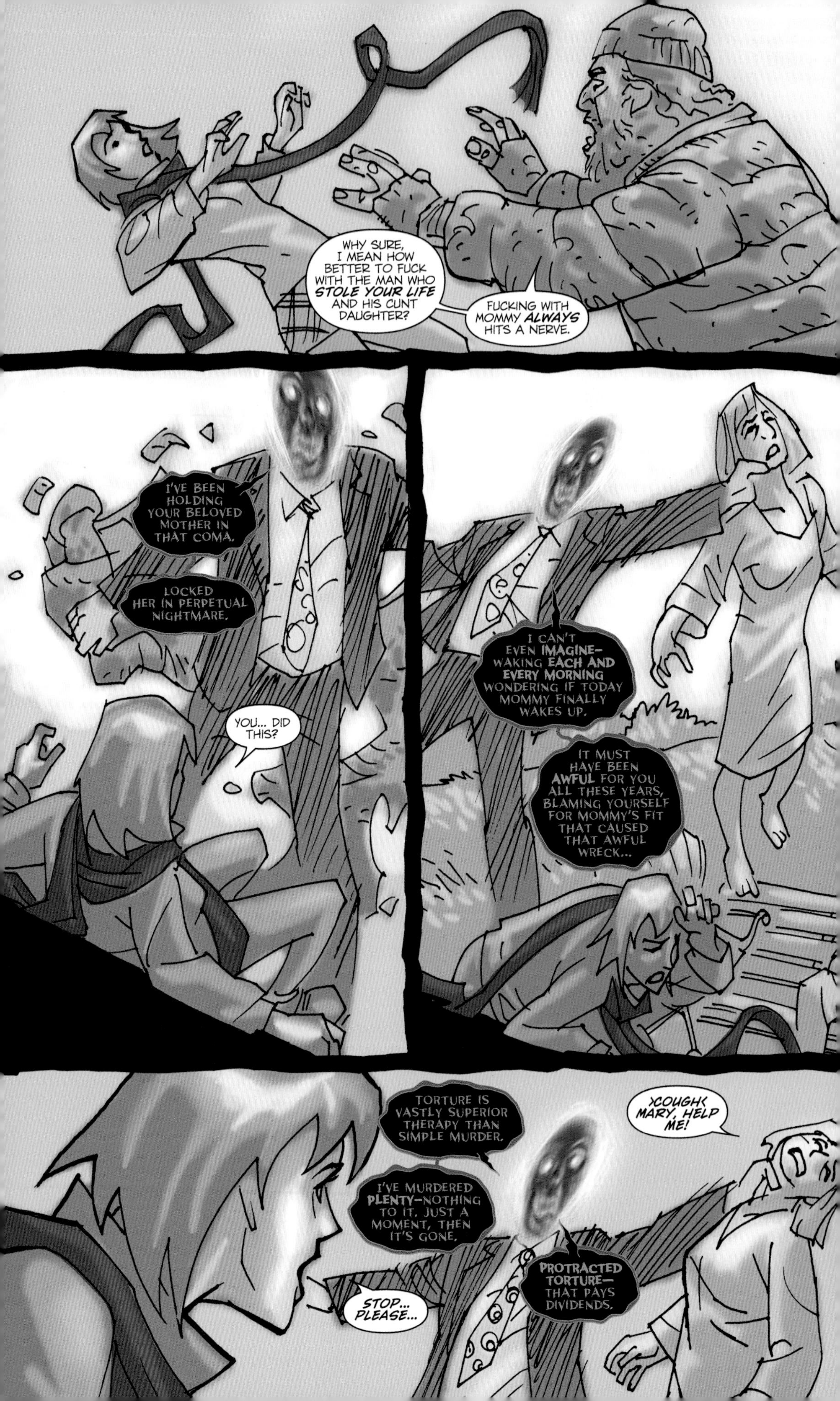

WHY SURE, I MEAN HOW BETTER TO FUCK WITH THE MAN WHO STOLE YOUR LIFE AND HIS CUNT DAUGHTER?
FUCKING WITH MOMMY ALWAYS HITS A NERVE.
I'VE BEEN HOLDING YOUR BELOVED MOTHER IN THAT COMA.
LOCKED HER IN PERPETUAL NIGHTMARE.
YOU... DID THIS?
I CAN'T EVEN IMAGINE-- WAKING EACH AND EVERY MORNING WONDERING IF TODAY MOMMY FINALLY WAKES UP.
IT MUST HAVE BEEN AWFUL FOR YOU ALL THESE YEARS, BLAMING YOURSELF FOR MOMMY'S FIT THAT CAUSED THAT AWFUL WRECK...
TORTURE IS VASTLY SUPERIOR THERAPY THAN SIMPLE MURDER.
I'VE MURDERED PLENTY--NOTHING TO IT. JUST A MOMENT, THEN IT'S GONE.
PROTRACTED TORTURE-- THAT PAYS DIVIDENDS.
>COUGH< MARY, HELP ME!
STOP... PLEASE...

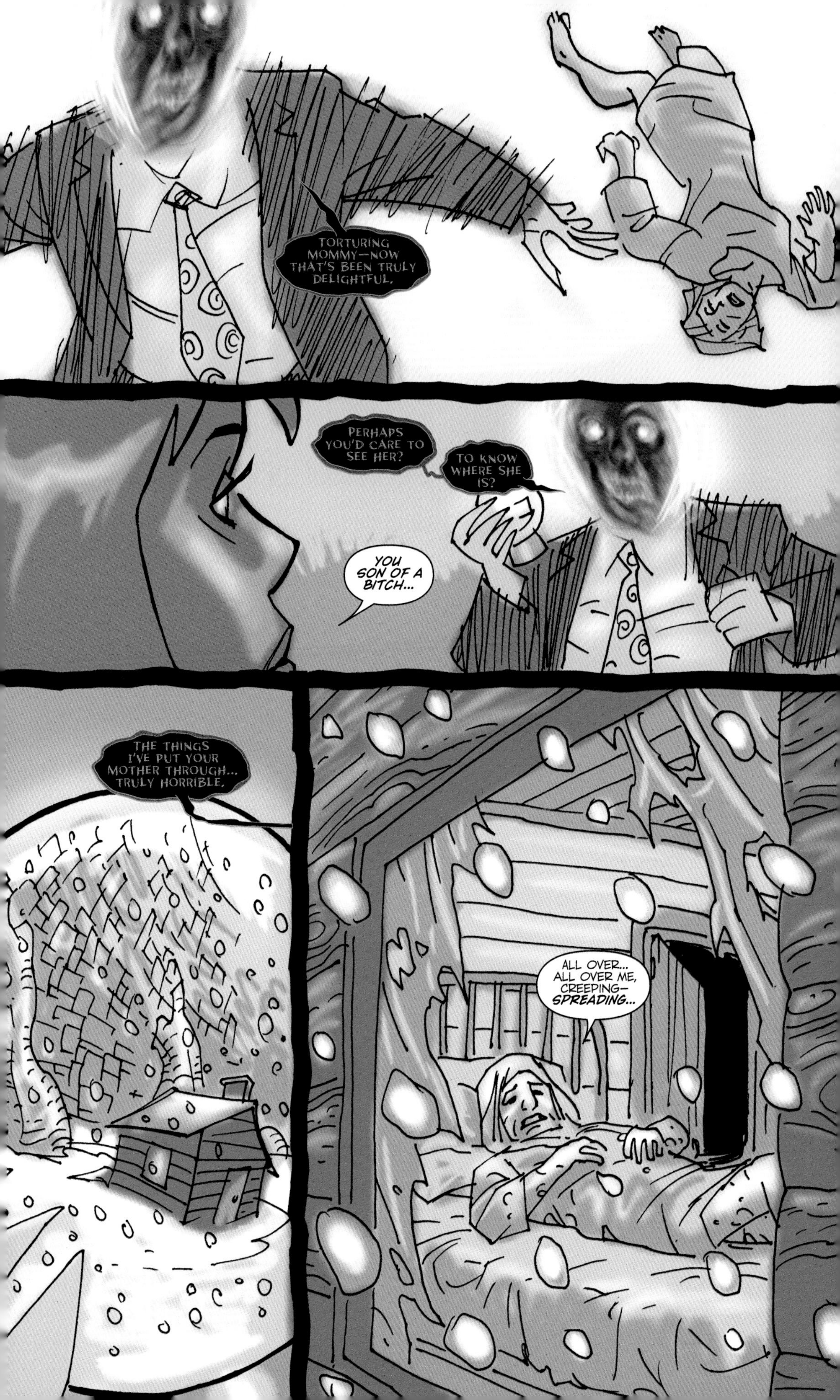
TORTURING MOMMY—NOW THAT'S BEEN TRULY DELIGHTFUL.
PERHAPS YOU'D CARE TO SEE HER?
TO KNOW WHERE SHE IS?
YOU SON OF A BITCH...
THE THINGS I'VE PUT YOUR MOTHER THROUGH... TRULY HORRIBLE.
ALL OVER... ALL OVER ME, CREEPING— *SPREADING*...

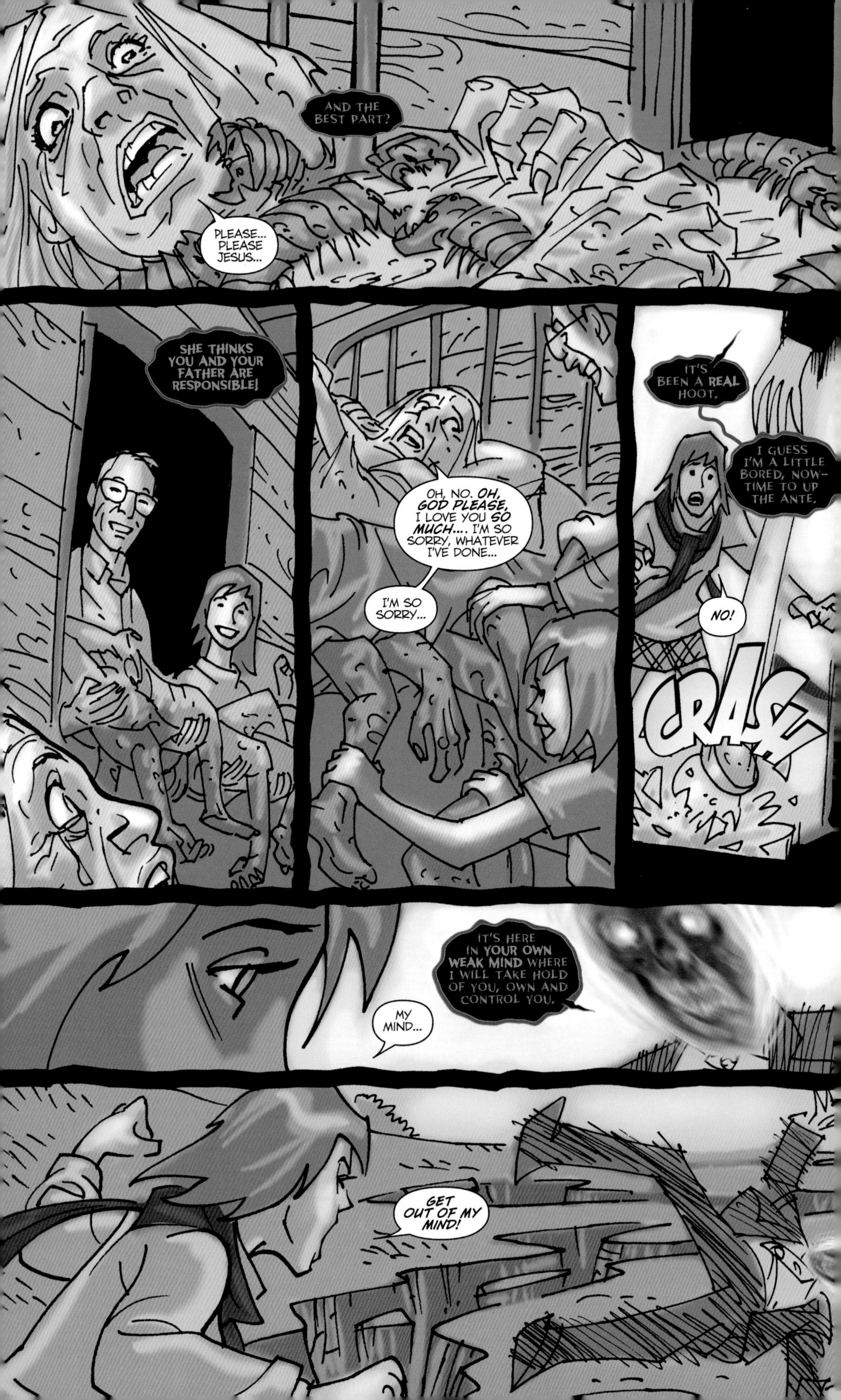
AND THE BEST PART?
PLEASE... PLEASE JESUS...
SHE THINKS YOU AND YOUR FATHER ARE RESPONSIBLE!
OH, NO. OH, GOD PLEASE, I LOVE YOU SO MUCH.... I'M SO SORRY, WHATEVER I'VE DONE...
I'M SO SORRY...
IT'S BEEN A REAL HOOT.
I GUESS I'M A LITTLE BORED, NOW-TIME TO UP THE ANTE.
NO!
CRASH
IT'S HERE IN YOUR OWN WEAK MIND WHERE I WILL TAKE HOLD OF YOU, OWN AND CONTROL YOU.
MY MIND...
GET OUT OF MY MIND!

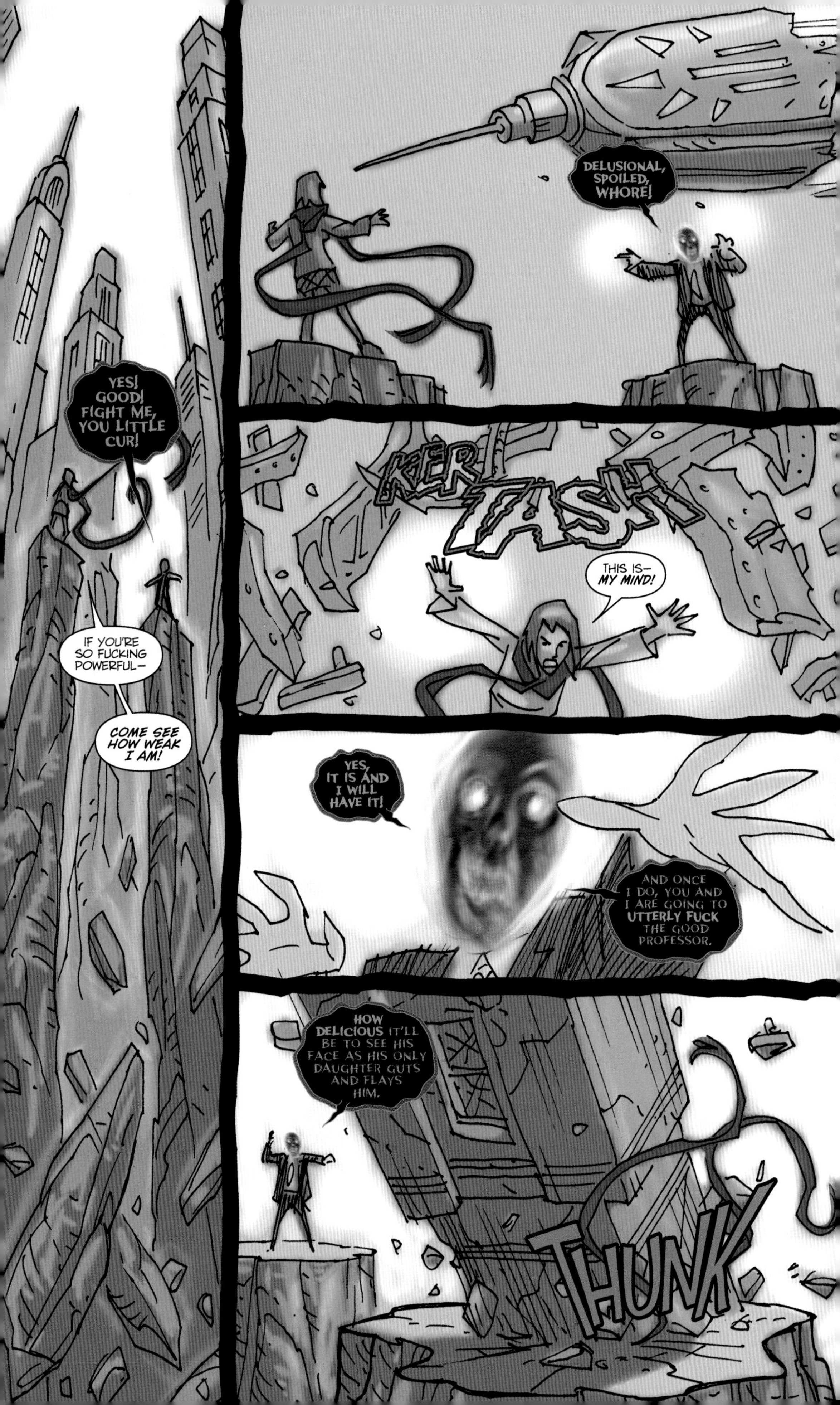

YES! GOOD! FIGHT ME, YOU LITTLE CUR!
IF YOU'RE SO FUCKING POWERFUL–
COME SEE HOW WEAK I AM!
DELUSIONAL, SPOILED, WHORE!
KER-TASH
THIS IS– MY MIND!
YES, IT IS AND I WILL HAVE IT!
AND ONCE I DO, YOU AND I ARE GOING TO UTTERLY FUCK THE GOOD PROFESSOR.
HOW DELICIOUS IT'LL BE TO SEE HIS FACE AS HIS ONLY DAUGHTER GUTS AND FLAYS HIM.
THUNK

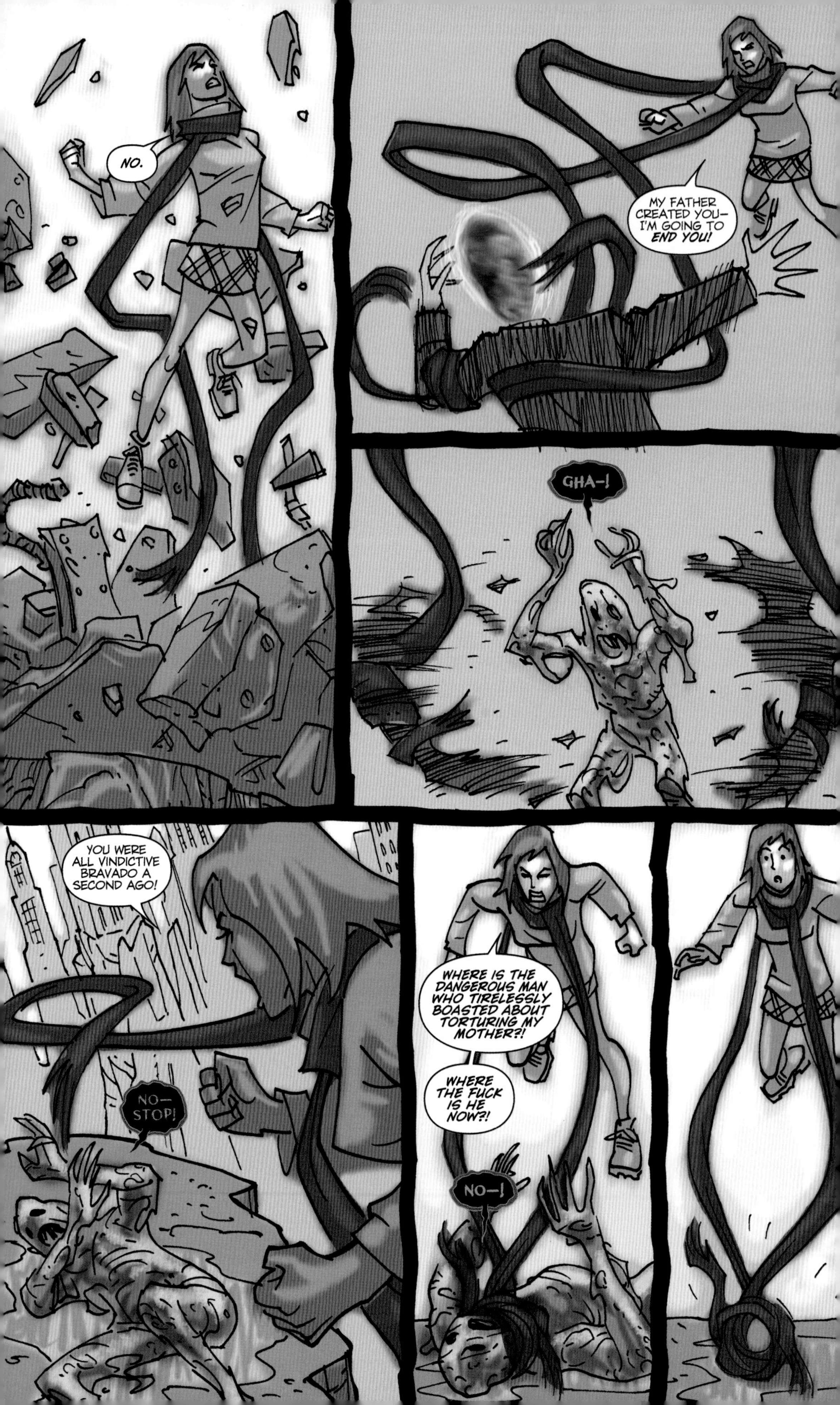
NO.
MY FATHER CREATED YOU— I'M GOING TO *END YOU!*
GHA-!
YOU WERE ALL VINDICTIVE BRAVADO A SECOND AGO!
NO— STOP!
WHERE IS THE DANGEROUS MAN WHO TIRELESSLY BOASTED ABOUT TORTURING MY MOTHER?!
WHERE THE FUCK IS HE NOW?!
NO—!

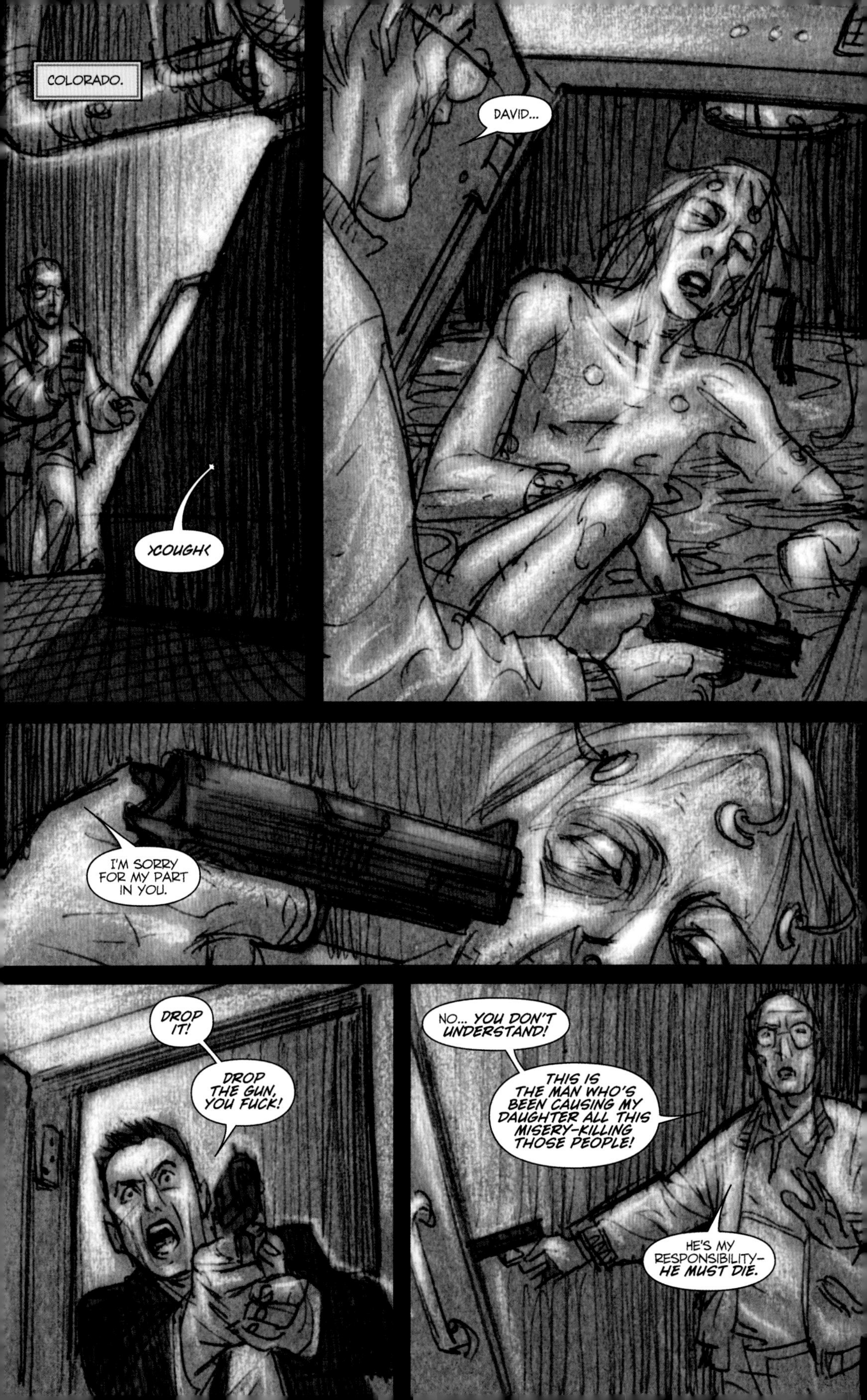
COLORADO.
>COUGH<
DAVID...
I'M SORRY FOR MY PART IN YOU.
DROP IT!
DROP THE GUN, YOU FUCK!
NO... YOU DON'T UNDERSTAND!
THIS IS THE MAN WHO'S BEEN CAUSING MY DAUGHTER ALL THIS MISERY--KILLING THOSE PEOPLE!
HE'S MY RESPONSIBILITY-- HE MUST DIE.

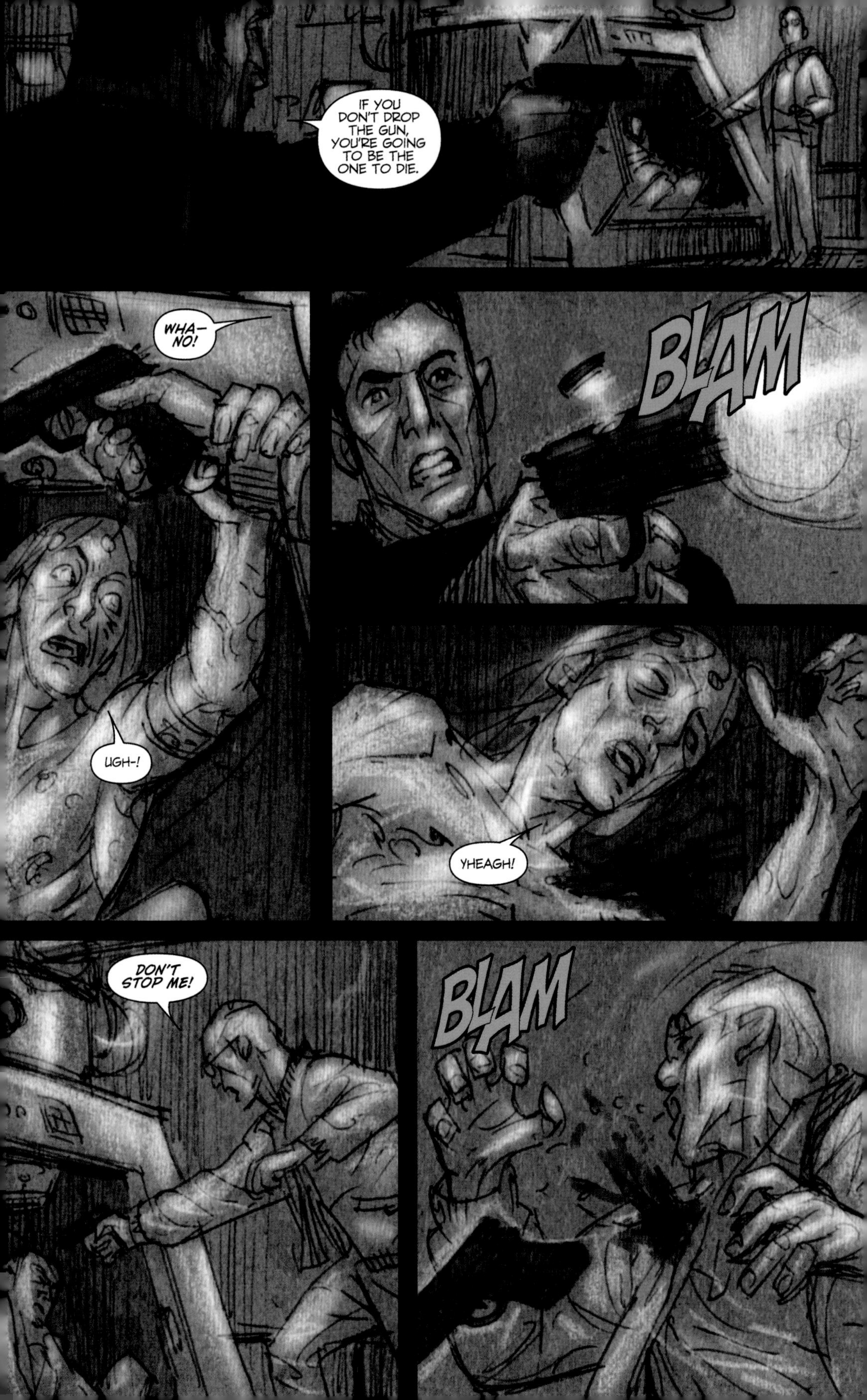
IF YOU DON'T DROP THE GUN, YOU'RE GOING TO BE THE ONE TO DIE.
WHA– NO!
BLAM
UGH–!
YHEAGH!
DON'T STOP ME!
BLAM

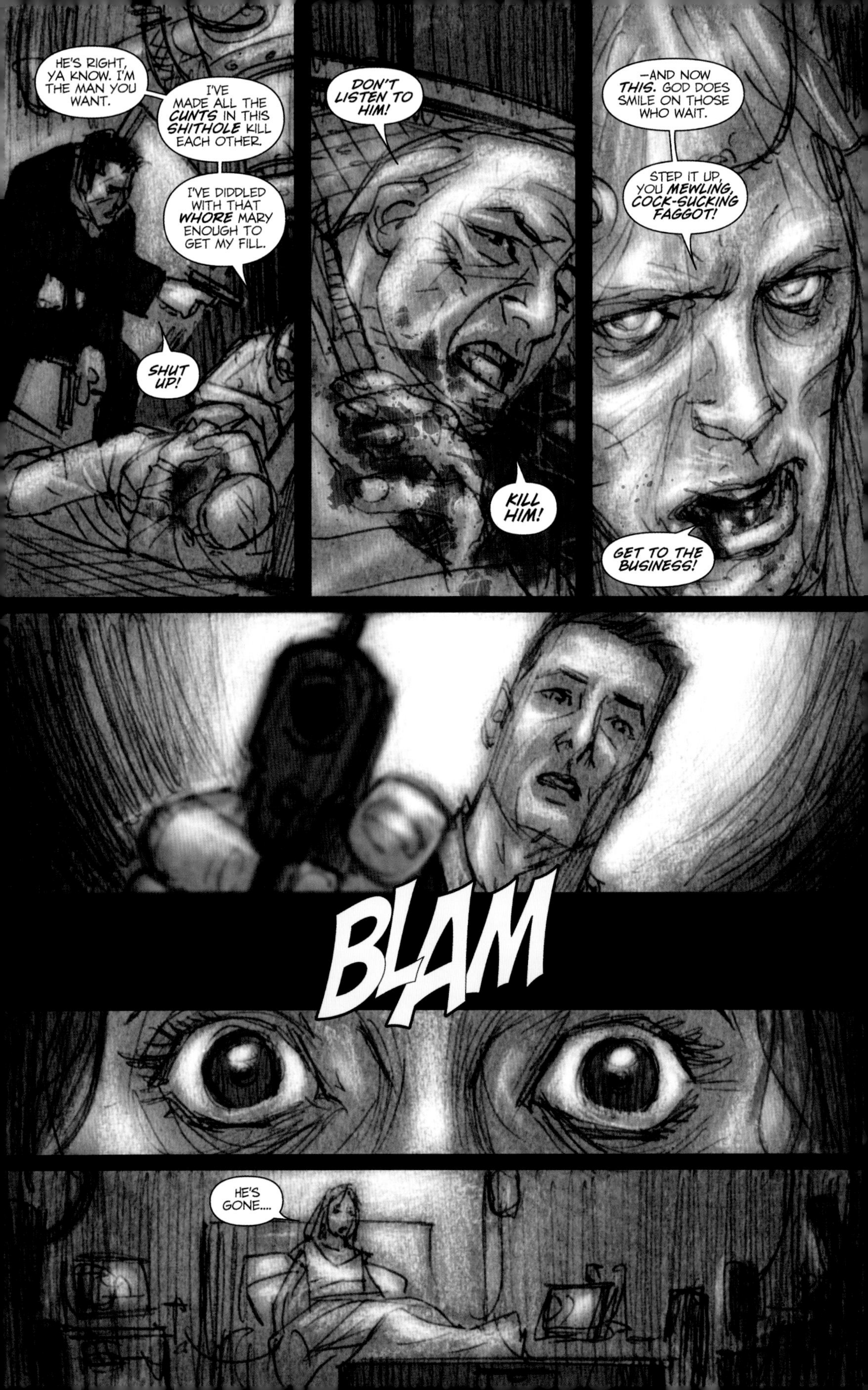
HE'S RIGHT, YA KNOW. I'M THE MAN YOU WANT.
I'VE MADE ALL THE CUNTS IN THIS SHITHOLE KILL EACH OTHER.
I'VE DIDDLED WITH THAT WHORE MARY ENOUGH TO GET MY FILL.
SHUT UP!
DON'T LISTEN TO HIM!
KILL HIM!
—AND NOW THIS. GOD DOES SMILE ON THOSE WHO WAIT.
STEP IT UP, YOU MEWLING, COCK-SUCKING FAGGOT!
GET TO THE BUSINESS!
BLAM
HE'S GONE....

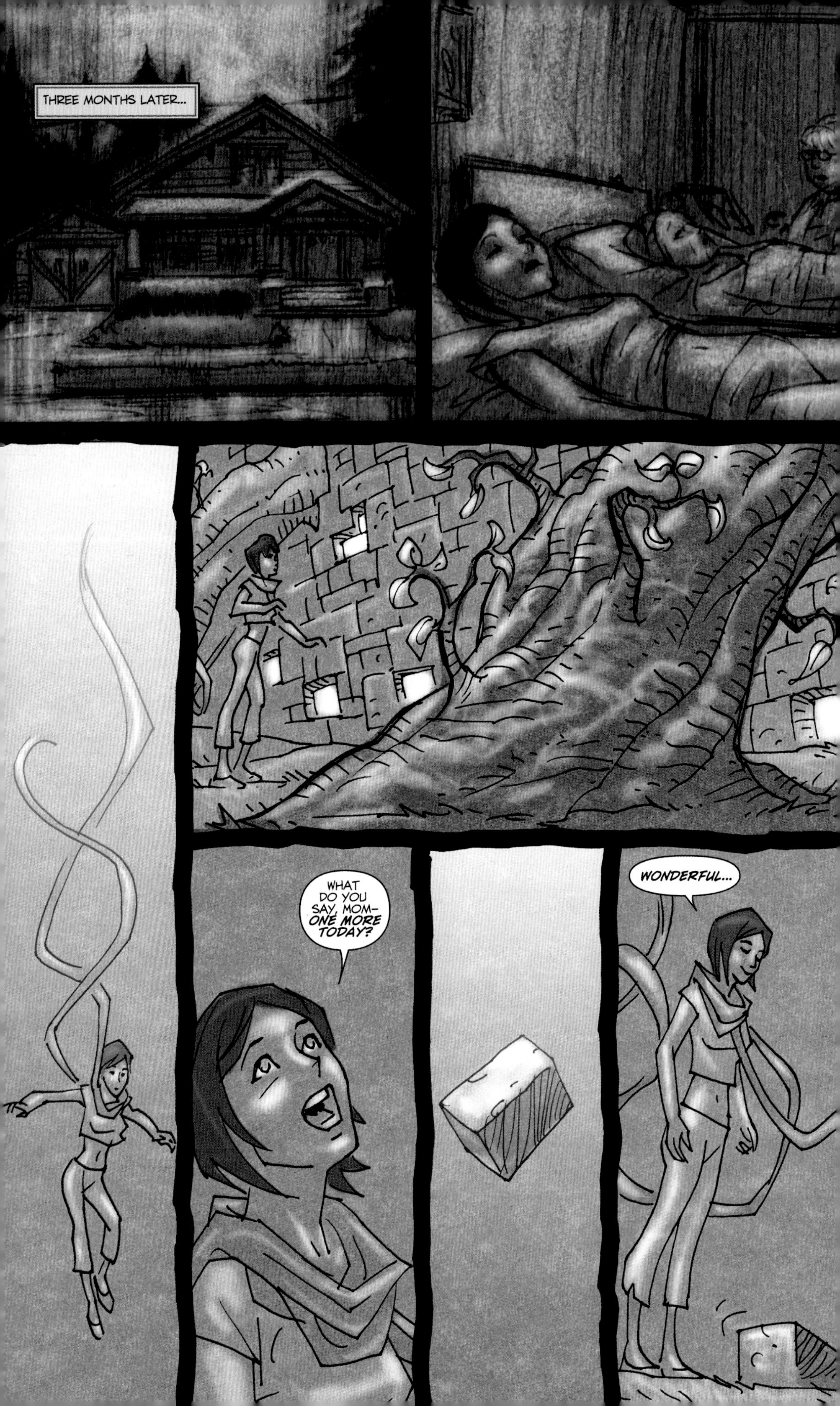
THREE MONTHS LATER...
WHAT DO YOU SAY, MOM– ONE MORE TODAY?
WONDERFUL...

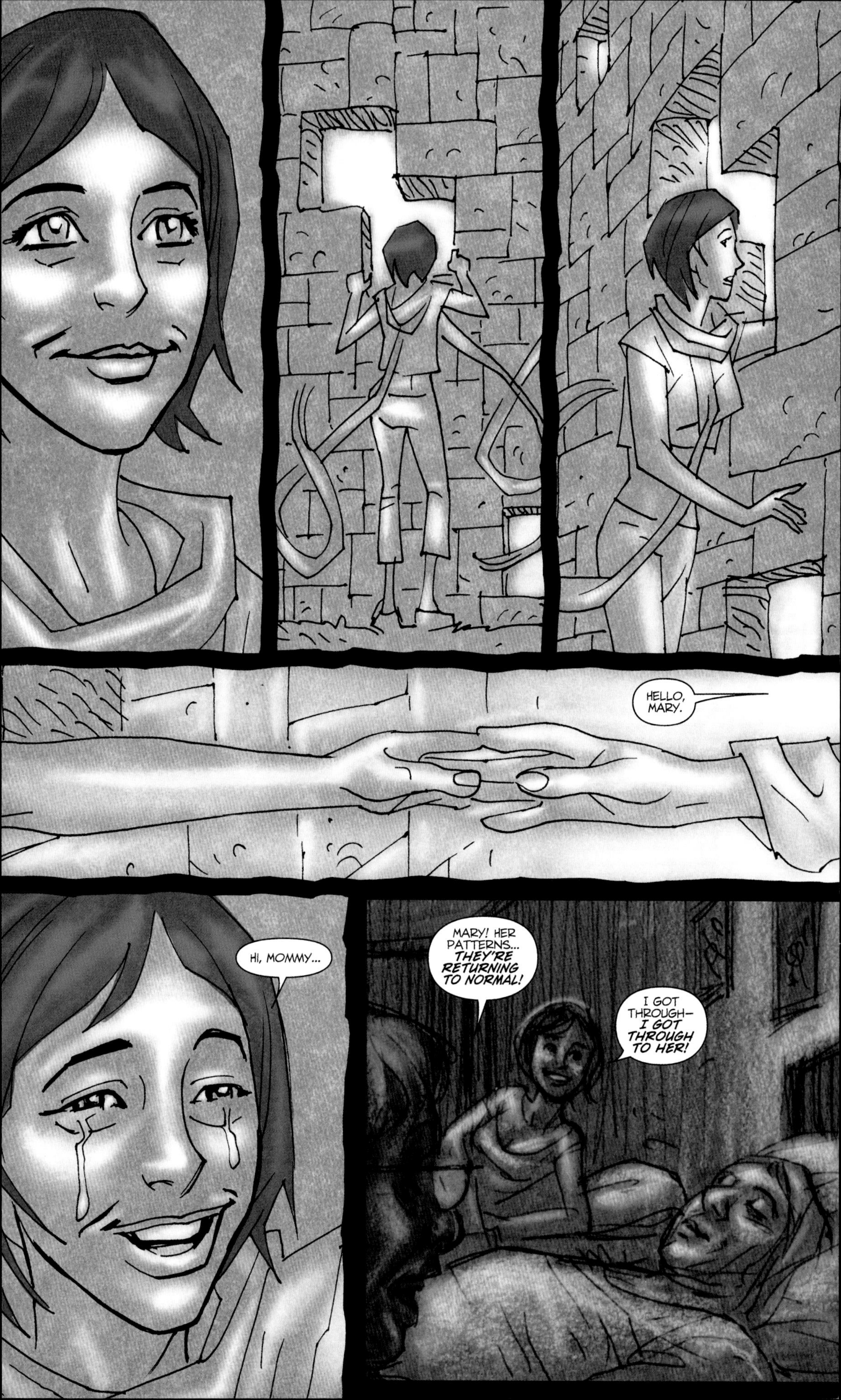
HELLO, MARY.
HI, MOMMY...
MARY! HER PATTERNS... THEY'RE RETURNING TO NORMAL!
I GOT THROUGH— I GOT THROUGH TO HER!

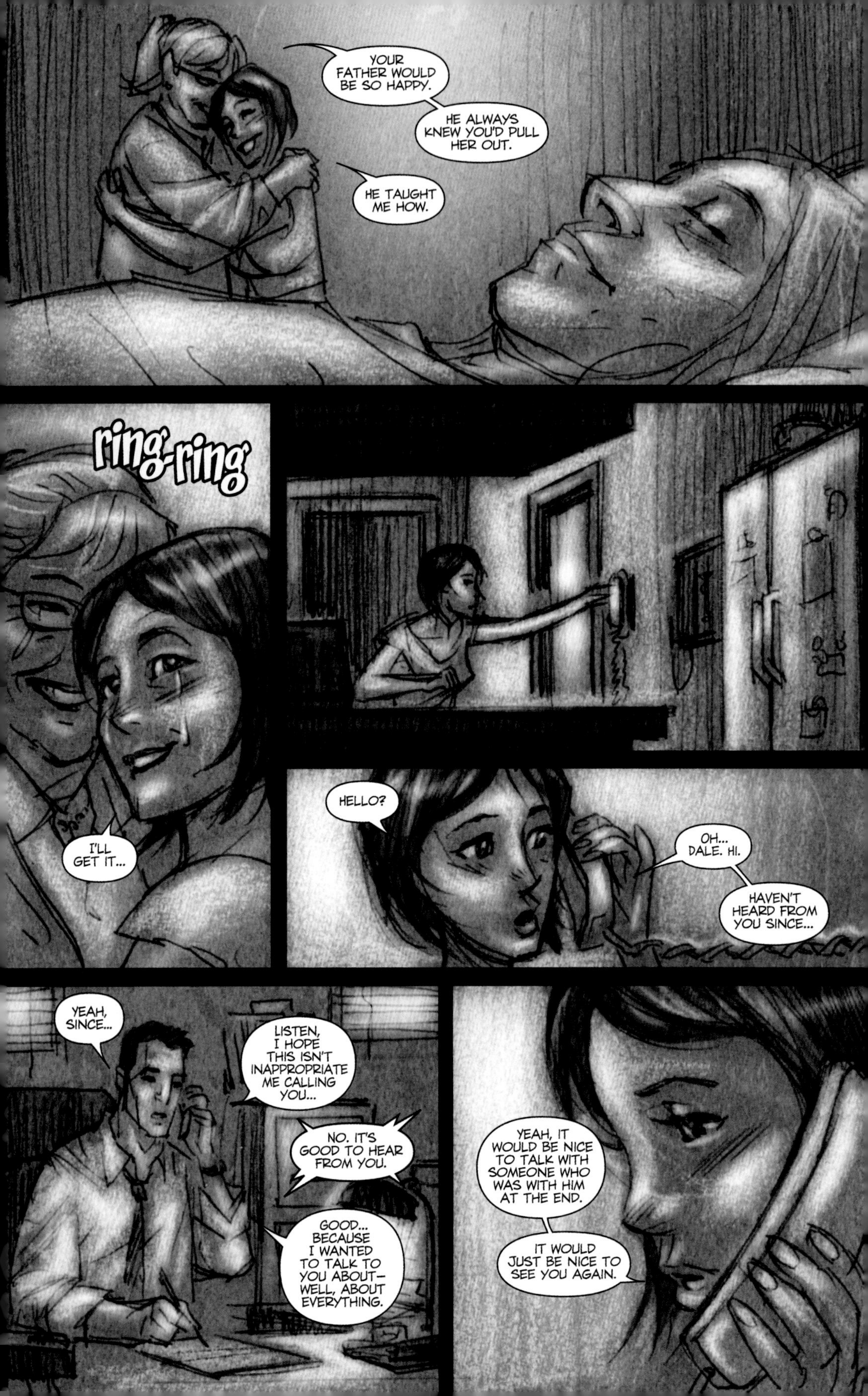
YOUR FATHER WOULD BE SO HAPPY.
HE ALWAYS KNEW YOU'D PULL HER OUT.
HE TAUGHT ME HOW.
ring-ring
I'LL GET IT...
HELLO?
OH... DALE. HI.
HAVEN'T HEARD FROM YOU SINCE...
YEAH, SINCE...
LISTEN, I HOPE THIS ISN'T INAPPROPRIATE ME CALLING YOU...
NO. IT'S GOOD TO HEAR FROM YOU.
GOOD... BECAUSE I WANTED TO TALK TO YOU ABOUT— WELL, ABOUT EVERYTHING.
YEAH, IT WOULD BE NICE TO TALK WITH SOMEONE WHO WAS WITH HIM AT THE END.
IT WOULD JUST BE NICE TO SEE YOU AGAIN.

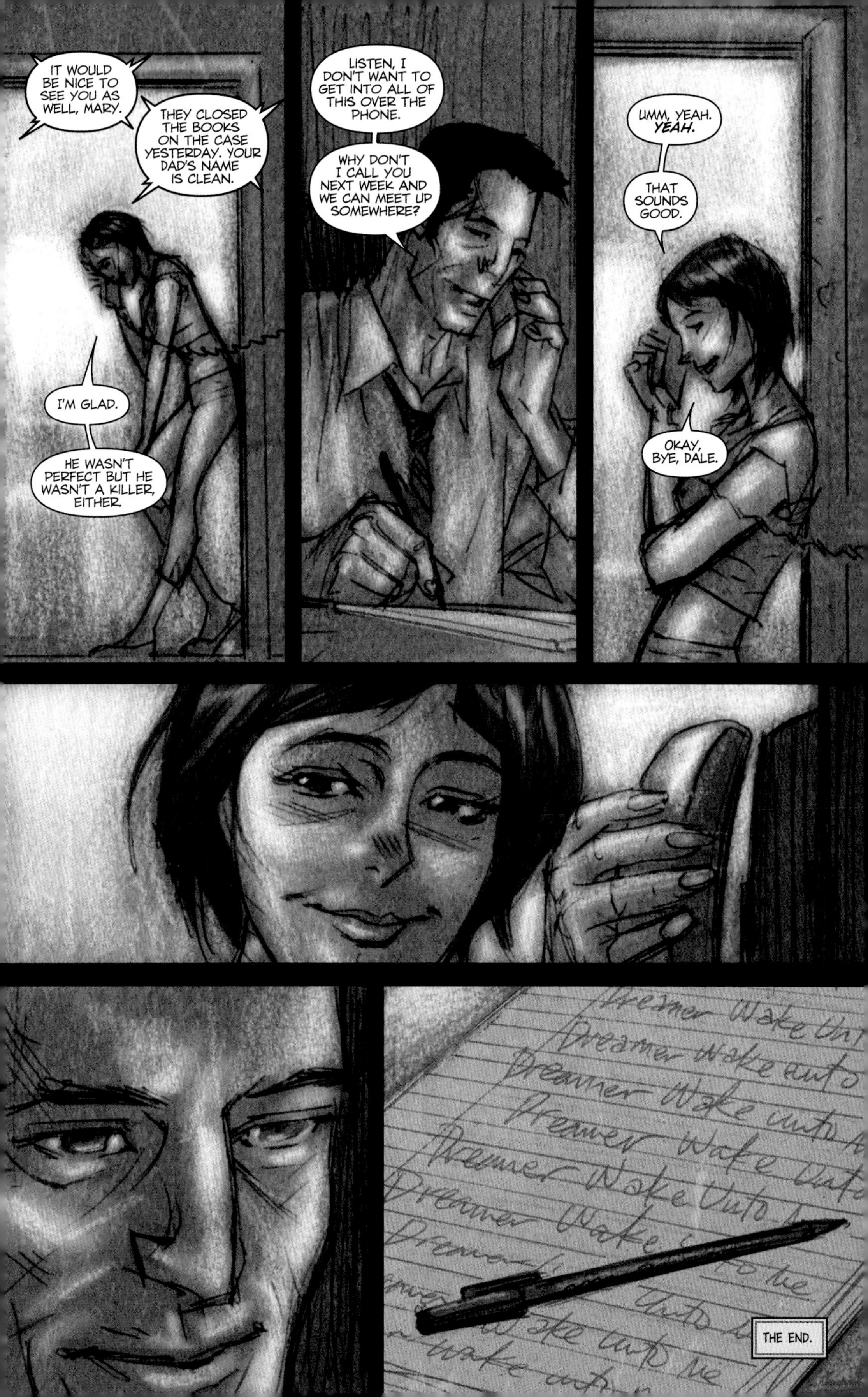
IT WOULD BE NICE TO SEE YOU AS WELL, MARY.
THEY CLOSED THE BOOKS ON THE CASE YESTERDAY. YOUR DAD'S NAME IS CLEAN.
I'M GLAD.
HE WASN'T PERFECT BUT HE WASN'T A KILLER, EITHER.
LISTEN, I DON'T WANT TO GET INTO ALL OF THIS OVER THE PHONE.
WHY DON'T I CALL YOU NEXT WEEK AND WE CAN MEET UP SOMEWHERE?
UMM, YEAH. *YEAH.*
THAT SOUNDS GOOD.
OKAY, BYE, DALE.
THE END.

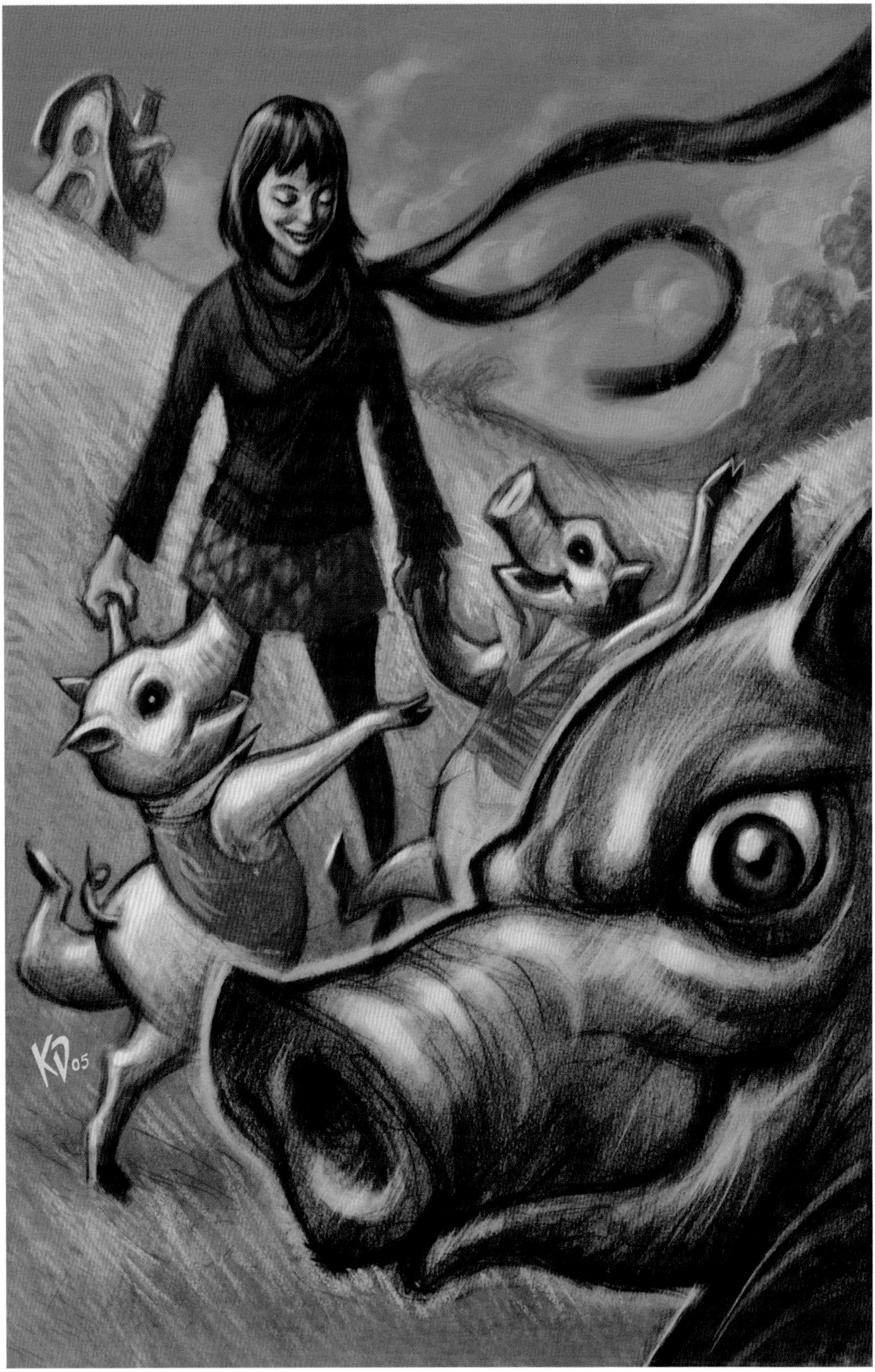
KD 05

NIGHT MARY ART GALLERY

ALL ART BY KIERON DYWER

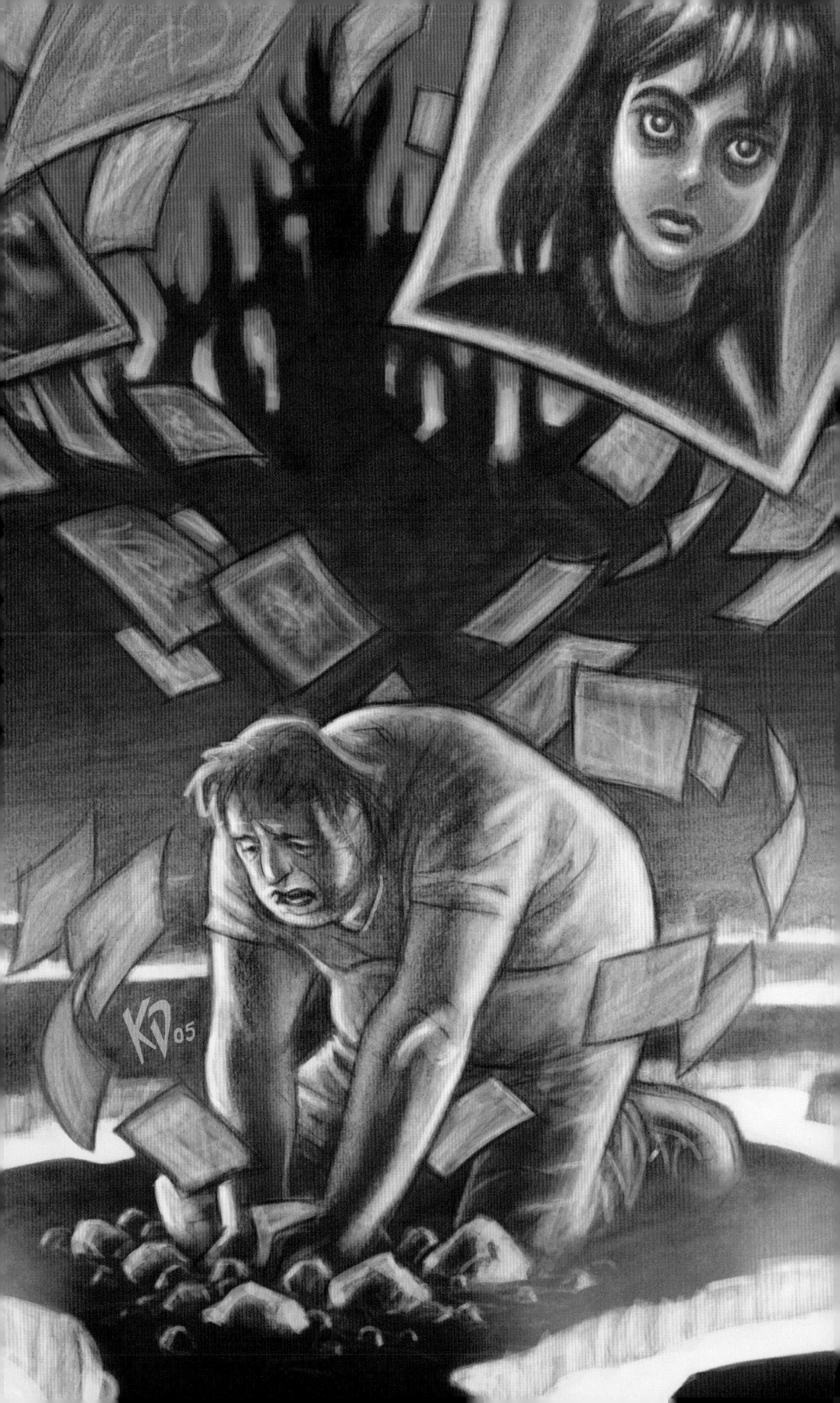

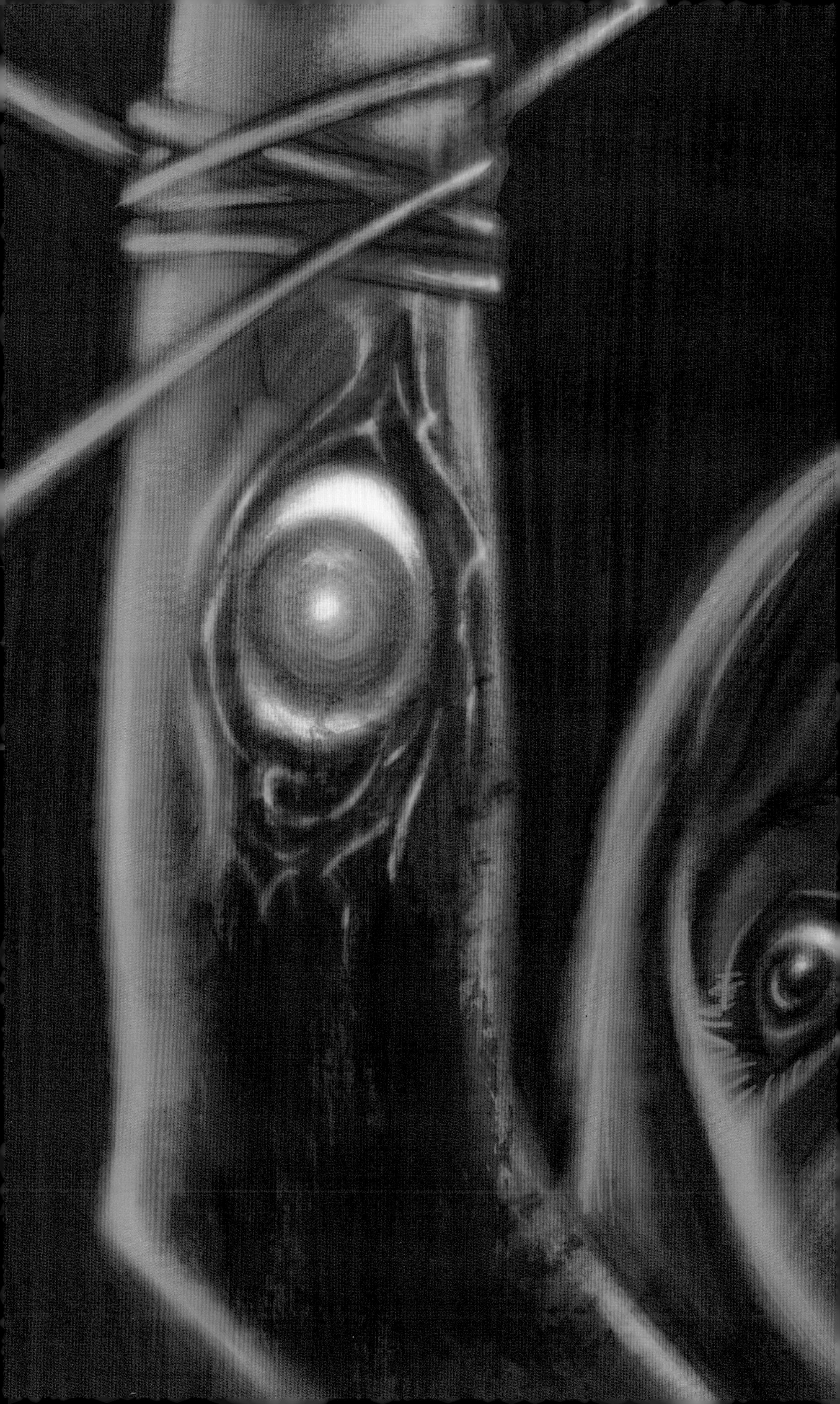

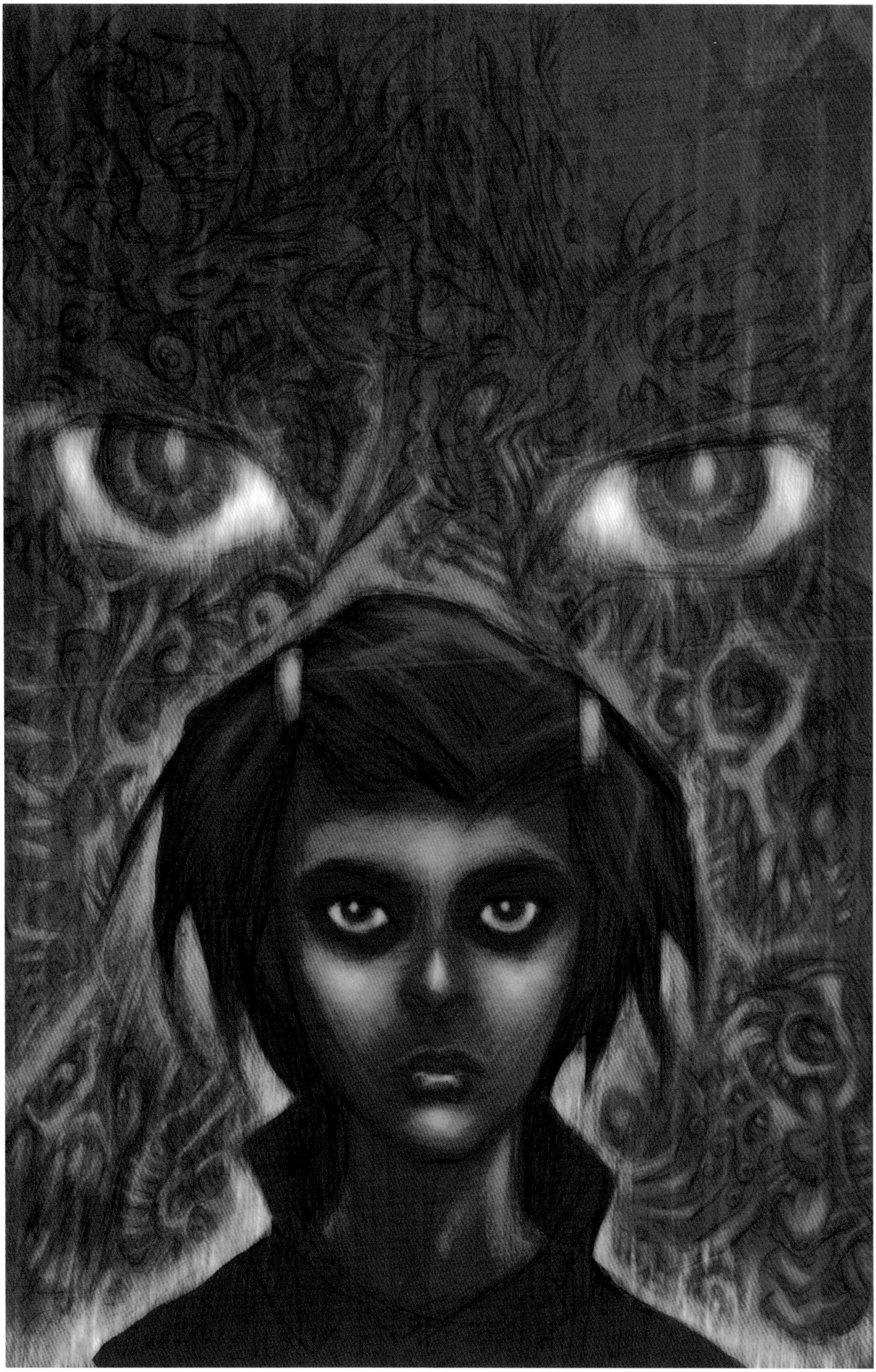

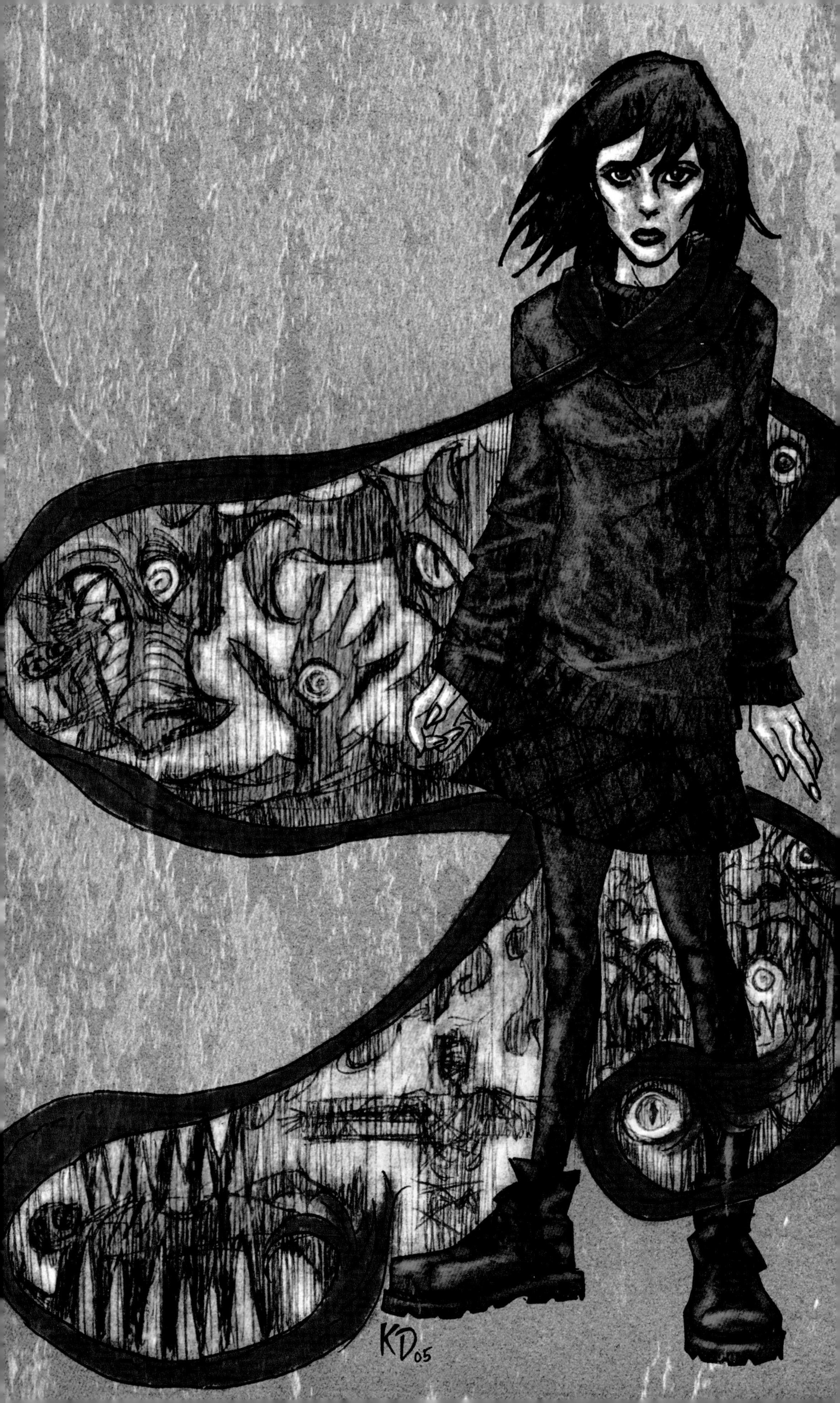
KD05